A Julema:
una mente brillante
y una mujer de lucha.
¡Por no dejarse vencer!
Adelante, con
abrazos
de Gladys

Delaware, marzo 2002

GLADYS M.
ILARREGUI

THE CUMAEAN SIBYL

SELECTED POETRY

A BILINGUAL EDITION
WITH LIFE AND CRITICAL INTRODUCTION

by

JUDY B. McINNIS

UNIVERSITY PRESS
OF THE SOUTH, Inc.

1999

Published in the United States by:
University Press of the South, Inc.
PMB 421, 5500 Prytania Street
New Orleans, LA 70115 USA
E-mail: unprsouth@aol.com Fax: (504) 866-2750
Visit our award-winning web page:
http://www.unprsouth.com
Visit our partner's web page: http://www.punmonde.com
Acid-free paper.

Gladys M. Ilarregui.
The Cumaean Sibyl. Selected Poetry. A Bilingual Edition with Life and Critical Introduction by Judy B. McInnis.
First edition. Latin American Studies, 10.
Xvi + 359 p. cm.
Includes index and bibliography.
Front cover photos: *Flower of Life* (Frida Kahlo, 1944); *Winter on Tawah Creek, Alaska* (Photo Doug and Carolyn Beaudoin).

1. Ilarregui, Gladys. 2. Poetry. 3. Women poets. 4. Latin American poetry. 5. Ethnic studies. 6. Spanish poetry. 7. Latin American culture. 8. American poetry.
ISBN 1-889431-61-3 (pbk.)
Library of Congress Catalog Card Number:

Dedication

For my daughter, Meghan Emily McInnis,

as she begins her career as a Hispanist.

CONTENTS

PREFACE: GLADYS M. ILARREGUI, A BIO-BIBLIOGRAPHICAL SKETCH

A life is a life is a life."

My first encounter with Gladys M. Ilarregui occurred in a Folger Library Seminar on the Andean Indians, given by Irene Silverblatt in the academic year 1993-1994. A tall, slender brunette, Ilarregui reminded me of portraits of Virginia Woolf--not just the large intelligent brown eyes, which she turned attentively to those she engaged in animated conversation, nor the long straight nose--a nose of character--certainly not the wide curving lips (for Woolf's mouth lacked such generosity of proportion), but rather the assurance and purposefulness emanated by the creative person who contemplates the self and others and then seeks to define and communicate that unique perspective. Here was a young woman who took herself seriously and assumed that others regarded her and themselves with equal seriousness. She combined femininity with forthrightness in the blend peculiar to Argentine women, who match North American women in their assurance, the assumption of sexual equality, their frank openness, and their self-confidence. Gladys Ilarregui wore those attitudes as easily as the stylishness and courteous deference which are more often associated with Hispanic women.

Ilarregui's seriousness is not incompatible with a certain ruefulness when she considers her standing among the aspiring writers and academics in the intensely competitive intellectual life of the capitol, where too many candidates are seeking too few positions and where, unfortunately, the institutions of higher learning use and abuse young professors. Her sense of humor never fails as she endeavors to survive and create a space for herself and her work: to realize her "potencias." Since that first meeting in 1993, Ilarregui and I have frequently met again--at first, fortuitously, then deliberately--in the many academic meetings, conventions, and congresses of our mutual specializations:

Loyola University in Chicago in 1994, where she gave a paper on the Florentine Codex of the sixteenth century for the Asociación de Literatura Femenina Hispánica;

Kean College, New Jersey, in April 1994 for the Mid Atlantic Council on Latin American Studies where she organized a panel on Malinche;

Davidson College, North Carolina for the ALFH in October, 1994 where she presented a paper on feminine autobiography in the post-Conquest period;

Albright College, Pennsylvania in March 1995 where she read a paper on colonial women and Marjorie Agosín for MACLAS;

Barnard College, New York City in November, 1995 where she compared Frida Kahlo's work to the weaving of colonial women for the ALFH conference;

the Naval Academy in Annapolis, Maryland in April, 1997 for the annual MACLAS meeting where she presented a paper on four contemporary Latin American poets;

Guadalajara, Mexico in April, 1997 for the Twentieth International Congress of the Latin American Studies Association where she presented a paper about the relevance of colonial texts in the new millennium;

George Washington University in Washington D.C. for her own conference on women and illness, sponsored by the Fundación Cultural Iberoamericana, in October, 1998;

University of Puerto Rico at Bayamón, San Juan, P. R. in November, 1998 for their Fourth Congress of Feminine Creativity where she gave readings of her poetry and attended a session dedicated to that poetry;

Ursinus College in Collegeville, Pennsylvania for the annual MACLAS meeting where a session was dedicated to her work in April, 1999.

This list represents but a half of the numerous meetings Ilarregui participated in during this period. While her topics represented a range of colonial and contemporary Latin American figures, my own became increasingly focused on the work of Ilarregui herself. From writing a review of *Oficios y personas / Guía para perplejos* for *Letras femeninas* I had moved to translating and commenting upon her poetry, a task that has provided me with the highest degree of aesthetic pleasure and intellectual stimulation in the last two years. As I studied her poetry, I became ever more avid to discover the background which formed her. Finally I journeyed to her home in Alexandria where we spent an afternoon, evening, and following morning recording her reminiscences. These, along with her poems, supplied the material for the following biographical sketch.

***

Gladys Ilarregui and her husband Carlos arrived in the United States on July 4, 1983 with three suitcases. One contained their clothing, another held her typewriter, and the third was filled with paper. She had heard that paper was exorbitantly expensive in the United States and had provided against this contingency by bringing her own supply. Even as she entered a new country and a new language, filled as she was with apprehension, she was determined that she would continue in her chosen vocation of Hispanic poet. The German typewriter whose clacking resounded through her home in Buenos Aires ("El poema en mangas de camisa / The Poem in Shirt Sleeves") would continue sounding in Alexandria. Indeed, she was more concerned with the reception of her poetry in her new country than she was with her own welcome as the poem "4 de julio / 4 of July" illustrates. As a new immigrant she had to forge a new identity in the United States--learn a new etiquette, a new geography, a new bureaucracy: as a practicing poet she had only to deepen and elaborate the self or selves that she had depicted in her poetry from her school days. Writing pieces for publication from the age of eight years, she had been gratified to discover that her verses could bring recognition and even monetary compensation. The literary prizes she has continued to win as an adult have helped to confirm her in her poetic vocation. The Spanish Embassy in the United States awarded the "Premio Federico García Lorca 1994" to *Oficios y personas / Roles and Persons*. She received the "Premio Plural 1993" (first prize) from the Editorial Excelsior in Mexico for her collection *Indian Journeys*. She perfected her English and familiarized herself with English literature through study for the B.A. degree (1989) in Philosophy and English at George Mason University. She continued her studies there to earn the M.A. (1990) in Contemporary Latin American Literature. Since receiving her Ph.D. in Colonial literature and Historiography from the Catholic University of America in 1995, she has taught at various colleges and universities in the Washington area and now serves as president of the Fundación Cultural Iberoamericana.

She was born Gladys Blanco in 1958, the first child of a middle class family whose ancestors had immigrated from Spain to Buenos Aires three generations earlier. Her father, José Eduardo, worked as a "literario de comercio" or sales representative, while her mother, Gloria, kept house for the extended family, consisting of Gladys, her younger brother Eduardo, her uncle, and her paternal grandfather. Although her grandfather died when Gladys was only four years old, he remained an influential figure in her development. A failed poet, he appealed to the young girl's imagination; as an adult Ilarregui continues to see her own poetry as a kind of vindication of that grandfather, whose sensitivity and warmth won him many friends and earned the love of his family. She gives a sympathetic depiction of her grandfather "con su cara de Beckett / with his face of Beckett" in the poem "Focusing." She was equally attached to her uncle, a tutor to whom she attributes both her own love of learning and her first awakening to metaphysics in the poem "Cool Memories: la piel de un globo / Cool Memories: The Skin of a Balloon." She has enjoyed the loving attention and support of her father throughout her life as the poem "Cambio de palabras: Final de juego / Exchange of Words: End of the Game" reveals: for him she is ever the "niña, la chica de ojos negros, Marcelita / the child, the girl with dark eyes, Marcelita."

The strongest influence in Ilarregui's life is undoubtedly her mother to whom references frequently surface in these poems. Ilarregui attributes the unusually strong bond she formed with her mother to four things: (l) being the eldest child and a girl; (2) being a sickly child who required her mother's constant nursing; (3) being the vehicle through whom her mother might realize her own frustrated ambition; and (4) being the means through which her mother could create a unique mother-daughter bonding. Ilarregui's maternal grandmother died when her mother was too young to accomplish such bonding. As a child Ilarregui used to imagine the lives of this grandmother as well as that of her paternal grandmother, both of whom she knew only from photographs. Perhaps Ilarregui's profound desire to trace roots and to find them in wise old men and women of Indian tribes stems from the absence of these figures in her family life.

The firstborn child usually holds a special place in his/her parents' hearts, if for no other reason than the child for a period enjoys the parents' exclusive attention. Firstborn children tend to be achievers, even over-achievers, who are eager to live up to their parents' expectations. As a poet who has earned her doctorate in a foreign land, Ilarregui has certainly fulfilled her parents' wishes. As a child she suffered from critical disease of the kidneys. She was frequently hospitalized, hooked up to life support machines, dependent upon nurses, doctors and her mother. She depicts this childhood illness in many poems, perhaps most poignantly in the section of four poems entitled "A la manera de Frida Kahlo / In the Manner of Frida Kahlo" from the book *Guía para perplejos / Guide for the Perplexed.* She recalls a healthier adolescence of intense discussions with youths of her own age and the awakening of her poetic vocation. At the age of twelve she began high school at the Regina Apostalorum School for Girls in the suburbs of Buenos Aires. At thirteen she began submitting poems to a literary journal. This was a period too when her deepest friendships were formed. She studied the usual courses in high school: mathematics, science, health, religion, history, foreign languages, and Spanish grammar, literature, and composition. Her foreign languages included French, English, and a little German. After graduation from high school, she studied music, German, and creative writing. She attended a seminar on James Joyce and also studied numerous other European writers, including Nietzsche, Chekhov, and Tolstoy. She also worked in a school for special children where she learned Piaget's principles of child development.

As a student Ilarregui participated in Buenos Aires' active café society. Cultural life was highly developed in the city and she took full advantage of public concerts of classical music, informative lectures, and readings of creative work. Immigrants from Germany, France, Italy and Spain invigorated the city; the student of foreign languages had ample opportunity to hear masses, obtain newspapers, and attend lectures in the several languages of Western Europe. At the same time the country suffered under a military government that fomented fear and suspicion among the citizenry. This ambiance, combined with the economic stagnation in Argentina, prompted Ilarregui to join the ranks of the many Argentines who sought a way out of the coutry. During this intense period the poet met and married Carlos Ilarregui, an engineer in computer science. His specialization, then as now so much in demand, provided the means for the young couple to emigrate from Argentina to the United States.

Like most new immigrants Ilarregui then learned how different "school" English is from the English spoken in the streets. With some trepidation she began the process of enrolling in the university, fearful that among all the forms she had to file she might have been signing her life away. Most difficult was the loss of old friends and family who provided guidance in the homeland. This loss of an established network as she uprooted herself helped Ilarregui relate to American Indians and encouraged her to investigate the strategies they used to keep their own minority traditions alive within a dominant society with different customs, beliefs, and language.

To establish life in a new land is to redefine oneself and fashion a new identity. As an immigrant Ilarregui was no longer surrounded by people who knew her and her history. Eager to act in the proper way in a new and strange situation, unsure of what was expected, unfamiliar with customs and with the new geography and the new language, Ilarregui endeavored to learn the new mentality and point-of-view during a two year period in which she never fully relaxed. On the other hand, the adjustment was a challenge and she enjoyed proving herself as she forged a place for herself. Fortunately, most of Ilarregui's encounters with North Americans have been positive; she praises the patience and friendliness of people willing to help the visitor or the new immigrant in all the small tasks of daily living.

Ilarregui had to wait for two years because of visa restrictions before beginning her university studies. At George Mason University she repeated much subject matter she had already studied in Argentina, but the work was useful in improving her command of English as she "went through the system." During her experience as a new immigrant she often found occasion to think of her mother with gratitude for her lessons in perseverance.

Travel to the United States has opened the door to travel around the world for Ilarregui. Ever curious about different cultures, she and her husband have visited Europe, Russia, China, and Africa. In addition they have explored the Americas from Alaska to Argentina. She is struck by the variety of cultures within the United States--the differences between Ohio and New York, between Florida and Boston--as well as by the larger differences of cultures across the continents. Yet she has also had the opportunity to observe first-hand how rapidly the world is moving towards a global culture. She welcomes this change, on the one hand, as an improvement for human beings, but regrets it, on the the other hand, for the loss of local traditions. To maintain and foment Hispanic culture in the United States Ilarregui joined with a group of residents in the greater Washington D.C. area to form the Fundación Cultural Iberoamericana, of which she presently serves as president. In her poetry Ilarregui balances the local perspective of the Hispanic experience in Argentina and the United States with the global perspective of a late twentieth-century citizen of the world. This translation makes her poetry available to English-speaking as well as Spanish-speaking readers.

***

Ilarregui's bibliography includes the following works of poetry:

Books

Ilarregui, Gladys. *Indian Journeys* in *Plural: Revista cultural de Excelsior*, March, 1994, pp. 4-15.

----------. *Indian Journeys: poems/ poemas.* Translated by Judy B. McInnis. Alexandria: Los Signos del Tiempo, Editores, 1998.

----------. *Oficios y personas / Guía para perplejos.* Alexandria: Los Signos del Tiempo, Editores, 1996.

----------. *Reuniones.* Salta, Argentina: Editorial Biblioteca de Textos Universitarios, forthcoming.

----------. *Refugios contra el mar.* Guadalajara, Mexico: La Luciérnaga, Editores, forthcoming.

----------. Editor of *Solo de Piano: Poemario para Músicos y Pintores de Consuelo Hernández.* Alexandria, VA: Los Signos del Tiempo, 1997.

----------. Editor of Forthcoming Virtual Literary Magazine for the Hispanics in the Arts. http://www.iberoamerican.org

Poems

----------. "A la manera de Frida Kahlo: Retrato con mariposas." *Horizonte 21: Revista de poesía de Estados Unidos en español* Vol I, No. 4 (Verano, 1996), p. 13.

----------. "Loose Hair" and "Time of the Object." *Poet Lore* Vol. 94, No. 2 (Summer, 1999), forthcoming.

----------. "Me distraje" (*Plural* prize poems translated into Portuguese by Amadeu Baptista). *Cadernos de Tomega: Revista semestral de cultura* No. 12 (Dezembro, 1994). Portugal.

----------. "Poema con los ojos lejos." *Hispanic Culture Review* Vol. I, No. 2 (Spring, 1991), p. 88.

----------. "Zonas prohibidas" and "Textos ficticios" (Two Prose Poems). *Letras femeninas* Vol. 19 (Primavera-Otoño, 1993), p. 170. University of Nebraska.

----------. "Prefacio al infierno" and "Autorretrato." *Horizonte 21: Revista de poesía de Estados Unidos en español* Vol. I, No. 5 (Otoño, 1996), p. 8.

----------. "Si me rompo." *Society for Latin American Studies Newsletter* No. 59 (London: January, 1998).

----------. "Sostengo este rostro." *Les portes des poetes*, April, 1993. Paris.

----------. "'El tiempo del objeto' and Comments on My Book *Oficios y personas.*" *Periplo* (magazine of the Pen Club International) (Sept. 1997), Mexico.

Publications about Gladys Ilarregui

McInnis, Judy B. "Review of *Oficios y personas/ Guia para perplejos*." *Letras femeninas* Vol. 24 (Números 1-2) (Spring-Fall, 1998), pp. 208-209.

----------. "Enfermedad de la niñez y desarrollo poético en *Guia para perplejos* de Gladys M. Ilarregui." *66 Escritoras hispanoamericanas contemporaneas*. Edited by Priscilla Gac-Artigas. Forthcoming.

----------. "Gladys M. Ilarregui and the Poetics of Transparency." *MACLAS: Latin American Essays* Vol. 12 (1999), pp. 83-96.

Academic Conference Sessions and Presentations about Gladys Ilarregui

Millicent Bolden. "La Infinita Canción Autumnal de Gladys Ilarregui." Cuarto Congreso de Creación Femenina. Nov. 16, 1998. Universidad Central de Bayamón.

Judy B. McInnis. "'Estos borrones / que hijos del alma son, partos del pecho': Gladys Ilarregui as Successor to Sor Juana Inez de la Cruz." Mid Atlantic Council of Latin American Studies, March 27, 1998 at The College of New Jersey, Trenton, New Jersey.

----------. "Gladys M. Ilarregui and the Poetics of Transparency." American Association of Teachers of Spanish and Portuguese, August 3, 1998 Convention in Madrid, Spain. The paper was read at the Session on Hispanic Literature of the United States, Chair, chaired by Edra P. Staffieri.

----------. "De Madres, Malestares, y Mariposas." Conference on "Madness, Illness, Bodies: the Hispanic Woman Writer and Her Fragmented World," sponsored by George Washington University and the Fundación Cultural Iberoamericana. Oct. 15, 1998.

----------. "Gladys Ilarregui: Fragmented Experience, Fragmented Voice." Cuarto Congreso de Creación Femenina. Nov. 16, 1998, Universidad Central de Bayamón, Puerto Rico.

----------. "Gladys Ilarregui: 'En la manera de Frida Kahlo.'" Mid Atlantic Council of Latin American Studies, Ursinus College, Collegeville, Pennsylvania, March 26, 1999.

----------. "Gladys Ilarregui as Cumaean Sibyl." X Congreso Internacional de la Asociación de Literatura Femenina Hispánica. Querétaro, México, Sept. 24, 1999.

ACKNOWLEDGMENTS

I have been fortunate to have enjoyed the poet's collaboration throughout this project. My thanks to Gladys M. Ilarregui for making herself available for my endless questions and verifications.

My heartfelt thanks also go to two efficient graduate assistants who prepared parts of this manuscript: Kimberly Ekstam and Elizabeth D. Oehrlein. They and I enjoyed the unfailing assistance of our two computer experts in the Foreign Language Media Center, Tom McCone and Rae Stabosz. Kudos to Diego Domínguez for his computer expertise.

For the actual publication of the manuscript, I wish to thank Alain Saint Saens and his assistant Jennifer Link, both of University Press of the South, as well as my chairman Richard Zipser and the Dean of Arts and Science, James Mehl, both at the University of Delaware. For their excellent advice on placing my manuscript I am endebted to Elizabeth Espadas and Tom Lathrop.

I am most grateful to four poet-scholars who read and commented upon the manuscript: Nela Río, Adaleida Martínez, Priscilla Gac-Artigas, and Lilianet Brintrup. I wish to thank Marie E. Castro DeMoux, Sharon Voros, and Edward Freidman for their support.

Finally, I thank my husband, Clay W. McInnis, for his advice in choosing exactly the right word in many poetic passages.

jbm
Newark, Delaware
July 23, 1999

GLADYS M. ILARREGUI: POST MODERN FRAGMENTATION WITHIN THE ANCIENT POETICS OF THE CUMAEAN SIBYL

In her first three books of poetry, *Indian Journeys, Oficios y Personas (Roles and Persons)* and *Guía para perplejos (Guide for the Perplexed),* Ilarregui reinterprets for a modern age a sibylline poetics in which, properly organized, the fragments of poetic insight yield a worldview useful to readers in guiding them into the future. In her own scholarly papers[1] Ilarregui frequently juxtaposes modern and ancient texts. In this paper I shall adopt her strategy to her own poetry by presenting Virgil's and Dante's conception of the Cumaean Sibyl as a background for Ilarregui's poetics.

The purpose of this essay is to situate Ilarregui's work within Western literature by identifying sources of her ideas and the poetic vocabulary which she uses to express her principle themes. Ilarregui knows not only the Hispanic and English traditions but also continental literary and philosophic currents. She alludes to the German philosophers Martin Heidegger and Martin Buber, the German writer Heinrich Böll, as well as to the French poet René Char, the Russian artist Wassily Kandinsky, the Mexican artist Frida Kahlo, the Italian novelist Italo Calvino, and the Swedish poet Tomas Tranströmer. Sylvia Molloy discovered that after Sarmiento:

> the scene of reading will continue to mark Spanish American autobiographical writing, either through its obsessive presence, as in the constant references to the European text that double Victoria Ocampo's autobiographical exercise (a sort of 'I quote therefore I am') or through its forceful omission, as in Neruda's vehement

---

[1] "Discursos contra el silencio: los textiles mexicas y Frida Kahlo" ("Discourses against Silence: the Mexica Textiles and Frida Kahlo"), *Letras femeninas* 22: 1-2 (Spring-Fall, 1996), 9-18; "La metáfora del mercado: el intercambio prehispánico en los poemas de Marjorie Agosín" ("The Metaphor of the Market: the Prehispanic Interchange in the Poems of Marjorie Agosín"), *MACLAS: Latin American Essays* 9 (1995), 18-35; and a chapter in a *Twice-Told Tale: Essays on Contemporary and Colonial Literature and Historiography*, edited by Santiago Juan Navarros, scheduled for publication in 1998.

> protestations--'*Libro, déjame libre*' ['Book, leave me alone']--in his memoirs and in his poetry. A mirror for the autobiographer, the book will, like a mirror, reflect, comfort, augment, distort: what it exhibits will be, nonetheless, the spectator's own image.[2]

In the autobiographical writing of these three volumes of poetry Ilarregui defines herself through her own texts which sometimes adapt the texts of other writers. I shall identify some major influences.

My method is a poem by poem exegesis which allows the reader easy access to commentary on a single poem or on all of them. This exegesis grew out of my efforts to translate each poem accurately, taking into account mood and voice as well as the literal significance of the vocabulary and structure. Rather than offering exhaustive commentary, I outline major motifs to engage the reader's own interpretative impulse.

In his long narrative of Troy's fall and his journey to Carthage, Aeneas tells Dido of his meeting with Helenus, priest-prophet of Apollo. The former urged Aeneas to consult the Cumaean Sibyl to discover the course to be followed in founding Rome. It was essential to bypass her oracles and insist on a personal interview with the Sibyl herself. Only she could reveal the proper order of the prophecies which she wrote on leaves to be tossed by the wind and gathered piecemeal by her oracles:

> "When on your way you reach the town of Cumae,
> the sacred lakes, the loud wood of Avernus,
> there you will see the frenzied prophetess.
> Deep in her cave of rock she charts the fates,
> consigning to the leaves her words and symbols.
> Whatever verses she has written down
> upon the leaves, she puts in place and order
> and then abandons them inside her cavern.
> When all is still, that order is not troubled;
> but when soft winds are stirring and the door
> turning upon its hinge, disturbs the tender
> leaves, then she never cares to catch the verses
> that flutter through the hollow grotto, never

---

[2] *At Face Value: Autobiographical Writing in Spanish America* (Cambridge: Cambridge U P, 1991), p. 35.

> recalls their place or joins them all together.
> Her visitors, when they have had no counsel,
> depart, and then detest the Sibyl's cavern.
> Let no expense of time be counted here,
> though comrades chide and though the journey urge
> your sails to take the waves or favoring
> sea breezes swell their folds for voyaging.
> But visit her, the prophetess, with prayers,
> that she reveal the oracles herself
> and willingly unlock her voice and lips.
> She will unfold for you who are the peoples
> of Italy, the wars that are to come,
> and in what way you are to flee or face
> each crisis. Worshipped properly, she grants
> prosperous voyages. These things are all
> the gods allow my tongue to chant and tell.
> Now go your way, and with your acts exalt
> the mightiness of Troy as high as heaven."[3]

In the final canto of *The Divine Comedy* Dante alludes to this scene when he, the new Aeneas intent on inspiring Italians with his vision of religious and national destiny, receives instruction from Bernard. As Helenus had counseled Aeneas on how to approach the Sibyl, Bernard counsels Dante on how to approach the Virgin. Dante's sight pierced through a ray of light to a vision of the deity that vanquished speech and defied his memory. He remembers the vision as one remembers a dream: the passion it inspires remains clear, its effects upon "the inmost soul," but its intellectual content becomes fragmented:

> So the sun melts the imprint on the snow,
> Even so the Sibyl's wisdom that was penned
> On light leaves vanished on the winds that blow.[4]

Dante invokes the Supreme Light to restore a glimpse of that glory:

---

[3] *The Aeneid of Virgil*, translated by Allen Mandelbaum (New York: Bantam, 1972), pp. 71-72; Book III, lines 576-606 (lines 441-451 in the original Latin).

[4] Translated by Dorothy L. Sayers and Barbara Reynolds (Baltimore: Penguin, 1962), p. 345 (Canto 33, lines 64-66).

Make strong my tongue that in its words may burn
One single spark of all Thy glory's light
For future generations to discern.[5]

He returns to the comparison with the Sibyl's leaves to describe the epiphany of eternal beauty and goodness that was his. The universe itself became a book whose leaves consisted of all phenomena, now comprehensibly ordered because the forms themselves of things, behind the accidents of matter and substance, were revealed:

In that abyss I saw how love held bound
Into one volume all the leaves whose flight
Is scattered through the universe around;

How substance, accident, and mode unite
Fused, so to speak, together, in such wise
That this I tell of is one simple light.

Yea, of this complex I believe mine eyes
Beheld the universal form--in me,
Even as I speak, I feel such joy arise.[6]

There he reached the perfect end of his quest. "But as my sight by seeing learned to see," he forged the image of the three spheres superimposed upon one another. Unable as the geometrician to square the circle, he discerned the final mystery in a "flash" of the understanding which revealed "the love that moves the sun and the other stars."[7]

Of such stuff does Gladys Ilarregui forge her poetry for citizens of the world who are endeavoring to assimilate Einstein's vision of the universe. Her first three books of poetry trace a trajectory from examination of maternal roots in the Indian cultures of the Americas, to consideration of paternal roots in European culture, to the triumphant definition of her own "particular" persona.

---

[5] *Ibid.* (Canto 33, lines 70-72).

[6] *Ibid.* (Canto 33, lines 85-93).

[7] *Ibid.*, p. 346 (Canto 33, line 125).

In this scheme the emotional, the subjective, affinity with Nature, familial and tribal bonding are associated with the feminine while reason and separation of the individual, which has resulted in the isolation of existential man with his consequent angst, tend to be associated with the masculine. Ilarregui exemplifies the process of "individuation" as defined by Carl Gustav Jung in the effort to discover and then to reconcile the anima (female) and the animus (male) aspects of the soul. Her treatment of Indian culture reveals her belief that "primitive" indigenous cultures retain closer links to the unconscious and to the Jungian archetypes which inform it. She believes that poets, oracles, the wise old men and women of the tribe, and children have special access to the archetypes buried in what Jung called the "collective unconscious." She also subscribes to the theory that children in their psychic development recapitulate the history of the race.

Resting on this Jungian substratum is a Lacanian identification of the feminine/maternal with the sphere of the Imaginary and the masculine/paternal with the sphere of the Symbolic. Mirrors figure prominently in Ilarregui's poetry. Lacan theorized that the child comes into existence as a separate psychic being upon recognizing his image in a mirror. This mirror may be the image of himself that his parents and his culture reflect back to him or try to impose upon him. The ego projects an image of itself that will be loveable to the Other; only through such images can the ego become self-conscious and define itself. For Ilarregui the psyche always exists in process, never as a finished product. It defines itself by considering the images of the former selves of its own autobiography and the roles which its society allows.

BOOK I: *INDIAN JOURNEYS*

"Los antepasados / Ancestors"

This poem opens with a Picasso-like image of "fractured faces." Breaking up the object so the spectator could view it from several perspectives simultaneously characterizes Picasso's cubist period; among the objects so broken up were faces. Looking at her image in numerous mirrors, looking at previous manifestations of herself in photographs kept in the attic, Ilarregui searches for the one continuous self beneath all these manifestations. The word "fracturadas/fractured" implies that her psyche has been wounded or damaged by the world; it is broken and lacks wholeness. Her portrait of herself recalls the existential angst of Neruda in the Vanguard mood of the first *Residencia en la tierra:*

> *Innecesario, viéndome en los espejos,*
> *con un gusto a semanas, a biógrafos, a papeles,*
> *arranco de mi corazón, al capitán del infierno,*
> *establezco cláusulas indefinidamente tristes.*[8]
>
> (Unnecessary, seeing myself in the mirrors,
> with a taste of weeks, of biographies, of papers,
> I wrest from my heart, the captain of hell,
> I establish indefinitely sad clauses.)[9]

It also recalls the T.S. Eliot of "The Wasteland":

> What are the roots that clutch, what branches grow
> Out of this stony rubbish? Son of man,
> You cannot say, or guess, for you know only
> A heap of broken images, where the sun beats,
> And the dead tree gives no shelter, the cricket no relief,
> And the dry stone no sound of water.[10]

---

[8] Pablo Neruda, "Caballo de los sueños" in *Residencia en la tierra (1925-1935)* (Buenos Aires: Editorial Losada, S.A., 1958), Sexta Edición, p. 13.

[9] My translation. Unless otherwise noted, all translations are my o\

[10] T. S. Eliot, *The Complete Poems and Plays* (New York: Harcourt, Brace & World, Inc., 1962), p. 38.

Ilarregui speaks of her "caras anteriores / earlier faces" and associates them with "gestos / gestures" which she has treasured. Lacan describes how the self-image becomes a role that the ego represents to itself:

> As long as the image of the counterpart plays only its primary role, limited to the expressive function; it triggers similar emotions and postures in the subject.... But when he submits to that emotional or motive suggestion, the subject is not distinguished from the image itself.[11]

In this first poem of *Indian Journeys* Ilarregui embarks on an initiation journey; here she begins the phase of separation and withdrawal from society to subject herself to self-examination. Discovery of her psyche commences with reflection upon images she has used to structure that psyche. In the course of the book she will experience transformation through exposure to Indian culture and will finally return to her modern urban culture reconciled to her role as poet and confident of her poetic vocation.

She starts with the realization that meaning depends upon perspective and that multiple meanings may mean no fixed meaning. She exhibits a sense of being "de-centered." The textualization of self that will continue to pervade Ilarregui's poetry begins here where she switches from talking about herself to talking about literature as if they were one and the same: "where literature is a deconstructing to find oneself." She is her own book which she tries to read and "deconstruct" as Jacques Derrida deconstructed the texts he interpreted. She is willing to defer meaning to allow the play of difference in Derrida's terms.[12] She "empties" the trunk of her memories as he emptied the text of meaning.

---

[11] Jacques Lacan, *Les Complexes familiaux dans la formation de l'individu*, p. 45; cited and translated by Mikkel Borch-Jacobsen in "The alibis of the subject: Lacan and Philosophy," in *Speculations after Freud: Psychoanalysis, philosophy and culture*, edited by Sonu Shamdasani and Michael Münchow (London: Routledge, 1994), p. 85.

[12] See Jacques Derrida, *Writing and Difference*, translated by Alan Bass (Chicago: U of Chicago P, 1978).

The images she finds in her trunk are fragments: they exist like the leaves of the Cumaean Sibyl, enigmatic and open to interpretation. Thus Ilarregui begins in the mode of deconstruction. However, although she believes the self continues to evolve, she has faith in the development of a coherent self which she can communicate through poetry. Throughout these three books she will forge a special vocabulary whose terms become clear to the reader. By going back to her American and European roots, she will gain the knowledge to order her memories and hence to restore order to the Cumaean Sibyl's leaves. An appreciation of the distance covered in these three books can be gained by comparing this poem with "**Época**: Rostro sobre rostro / **Epoch**: Face on Face" *Guide for the Perplexed* (see below).

"Me distraje / I Grew Distracted"

This poem begins in rain and proceeds into light, indicating a journey from the unconscious into consciousness. Ilarregui shows how poetic creation takes place in the process of creating this poem. She evokes a scene of walking along a road, then simultaneously presents two variations of such a scene: an urban street or a rural Indian road. In the process of creation as Ilarregui experiences it, she joins images together, or superimposes one upon another. This doubling absorbs her psychic energy and she withdraws into her interior world, in a kind of *ensimismamiento* or engrossment or self-absorption where she is open to contradictory emotions and images. It allows her to combine images from distinct strata: the earth, the heavens, and time. The objects of Nature take on human characteristics: the stones sing like girls and they have eyes that look at her before they resume their usual aspect of "permanent" objects lying on the road, impervious to time's passing. She perceives a passing bird as an electric slingshot. Thus, she mixes spheres and crosses boundaries between categories to create similes and metaphors. She associates writing with giving birth, with dying, and with making love. These are the three most intense and universal of human experiences, occupying the beginning, the middle, and the end of life. Poetic creation necessitates the mind's constant movement and risk taking, for the poet may fail and produce, instead of living words, stillborn images. She also associates poetic creation with the forbidden or the taboo. This feeling recalls Freud's theory that artistic creation is a sublimation of sexual desire and Lacan's association of the Symbolic realm with the child's learning of language to express his desire for what is absent. Her goal is to create her own poetic medium: "my words, my time." Finally, she cannot be certain whether inspiration comes from within or is visited upon her from without by the sun. Ilarregui's textualization of self and nature can be seen where the road becomes the road of life and she equates "turning a page" with a change of scene. Forms become spaces into which she can pour her poetic insights.

"Conversaciones / Conversations

The quotation which opens this poem assumes the scene of a person interrogating an oracle; the relationship between the two depends on the sincerity of both. The quotation indicates that Ilarregui as poet perceives herself as an oracle and that she also perceives poetry as a conversation between writer and reader. The image of the buffalo dominates this poem where Ilarregui translates to an American context Aleixandre's evocation of the bull in his poem "Toro" where he presents the bull as the universe, the world, the sky, sea, time, and power. He uses the creature to symbolize his own desire to live on the edge of life's struggle ("sólo quiero los bordes de la lucha" / "I only want the edges of the struggle").[13] Aleixandre too began with the question of sincerity, questioning whether the bull is a false or a true symbol: "esa mentira o casta (that lie or thoroughbred)." Ilarregui associates the buffalo with burgeoning life, fertility, time, and power. She also conjoins the buffalo with Spring and its burgeoning growth and sexuality in the insect and plant worlds. Specifically she equates the buffalo with psychic growth and adapts it to a the literary context of creating poetry. The buffalo is "running in the page's meadow;" as growth "it spills out blue between words;" as night "it passes over the keys of

[13] Vicente Aleixandre, *Mis poemas mejores* (Madrid: Editorial Gredos, 1976), p. 63.

the typewriter." She increases the allusions to time, associating the buffalo with night and dawn, with the present and the future, and with her own time on earth. Ilarregui might be said to "feminize" Aleixandre's poem for she emphasizes the moon, seeds, flowers' petals (the more diminutive) as well as the domestic ambiance (houses and doors, persons, an old man).

This is an important poem in Ilarregui's quest for individuation because she combines the power of the unconscious, the power of the buffalo, with her encounter with the old man. For Jung the "Wise Old Man" figured "knowledge, reflection, insight, wisdom, cleverness, and intuition on the one hand, and on the other, moral qualities such as goodwill and readiness to help."[14] It is important to note that Ilarregui's textualization of life works in both directions. Just as authors of fiction might invent a character to fulfill the function of the "Wise Old Man," Ilarregui presents herself seeking out in life, who is to say whether imaginatively or actually, such a character, and finding him on the Big Cypress Indian Reservation. This poem shows the process through which Ilarregui moves from the person who seeks the oracle to the poet who becomes the oracle herself in relation to her readers. She has returned to her American roots in Indian culture and has incorporated the energy of the buffalo, the huge, primitive animal which once ruled the prairies.

Ilarregui draws on Diane Glancy in her images of the buffalo and of Indians originating in what is now the United States. In the preface to *Claiming Breath* Glancy writes: "I would say a pencil is a buffalo migration under the sky with its stars turning like a jar-lid poked with holes."[15] Ilarregui could identify with Glancy's self-description of being "in the middle ground between two cultures, not fully a part of either."[16] While Ilarregui adopts her Indian ancestors

---

[14] C. G. Jung, *The Archetypes and the Collective Unconscious*, translated by R. F. C. Hull, 2nd ed. (Princeton: Princeton U P, 1968), p. 217.

[15] Diane Glancy, *Claiming Breath* (Lincoln: U of Nebraska P, 1992), p. xiii.

[16] Glancy, p. xiii.

as part of her American heritage, Glancy, a professing Christian, actually is a descendant of native Americans; her father belonged to the Cherokee tribe and her mother was a white. Ilarregui lives between her native Argentina and the culture of the United States. Both women write metapoetry in which the process of literary creation becomes the central topic.

"Autumn Prayer"

The quotation at the beginning of the poem expresses the Indians' faith that their people will endure and their feeling of participation in nature as the youngest members of the animal kingdom. In her prayer Ilarregui shows that the prayer-like posture that one assumes in kneeling before a stream to take water into one's hands is the essence of the sacred. Jung associated water both with the unconscious and with purification and rebirth; he believed that rivers or streams symbolize "death and rebirth (baptism)" and "the flowing of time into eternity."[17] Ilarregui draws on these deep symbolic levels in her development of "Autumn Prayer." The Indian silently worships nature for its gifts of water and air. At the same time that he takes nature's gift, he recognizes himself, his own face, in the stream. Instead of falling in love with his own reflection as Narcissus did in the European myth, the Indian sees both himself and nature in the stream. He becomes aware that he is part of the continuum of nature and time. He recognizes the particularity of each thing--each is a fragment like the fallen leaf on the stream's surface. Yet he still maintains the belief that the fragments join together to form a whole. He is aware of the fugacity of time but as a member of a continuing race feels forever young. He participates in nature rather than becoming her exploiter or her manager. Ilarregui commemorates the purity of the Indian worldview in her poem.

---

[17] Wilfred L. Guerin, Earle Labor, Lee Morgan, Jeanne C. Reesman, and John R. Willingham, *A Handbook of Critical Approaches to Literature* (Oxford: Oxford UP, 1992), p. 150.

"Criar espejos / Breeding Mirrors"

In this poem Ilarregui expresses a conflict between the natural mirror of the preceding poem and the literary mirrors that her poems constitute. Her desire to create an autonomous world within her poetry, to develop her own vocabulary to express that unique worldview, is a product of the ever-increasing emphasis on individual as opposed to tribal consciousness. The mirror does not capture the entire person even though the person recognizes enough of himself in the mirror to be able to identify himself. Thus, she may recognize herself in the mirror of Indian culture, yet she is not satisfied that the culture gives a full picture of herself. People change psychologically, emotionally and physically to such a degree that it is a shock that they continue to recognize the few basic elements that form the "bone structure" of their ongoing identity.

Lévi-Strauss theorized that man can recognize himself in the myths of diverse cultures because of the underlying structures common to all myths. Ilarregui wishes to return to Indian myth as an underpinning to which all readers can respond, but she recognizes the difference between myth and poetry. Lévi-Strauss has identified the difference: "Myth should be placed in the gamut of linguistic expressions at the end opposite to that of poetry. . . . Poetry is a kind of speech which cannot be translated except at the cost of serious distortions; whereas the mythical value of the myth is preserved even through the worst translation."[18]

Ilarregui refers to rain as a word which has changed over time and in different cultures. She calls upon the associations of rain or water with the unconscious and fertility to show that where it once was perceived as a positive force, it may now be associated with sadness. She herself resurrects the old meaning but she combines it with fire, symbol of the intellect. Rain may wash away memory, but in doing so it leaves a space for new inventions and a return to origins. She also relates rain/water with cleansing and fertility. Associating her own psychic processes with water, she declares that her mind can "spill out" images, can grow a text. She will create her own texts to

---

[18] Claude Lévi-Strauss, *Structural Anthropology* (New York: Basic Books, 1963), p. 210.

mirror herself and her world; texts which constitute a world in themselves. This ambition is perhaps the polar opposite of the anonymous, oral tradition of Indian poetry and myth. Yet she wishes to reincarnate the Indian oracle at the same time that she writes as a modern poet.

"Retrato de una mujer con un mensaje / Portrait of a Woman with a Message"

In this poem Ilarregui draws the portraits of two women with messages--herself as a poet and a pregnant Indian woman. As she will create poems with a message for the world, so the Indian woman will give birth to a child who may be a leader of his tribe. The poet remembers her own infancy and the precariousness of new human life as a baby in a cradle. When she appeared to sleep, she was remembering her prenatal existence and the birth experience. "Nacer / to be born" is an active rather than a passive verb in Spanish. Ilarregui pictures birth as a process in which the baby takes the active role, breaking the waterbag. She views this water as the sacred liquid of cosmic knowledge. Here Ilarregui expresses the Jungian idea that the child is born with the archetypes of his tribe encoded in his psyche. As a fetus she could already foresee her role as poet who would describe in a new way the "blue orbit" of prenatal experience. The present poem is a fulfillment of that promise made to herself then. Ilarregui's perception that all children have such prenatal experience becomes apparent in her reaction to the pregnant Indian woman. Within the womb the Indian child is traveling through the cosmos, "an astronaut of his tribe."[19] Ilarregui evokes what Lacan called the Imaginary state where the child exists in undifferentiated unity with the mother. This poem celebrates woman and her maternity; she is the vehicle through whom innate knowledge passes during the period she serves as a cradle for the fetus and during the postbirth period when she brings the child to the threshold of language.

---

[19] See below (p. 46) in the discussion of the poem "Personas perdidas / Lost Persons," the initial poem of *Guia para perplejos / Guide for the Perplexed*, Ilarregui's development of the Romantic view of the child's innate ideas and her affinity with the mystics Saint John of the Cross and Saint Teresa of Ávila in ascribing to infants a knowledge of the unity of creation.

"Wisdomkeepers"

On the level of psychological development this poem shows the transition from Lacan's Imaginary to the Symbolic phase. As a child Ilarregui's mother told her that she must "lose something in order to be able to speak." In Lacanian psychology, the loss of the mother, of her constant answering every wish of the child, triggers the child's development of speech. He must learn to name the absent object, the object of his desire. The poem also celebrates mothers as "wisdomkeepers" in the later development of the child. Ilarregui begins with a quotation from Uncle Frank, an Indian spiritual leader who attributes his wisdom to his mother. His recognition triggers Ilarregui's remembrance of her own mother's wisdom, exemplified in her theory of sacrifice and compensation. Thus the poet makes explicit her association of Indian culture with her own mother--with the feminine, maternal element.

Ilarregui joins the exchange of a present blessing for a greater one hereafter, specifically, to the ability to speak with authority. Emptiness and loneliness, the withdrawal from others to investigate one's own psyche, make room for new knowledge. The person who turns in upon himself/herself like a sweater turned inside-out discovers new resources which have space to grow in the area now vacated by the lost item. Ilarregui declares that her mother also taught her the patience needed to await fruition, a lesson women may know more intimately than men because of the ties to pregnancy and birth.

In this poem Ilararegui once more joins images of light and rain. She associates light with words and rain with silence, paralleling the association with consciousness and unconsciousness. She returns to the image of fallen leaves lying on the patio. These leaves, in association with the beginning line of the stanza ("there is a time for each word") suggest the equivalence of words and leaves brought together in the image of the Cumaean Sibyl. Subsequently, she associates creating a literary text with an Indian woman weaving a cloth filled with "voices that surge forth as in stories." As she had concentrated on the loss of prenatal knowledge in the previous poem, here Ilarregui emphasizes the loss of ancestors. Beloved persons who have died must be recreated by memory. She also recalls the losses these ancestors experienced. As the Indian tribes lost their land in the Americas, so the European immigrant forebearers had to give up their native lands and cultures as they made a home in the new world. The compensation for these losses was to form new dreams with new generations.

The poem ends with a paraphrase of Ecclesiastes: "Todo tiene su momento, y cada cosa su tiempo bajo el cielo / To everything there is a season, and a time to every purpose under the heaven."[20] This Biblical verse, used in Jewish and Christian funeral rites, comes at the exact center of *Indian Journeys*. Thus Ilarregui shows the union of Indian and Judeo-Christian religious insight into the ultimate reality that we are born and must die, both the foolish and the wise person.

"Contando cuentos / Telling Stories"

Ilarregui repeats the joining of water and fire in the definition of happiness which unites a form of fire to *spilling* (i.e. water) "joyously over onto others." She celebrates the Indians' communal life where they maintain intimate connections to each other and to their ancestors in life and in death. Their oral traditions provide both "a personal and tribal identity" as Diane Glancy observed.[21] Youth shares its joys and sorrows with age in an easy fraternization between generations which gives all a feeling of being whole and intact. This mindset contrasts with the fractured and fragmented psyche of the urban person, the poet herself, as she appears in the first poem of this collection. The Indians remain sensitive not only to each other but to nature--from the plants to the planets.

Ilarregui exemplifies her interpretation with a scene she witnessed where a girl regaled her family with her experience as a

---

[20] Chapter 3, Verse 1 in Biblia de Jerusalén (Bilbao: Desclee de Brouwer, 1975), p. 902. The English version is cited from Holy Bible: King James Version (Boston: Pathfinder Publications, Inc., n.d. [1611 Version]), p. 287.

[21] *Claiming Breath*, p. 103.

deer. The child chose the grandmother, the storyteller, as recipient of her experience, but the entire family participated in her fantasy. In the Indian tribe women keep stories in their heads--in memory kept alive in the oral tradition. Ilarregui expresses herself through her hands--with pen, paper, and the computer--but she, like them, wishes to impose herself upon silence.

"Las cuentas de un collar / The Necklace's Beads"

Ilarregui conceives her necklace as a kind of rosary, each of whose beads contains one of her secrets. A mnemonic device for remembering her own past, the necklace also connects her to the universe for the beads resemble planetary material of the moon and the stars. Comparing the beads to cosmic polar bears, the poet makes the necklace a talisman of psychic power. The poet then recalls Indian necklaces with beads in forms of stars and animals. The necklace which she wears, perhaps a souvenir of her visit to an Indian tribe, connects her to that tribe and the Indian cosmological point of view. The circle of the necklace symbolizes the Indians' view of cyclical time; the self-sufficiency of each round bead, the silence of the universe. A flight of butterflies and the coming on of night bring the poet back to the awareness of life's ephemerality and the approach of death.

"Mis tristezas / My Sadnesses"

Fray Bernardino de Sahagún collected over one thousand folios of Indian myths and poetry in Náhuatl transcribed to Latin letters in the seventy years following his arrival in Mexico in 1529. He used this material to write in Spanish his *Historia general de las cosas de Nueva España (General History of the Things of New Spain).* Especially relevant to Ilarregui's poem are several presages that the Indians had observed before the arrival of Hernando Cortés. Among these were the following:

> "*Primer presagio funesto*: Diez años antes de venir los españoles primeramente se mostró un funesto presagio en el cielo. Una espiga de fuego, una como llama de fuego, una como aurora: se mostraba como si estuviera goteando, como si estuviera punzando en el cielo....

Segundo presagio funesto que sucedió aquí en México: por su propia cuenta se abrasó en llamas, se prendió en fuego: nadie tal vez le puso fuego, sino por su espontánea acción ardió la casa de Huitzilopochtli....

Tercer presagio funesto: Fue herido por un rayo un templo....

Cuarto presagio funesto: Cuando había aún sol, cayó un fuego.

Quinto presagio funesto: Hirvió el agua: el viento la hizo alborotarse hirviendo....

Sexto presagio funesto: Muchas veces se oía una mujer lloraba, iba gritando por la noche; andaba dando grandes gritos:

–¡Hijitos míos, pues ya tenemos que irnos lejos!

Y a veces decía

–¡Hijitos míos, ¿a dónde os llevaré?

Séptimo presagio funesto: Muchas veces se atrapaba, se cogía algo en redes....

Octavo presagio funesto: Muchas veces se mostraban a la gente hombres deformes, personas monstruosas....

(*First fatal omen*: Ten years before the Spaniards arrived firstly a fatal omen shown forth in the sky. A spike of fire, one like a flame of fire, one like dawn: it shown forth as if it were dripping, as if it were puncturing the sky....

Second fatal omen that happened here in Mexico. On its own account it burst into flames, it was set afire: nobody perhaps set it on fire, but by its spontaneous action the house of Huitzilopochtli burned....

Third fatal omen: A temple was damaged by a lightning bolt....

Fourth fatal omen: When the sun yet shown, a fire fell....

Fifth fatal omen: Water boiled: the wind stirred it up, making .. . ..

Sixth fatal omen: Many times it was heard: a woman was weeping; she was going about screaming through the night; she was walking about giving great cries:

–My children, well now we have to go far away!

And at times she would say:

–My children, where can I take you?

Seventh fatal omen: Many times something was trapped, something was caught within the nets....

Eighth fatal omen: Many times deformed men, monstruous persons showed themselves to the people.)"[22]

---

[22] "Los presagios, según los informantes de Sahagún" in *Literatura del México antiguo: Los textos en lengua náhuatl*, edited by Miguel León-Portilla (Caracas: Biblioteca Ayacucho, 1978), pp. 366-367.

These omens help explain Moctezuma's fatal passivity at the beginning of his interaction with the Spaniards.

In her poem Ilarregui calls upon the powerful resonance in the Latin American consciousness of the legend of La Llorona (The Weeping Woman) as she becomes a modern manifestation of that woman. The latter served as an oracle foretelling the conquest of her people. Ilarregui transfers the great anguish the Mexican people felt upon seeing and hearing the evil omens to her personal, twentieth-century situation. The union of fire and water, which she has used throughout *Indian Journeys,* reappears here, both in her poem and in her source. Here they have become signs of doom, presaging death. On the personal level fire and water have been transformed into the light of the lamp and the tears in her eyes. Her present angst is an echo heard from the shadows of the past. "Desparramadas / spilled out" has also taken on a sad connotation as the poet sees the items most intimately connected to her persona lying scattered on the bedclothes: albums, photos, bracelets, purses, poems. She has returned to the anguish and fragmentation of the first poem of *Indian Journeys*. This sadness is a response not only to death but to the extirpation of Indian cultures in the Americas.

"Pinturas indias / Indian Paintings"

This poem contrasts with the previous one in the poet's affirmation that art overcomes death and the impermanence of history in which each event occurs and then recedes into the distant past, eventually to pass into oblivion. The Indians made sand paintings to express and eternalize their individuality. The poet meditates on the anomaly that the medium itself--elemental sand which can be adapted to any purpose and which is swept by the tides--can be made into a permanent image. In the reference to the sea Ilarregui relies upon its archetypal association with death and the unconscious. Ironically, the image that the painter wishes to eternalize in the tribal memory is a flower, itself a symbol of ephemeral beauty. The poet recalls small things from a variety of classes, the human mixed with the animal and the plant. She wishes such things as flowers, seagulls, lips, bottles, oysters be remembered against the eternity of sea and sand. In the description of "the tribe of memory" Ilarregui recalls Jung's theory of archetypes existing in the collective unconscious and the idea that the individual recapitulates the history of the race in his or her psychic development.

"Vasija de tierra / Earthen Vessel"

Ilarregui continues to develop the theme of how art creates objects which make the present moment eternal. The artist's feelings are so encased in his object that future spectators will immediately recognize and comprehend them. Ilarregui depicts a scene where she is herself a spectator who views an earthen vessel in a museum. This vessel was created during the Aztec empire with its powerful emperors, busy markets, and avid cultivation of flowers. The vase was broken and reconstructed by art experts cognizant of preColumbian history. Ilarregui makes a delightful comparison of the vessel to a wizened old woman curious to see the excavations. Despite its present importance as a venerable art object, it was probably an ordinary vessel that children used to carry water. In this contrast of the children and the old woman with the unchanging vessel, Ilarregui illustrates the permanence of art in relation to human ephemerality. Since fire has been used to create the earthen vessel that holds water, the reader can perceive once again the union of symbols of the conscious and the unconscious in the art object.

"De cómo perdimos las estrellas / About How We Lost the Stars"

The opening quotation from Louis Farmer contrasts the horizontal organization of technological man's communication--around the earth--with the vertical organization of the Indians' communication from the earth to the heavens, from man to the gods. Ilarregui suggests that time itself feels shame for the process through which one culture replaces another: the windows' shamefaced blush suggests the blood of battle. The poet identifies more with the religious values of the conquered Indian tribes than with secular modern values in her resolution to become a morally, physically, and emotionally stronger person and a better-integrated one. In her affirmation that the future holds promise, the poet paradoxically equates going forward with a return to the earlier Indian mindset. She feels that in the present people depend upon signs supplied by their technological culture; they exchange birds' wings for those of insects capable of occupying and seeing only a small part of a house rather than the universe entire.

"Indian Nations/partes de mí / Indian Nations/Parts of Myself"

The poet's admiration for Indian perception is evident in her association of the Indian festival with eagles. These birds of keenest perception are symbols of power as the highest-ranking animals within their family. She implicitly contrasts the birds' soaring spirit, with which the Indians are identified, with the Indians' being on foot. Their lack of technological progress has enabled them to keep a more intimate contact with the body and with the earth on which their feet dance. They celebrate their participation in the cosmos and with other animals by wearing birdfeathers on their foreheads, a symbol of the flight of their intelligence to higher spiritual realms. Ilarregui suggests that they also have a more intimate bond with the past in their cyclical view of history as opposed to the modern European view of linear history. The Indians believe they are children of the Creator who will bless them as he does other parts of Creation in the plant and animal kingdoms. They feel part of an integrated continuum from the flower, to the butterfly, to the person, to the universe, to the Creator. In the title of this poem Ilarregui explicitly states her belief in the Jungian theory of cultural recapitulation within each individual[23] in her perception of the Indians as her American ancestors, members of the mother culture.

---

[23] Jung states that people are subject to dreams of two types: personal and collective. The second type contains "peculiarly mythological, legendary, or generally archaic imagery. One must turn to historical or primitive symbology in order to explain such dreams." He goes on to state that these dreams tend to appear "from the third to the sixth year; at puberty, from fourteen to sixteen; in the period of maturity from twenty to twenty-five; in middle life from thirty-five to forty; and before death." In "On the Psychogenesis of Schizophrenia," *The Psychology of Dementia Praecox*, translated by R. F. C. Hull (Princeton: Princeton UP, 1974), p. 164.

"Calendarios / Calendars"

Again Ilarregui contrasts the Indian mythic sensibility with her own scientific sensibility. While the Indians held a cyclical view of time,[24] Europeans had a linear concept. The poet reviews the cycle of the seasons, a cycle that modern man still relates to, as a metaphor for periods in an individual's life and in that of cultures. She then imposes this annual cycle upon the whole of human history. She does not make it a cyclical sequence to be repeated every 50 or 100 or 1000 years, but a purely linear pattern. There will be only one spring, one summer, one fall, one winter for the human race before it becomes extinct.

Ilarregui perceives herself as being born in the autumn of the human race, near the end of its tenure on earth. The race has only the winter to anticipate. For Ilarregui this will be a sad period where the buffalo--symbol of creative power emanating from the unconscious--becomes an "afligido / afflicted" animal, which no longer has a place in the scheme of life. She laments the loss that the linear point of view heralds for the human psyche.

Once again Ilarregui turns to art as the means of redemption for the human race. She can relate to the Indians' wall painting from long ago as if it were a picture of herself. In Spanish the line "si yo hubiera nacido / dentro de mucho tiempo (if I had been born / encircled by a long time)" is ambiguous. It seems to refer to the past as though the poet herself were the subject of the ancient Indian wall painting, but it could also refer to the future. The poet then affirms her faith in poetry which can recapture the Indians' mythical perspective and keep it alive in the present like "un eco en la garganta / cósmica de una pradera (an echo in the cosmic / throat of a meadow)." The

---

[24] The best example of the Indian view of cyclical time can be seen in the Aztec calendar round: "The most important unit of time was a 52-year period, sometimes called the 'Calendar Round', which was arrived at by intermeshing the 260-day Almanac Year with the 365-day Solar one. Each of these cycles repeated itself endlessly throughout time, and any given day could therefore be expressed in terms of two quite different calendars....The year when Cortés landed in Mexico (1519 by our system) was 1 Reed in Aztec terminology. In other words, New Year's Day (Day 1 of the first month in the Solar Year) fell on the day 1 Reed of the Almanac Year, a combination which would not recur until 52 years had passed." In Warwick Bray, *Everyday Life of the Aztecs* (New York: Dorset Press, 1968), p. 168.

image of the throat of the meadow, a metonomy for the earth, at once frightens the reader in its devouring aspect and comforts him/her in its sound-producing aspect. The image portends the earth consuming humanity as the final devourer, a phenomenon we are all subject to individually. Yet the image also shows the earth reflecting the human psyche in the poet's return to the "pathetic fallacy." Affirming the continuance of the Indian or mythic point of view in poetry, Ilarregui perceives herself as inheritor of the mantle of the Indian oracle, another manifestation of the Cumaean Sibyl. Through her ongoing connection to the mythic past and the powerful archetypes of the unconscious, she can bring herself and her reader psychic wholeness.

Thus, Ilarregui completes her pilgrimage to the North American Indian tribes from Alaska to Mexico. As Neruda visited Machu Picchu to search out the roots of American culture, she has turned to the descendants of the original Americans to learn the myths and secrets of these lands.

BOOK II:
OFICIOS Y PERSONAS / ROLES AND PERSONS

This book begins as did *Indian Journeys* with the poet closed off to the world and herself, throwing herself against closed doors, which may briefly open to the outer world and to the inner.

"Poco a poco"/ "Little by Little"

The circular poem "Little by Little," which initiates the section "Roles and Persons" begins and ends with the lines: "from the heart beating so hard against the doors of oneself / a crack opens where a light says: *I was expecting you*." The light precipitates an epiphany where the poet perceives the union of a Surreal conglomeration of seemingly disparate things: "and rays of dead sunlight filter down, caressing things that we lose / splinters encrusted on tables and plates / the floor papered with one's little pieces: steps or gestures / worn out shoes and the eye of three-month old cats." These things trigger memory and allow the union of a moment from the past with the present over the divides of time and space. The self itself is shattered, broken up into fragments, "little pieces (pedacitos)" reflected in the paraphernalia of the things one collects. Like the leaves of the Cumaean Sibyl, the "little pieces" of the self contain messages waiting to be deciphered. As we grow older, "we are less certain in the world;" doubts increase as we confront "sparks of perplexity." We perform ritual actions, like putting the same tablecloth on the table, dream of our younger selves, and believe that our experience carries the sacred secret of the future. "A life is a life is a life," declares the poet, recalling Gertrude Stein's declaration of the final enigma of life in "A rose is a rose is a rose is a rose."

"Fragmentos del futuro" / "Fragments of the Future"

In "Fragments of the Future" the prophetic powers of the Cumaean Sibyl are again recalled as the poet seeks to decipher the future while her palm is being read. The fortune-teller's prophecy constitutes the poem. Although the fortune-teller is usually perceived as a modern, degraded form of the Cumaean Sibyl, Ilarregui's fortune-teller speaks in the poet's own language and shows a deeply intuitive understanding of nature. As Ilarregui had depicted sympathetically the Indian oracles--male and female--here she presents the fortune-teller as someone with real access to the future and real comprehension of her client. The poet evokes the tactile presence of the four elements as she speaks of

> the marine wind entangled in the birds' feathers
> the force of rocks that don't tremble when the wind passes
> the wind that runs toward an ocean of wet stars
> this time, someone will bring you fresh things.

Air and water--the ocean wind; earth--the force of indomitable rock; fire--the humid stars and, later, the burning moon. Like Virgil, Ilarregui emphasizes rock and marine wind as elements especially congenial to the poet/sibyl. Virgil located the Cumaean Sibyl "deep in her cave of rock" among "the sacred lakes, the loud wood of Avernus" (*Aeneid*, Book III, lines 577-579). Like Dante, Ilarregui awaits an epiphany that will release the significance of world and self, "crossing the solitude of your words." Dante requested divine inspiration that his word be: "One single spark of all Thy glory's light / For future generations to discern" (*Divine Comedy [Paradise]*, Canto 33, lines 71-72).

Echoes of more modern poets also infiltrate "Fragments of the Future." The poem recalls the Neruda of "Barcarola" in its lists of things piled upon one another:

> Si solamente me tocaras el corazón
> . . .
> Sonaría con un ruido oscuro, con sonido de ruedas de tren
> con sueño,
> como aguas vacilantes,
> como el otoño en hojas,
> como sangre,
> con un ruido de llamas húmedas quemando el cielo,
> soñando como sueños o ramas o lluvias,
> o bocinas de puerto triste [25]

[25] Pablo Neruda, *Residencia en la tierra (1925-1935)* (Buenos Aires: Editorial Losada, S.A., 1958), p. 78.

(If you would only touch my heart,
. . .
It would sound with an obscure noise, with the noise of train wheels

with dream,
with vacillating waters
with the autumn in leaf
with blood,
with a noise of humid flames burning the sky,
sounding like dreams or branches or rains,
or foghorns from a sad port).

The poem echoes Octavio Paz in the stress on the four elements, fragmentation, secrets, and the Sibyl's search for the key to understanding. In "Virgen / Virgin" from "A la orilla del mundo / At the Shore of the World" he writes:

Rocas y mar. El sol envejecido
quema las piedras que la mar amarga.
Cielo de piedra. Mar de piedra. Nadie.
. . .
Sobre la alfombra junta las figuras
de su rompecabezas infinito.
Y siempre falta una, sólo una,
y nadie sabe dónde está, secreta.
. . .
Está enterrada al pie del árbol. ¿Quién?
La llave, la palabra, la sortija ...

(Rocks and the sea. The sun in its old age
burns up the rocks embittered by the sea.
Sky of stone. Sea of Stone. No one.
. . .
On this carpet, she joins the figures of
an infinite puzzle of dismemberment.
And always one missing, always only one,
and no one knows where this one can be hidden.
. . .
Buried deep at the foot of the tree. Who is?
The one key, the one word, the ring ...[26]

---

[26] *Selected Poems of Octavio Paz: A Bilingual Edition with Translations by Muriel Rukeyser* (Bloomington: Indiana U P, 1963), pp. 106-107.

Luis Sáinz de Medrano points out that in "¿Águila o sol? / Eagle or Sun?", the fourth part of *Libertad bajo palabra / Liberty Under Word,* Paz endeavored to decipher the world, "un vasto sistema de señales, una conversación entre seres inmensas / a vast system of signs, a conversation between immense beings."[27] He sought to find the word of which he constituted a syllable, its speaker and its recipient. Ilarregui continues this textualization of the world and the self.

The poem too has something of the aura of Federico García Lorca's poetry: Ilarregui's depiction of the moon recalls "Romance de la luna, luna / Ballad of the moon, moon," while her insistence on the powerful wind brings "Preciosa y el aire / Preciosa and the Wind" to mind. Most evocative is Ilarregui's "newborn fish," an image Lorca used in "San Rafael / Saint Raphael"

> Un solo pez en el agua
> que a los dos Córdobas junta[28]
>
> (Only one fish in the water
> that joins the two Cordobas).

Lorca used the image of the fish again in "Romance sonámbulo / Sonambulant Ballad", where the fish appears in conjunction with dawn as in Ilarregui's poem:

> Verde que te quiero verde.
> Grandes estrellas de escarcha,
> vienen con el pez de sombra
> que abre el camino del alba.[29]
>
> (Green that I want you green.

---

[27] Luis Sáinz de Medrano, *Historia de la literatura hispanoamericana (Desde el Modernismo)* (Madrid: Taurus, 1989), p. 529.

[28] *Romancero gitano* in *Obras completas,* Edited by Arturo del Hoyo (Madrid: Aguilar, 1988), I: 413.

[29] *Ibid.*, I: 400.

Great stars of frost,
they come with the fish of shadow
that opens the door of dawn.)

Ilarregui has transposed the fish and the man that Lorca described in "Canción inútil / Useless Song" to "newborn fish" and "children that breath." Lorca wrote:

Hombre y pez en sus medios,
        bajo cosas flotantes,
esperando en el alga o en la
        silla su noche.[30]

(Man and fish in their environments
        beneath floating things
awaiting in the algae or in the
        chair their night.)

Ilarregui evokes the wonder of newborn things--the placenta, fish under water, the phases of the moon; the birth prefigured is that of the poem itself and of the poet who travels towards the dawn whose arms are outstretched in maternal embrace.

"Fotos viejas / Old Photos"

In "Old Photos," the third poem of *Roles and Persons*, Ilarregui depicts a scene in which a woman is cutting up and rearranging photographs while a scissors-sharpener walks by, whistling, beneath her window. The particular circumstance of a woman, obviously moved by anger and despair to destroy her mementos, has universal implications. The situations of the female and the male in this poem suggest the classic scene of the woman waiting on the balcony while the knight passes on the street below. The woman is confined to the house and spends her time waiting for the male and thinking about her relationship with him. The male engages in work outside the home (sharpening scissors) and happily pursues his course, oblivious to her suffering and free of dependence upon emotional ties. He is full of potential or the power to affect her life; in

---

[30] *Canciones para terminar* in *Obras completas* I: 385.

other poems Ilarregui will also describe leaves of trees ("Corte de pelo / Haircut," final poem of *Roles and Persons*) and the words of her poetry ("Época / Epoch" in *Guide for the Perplexed*) as full of "potencias" / "power-potential." Symbolically his freedom and indifference serve to sharpen the instrument, the mind, which he can use "to divide, to cut, to injure, to organize in another way, / the puzzle of lines that climb and go down, little pieces of herself." The photos are a modern equivalent of the Cumaean Sibyl's leaves: they contain images of the past which one carries into the future, and they can be dispersed, rearranged, and even cut up and destroyed in this image of the woman's fragmented mind. The poet combines the offices of the female and the male, of the subjective and the objective, for her emotional experience provides the raw material from which she, as poet, selects particular images which she heightens with the sharpness of a mind constantly filed by the craft of the poet's language--images, metaphors, rhythm, and other poetic devices. The modernity of the poem stems from the fact that the woman has taken it upon herself to reorganize her own psychic history rather than to accept a male's interpretation of that history. Ilarregui uses the word "pájaras" as a metaphor for scissors which resemble "paper birds" kept in a box. The word also means "crafty female," thus reinforcing the image of the Cumaean Sibyl. Finally the word "pájara" may refer to the female partridge or to a child's kite. From these diverse meanings I have selected "paper rooster" and the genderless "bird" in the poem's translation because the scissors' blades resemble birds' beaks: "beaks that jabber in silence, or go to sleep sealess."

"Transparencias / Transparencies"

Ilarregui opens "Transparencies" with a quotation from *Yo el supremo / I, the Supreme*, novel (1974) of the Paraguayan Augusto Roa Bastos,[31] to the effect of inventing a language in which there is no

---

[31] (Mexico, Madrid, Buenos Aires: Siglo Veintiuno de España Editores, 1976), p. 66. El Supremo finishes his lecture on writing with these words: "Olvida tu memoria. Escribir no significa convertir lo real en palabras sino hacer que la palabra sea real. Lo irreal sólo está en el mal uso de la palabra en el mal uso de la escritura" / "Forget your memory. Writing does not signify converting the real into words but rather making the word be real. The unreal is only in

distance between sign and signified, word and thing. Striving to restore language to a primal purity in which an innate relationship obtains between sign and signified defines the poet's office. Juan Ramón Jiménez sought to realize this goal as he explained in "Seré yo solo / I Shall Be Alone":

> Una exacta palabra
> Es toda la palabra. Todo velo
> Cubre un secreto solo.
>
> Si cojo todo el cielo,
> Aunque todos lo cojan, seré apolo
> yo solo.[32]
>
> (One exact word
> Is the word entire. Each veil
> Covers only one secret.
>
> If I capture the sky entire,
> Although others may capture it, I shall be Apolo
> I alone.)

This goal motivated Dante and Virgil as much as Neruda and Gabriela Mistral. There are echoes of both these Chilean poets in Ilarregui's poem. The water imagery especially recalls Neruda's "Arte poética / Poetic Art":

> *Entre sombra y espacio, entre guarniciones y doncellas,*
> *dotado de corazón singular y sueños funestos,*
> *precipitadamente pálido, marchito en la frente*
> *y con luto de viudo furioso por cada día de vida,*
> *ay, para cada agua invisible que bebo soñolientamente*
> *y de todo sonido que acojo temblando,*
> *tengo la misma sed ausente y la misma fiebre fría,*
> *un oído que nace, una angustia indirecta,*
> *como si llegaran ladrones o fantasmas,*
> *y en una cáscara de extensión fija y profunda,*
> *como un camarero humillado, como una campana un poco ronca*

---

the bad use of the word in the bad use of writing" (p. 67).

[32] *Selección de poemas*, Edited by Gilbert Azam (Madrid: Editorial Castalia, 1987), p. 207.

como un espejo viejo, como un olor de casa sola
en la que los huéspedes entran de noche perdidamente ebrios,
y hay un olor de ropa tirada al suelo, y una ausencia de flores,
--posiblemente de otro modo aún menos melancólico--,
pero, la verdad, de pronto, el viento que azota mi pecho,
las noches de substancia infinita caídas en mi dormitorio,
el ruido de un día que arde con sacrificio
me piden lo profético que hay en mí, con melancolía,
y un golpe de objetos que llaman sin ser respondidos
hay, y un movimiento sin tregua, y un nombre confuso.

(Between shadow and space, between garrisons and damsels,
endowed with singular heart and sorrowful dreams,
Suddenly pale, withered in the forehead
And with the widower's weeds for each day of life,
Oh, for each invisible water that I drink dreamily
And of each sound that I catch trembling,
I have the same absent thirst and the same cold fever,
An ear that is born, an indirect pain
As if thieves or ghosts were arriving,
And in a shell of fixed and deep extension,
Like a humiliated waiter, like a bell a little hoarse,
Like an old mirror, like a smell of a lonely house
In which the guests enter at night hopelessly drunk,
And there is a smell of clothes thrown on the floor, and an absence of flowers,
--possibly in another way even less melancholy--,
But, the truth, all of a sudden, the wind that whips my breast,
The nights of infinite substance fallen in my bedroom,
The noise of a day that burns with sacrifice
Ask me for the phophetic that there is in me, with melancholy,
And there is a blow of objects that call without being answered
And a movement without respite, and a confused name.

While the Chilean poet evokes the melancholy frustrations of a shoddy ambiance (the humiliated waiter who awaits the orders of imperious clients, the flophouse with its drunken inhabitants, the scent of dirty clothes thrown on the floor) and speaks of "*cada agua invisible / each invisible water*" and "*sed ausente / absent thirst,*" Ilarregui evokes a genteel atmosphere of the poet typing her poems as she looks through the window upon a rainy winter day filled with day-soaked birds and solitary pedestrians and bicyclists. Like Jiménez, both Neruda and Ilarregui perceive the poet as one who gathers together images and memories. Neruda speaks "*de todo sonido que acojo temblando / of each sound that I gather trembling."*[33] Ilarregui uses variations of the verb "recoger / to collect" four times: the typewriter keys "collect parts of old windows;" the mirror (Neruda too used the image of *"un espejo viejo / an old mirror"* in his poem) possibly "collects your face" as it also collects nature (in the window / the fresh surface of a winter's day") and the poet's interior reality ("may collect also / this way of saying from within, secretly)." Finally Ilarregui makes the act of gathering together an explicit element of the poetic office: texts emerge from the typewriter, "key by key, hour by hour, / may make producing poetry a transparent job, as if one / might go to collect something: water in open hands, the lustre / of hidden desires." Ilarregui emphasizes the secrecy of the world and of desires, as well as of the words that briefly break the silence; Neruda emphasizes more the world of dream and night from which "un nombre confuso / a confused name" finally emerges.

Clarity, confidence, tranquillity, exactness characterize Ilarregui's poem, though it emerges with the clarity of rain rather than of sun, while uncertainty, amorphousness, confused consciousness, and a sudden violent insight emerge from Neruda's description of the poet's struggle towards expression. Most surprizing in Ilarregui's poem is the assimiliation of technology, the typewriter and the computer, into the intimate act of writing poetry; technology does not alienate, but rather enhances the creative process.

Ilarregui's calm tone more closely approximates that of Jiménez in "Seré yo solo / I Shall Be Alone" (see above). However, in his Modernist poem Jiménez underscores his own role in the creative process; he insists on "yo solo" both in the poem's title and in its concluding line. In this, he followed Vicente Huidobro, who also insisted that the poet was "un pequeño Dios / a small God," who creates all things by seeing them. Huidobro opened his "Arte poética" with images to which Ilarregui frequently recurs:

> Que el verso sea como una llave
> Que abra mil puertas.

Neruda, *Residencia*, p. 39.

Una hoja cae; algo pasa volando;[34]

(Let the verse be like a key
That opens a thousand doors,
A leaf falls; something passes by flying.)

The legislative tone of Huidobro's poem, like the self-affirmative one of Jiménez, could not be further removed from Ilarregui's self-evasive tone. Ilarregui puts the creative process itself into the center and, like Jiménez, she emphasizes the secrecy of that process. She goes further than Huidobro, Neruda or Jiménez in the return to silence. Unlike these male poets, who speak in the first person, she speaks in the third person, from the periphery, describing herself from a distance. Only in the third stanza does she slide into the first person, and then it is to address her reader, to whom she speaks in the intimate *tú* form. Thus, she seems to place her reader, more than herself, in the center.

While Huidobro emphasizes invention, for Jiménez, Neruda, and Ilarregui the "collecting" of concrete images defines the poetic method. As Huidobro stressed brain over brawn ("El vigor verdadero / Reside en la cabeza" ["True vigor / Resides in the head"]), Jiménez identifies himself with Apollo, symbol of the light of reason and clear communication. Both Ilarregui's emphasis on the means of recording her poetry as well as her confidence in an everpresent inspiration of which she is merely the vehicle of communication align her with the image of the poet as Cumaean Sibyl. Neruda's images align him with the Bacchic poet subject to emotions, thoughts and an inspiration visiting him intermittently from without and with which he struggles desperately. The Post Modern poet, in the office in her house, looking out through windows and doors, as she types her poems on computer sheets becomes the contemporary reincarnation of the Cumaean Sibyl writing her messages on leaves.

Identifying with Christ, Gabriela Mistral carried the idea of the suffering poet further than Neruda as she wrote emotionally

[34] The poem is from *El espejo de agua*, 1916; Reprinted in *Huellas de las literaturas hispanoamericanas*, edited by Garganigo et.al. (Upper Saddle River, N.J.: Prentice Hall, 1997), p. 421.

intense poems which leave little room between the poet and her subject, nor between the poet and her reader. Taylor has studied Mistral's development of the Veronica motif in "Mis libros" and "Nocturno" where the poet declared: "Yo en mis versos el rostro con sangre / como tú sobre el paño, le di." As Taylor points out, Mistral perceived suffering, "the essence of life," as suffering for Christ, and transformed "el drama de Cristo y el sacrificio en inspiración poética."[35] Ilarregui sometimes associates herself with Christ. As a critically ill child, she experienced the crucifixion of lying flat on the bed with her arms, connected to life-support systems, extended in the poem "La edad de las muñecas / The Age of Dolls." In adulthood she experiences the fear of breaking apart in "Si me rompo / If I Break." (Both poems are from *Guía para perplejos / Guide for the Perplexed.*) More typically Ilarregui moves to the opposite end of this emotional trajectory; more often she echoes the cool distance of Jiménez as well as his pursuit of tranquillity and pristine clarity in her poetry.

Yet one line of "Transparencies" recalls a line from Mistral's "Recado para la 'Residencia de Pedralbes' en Cataluña / Message for the 'Pedralbes Residence' in Catalonia." As she records poetry's ability to evoke the residences of the past, people receding into the distance on a lonely street, Ilarregui observes: "un tocar puertas y ventanas que se despiden / a touching of doors and windows that bid farewell." She attributes to the doors and windows the human characteristic of leave-taking, while it is actually the people who take leave of them. In her poem Mistral recorded her sensations upon visiting the orphanage for Basque orphans of the Spanish Civil War in Catalonia. She speaks of her journeys with their restless nights spent in houses that did not belong to her, nights that sharpened her body. However, she wishes to leave her imprint upon those houses as she continues on:

> Pulpa de sombra de la casa

---

[35] Martin C. Taylor, *Sensibilidad religiosa de Gabriela Mistral* (Madrid: Editorial Gredos, 1975), p. 222.

tome mi máscara en carne viva.
La pasión mía me recuerden,
la espalda mía me la sigan.[36]

(Pulp of the house's shadow
take my mask in living flesh.
May they remember my passion,
May they follow behind me.)

Then, emphasizing her assimiliation to Christ, Mistral refers to herself as a "wounded deer," traditional image of Christ, and declares her desire that her image be imprinted on the house as the image of Christ's face was imprinted on Veronica's veil:

Pene en los largos corredores
un caminar de cierva herida,
y la oración, que es la Verónica,
tenga mi faz cuando la digan.

(May the walking of a wounded deer
grieve in the long corridors
and the prayer, that is called the Veronica,
have my face when they say it.)

After these injunctions, Mistral leaves the house, touching the stairway and kissing the door as she confronts her solitary anguish:

¡Volteo el ámbito que dejo,
miento el techo que me tenía,
marco escalera, beso puerta
y doy la cara a mi agonía!

(I turn above the limits that I leave behind,
I give the lie to the roof that held me
I mark the staircase, I kiss the door
and I turn my face to my agony.)

Both Ilarregui and Mistral evoke the reluctance of leavetaking and the sensuous stroking of that abode that at least briefly has provided refuge from the world. Both also record the projection of oneself into

---

[36] Penultimate poem of *Tala* (Buenos Aires: Editorial Losada, S.A., 1946), p.143.

one's surrounding, the becoming a part of the things that one touches daily. The caresses that women lavish not only on people but on beloved objects of the home will emerge again in Ilarregui's poetry where she will speak of "touching" doors and windows. That it is not a characteristic only of women can be seen in Neruda's loving lists of things from vegetables to mechanical objects in his poetry and his collections of things from ships' masts to books in Isla Negra. Doors, windows and locks also appear in quotations from René Char and Thomas Tranströmer, which Ilarregui uses to preface other poems.

The house with its windows and doors is an ancient symbol both for the body and the mind. Santa Teresa de Jesús used it in *Las moradas*, San Juan de la Cruz in his famous lyric poems, "Noche oscura, and the "Cántico espiritual." In the Christian tradition it can be traced back to Christ's declarations:

> I am the door: by me if any man enter in, he shall be saved, and shall go in and out, and find pasture / Yo soy la puerta: si uno entra por mí, estará a salvo; entrará y saldrá y encontrará pasto. (Book of John ch.10, v. 9)
>
> Behold, I stand at the door, and knock: if any man hear my voice, and open the door, I will come in to him, and will sup with him, and he with me. / Mira que estoy a la puerta y llamo; si alguno oye mi voz y me abre la puerta, entraré en su casa y cenaré con él y él conmigo (Revelations [Apocalipsis] Ch. 3, v. 20).

Ilarregui has moved farther than Mistral into a purely secular, philosophical rather than religious, use of this image. The realization that each of us exists on the periphery and hence has equal right to place himself/herself at the center is characteristic of the Post Modern ethos. Finding only her own creative process, rather than that of Christ (Santa Teresa) or of herself as Christ (Mistral), confirms Ilarregui's "anthropormorphic" Post Modern experience.[37]

---

[37] Four essays appearing in *Postmodernism: A Reader*, edited by Thomas Docherty (New York: Columbia UP, 1993), concur on the "decenterment" typical of Post Modernism. Ihab Hassan associates Post Modern indetermanacies with "ambiguity, discontinuity, heterodoxy, pluralism, randomness, revolt, perversion, deformation ... decreation, disintegration, deconstruction, decenterment" (p. 153). Charles Jencks, defining Post Modern Classicism in art and architecture, identifies eleven characteristics: disharmonious harmony, pluralism, urbane urbanism, anthropomorphism, anamnesis (suggested recollection), radical eclecticism, double-

"Verano, verano / Summer, Summer"

Like "Fragments of the future" and "Old Photos," "Summer, Summer" recreates a situation. The repetition of the word "summer" serves to bring the season more immediately to the reader's consciousness. Ilarregui uses the refrain of the passing of the lawnmower to evoke the brilliance of a sunlit day where birds, flowers, grass, insects and man are all penetrated by light and insect wings gleam in the water cast by a lawnsprinkler. The fragmentation that figures so prominently in Ilarregui's poetry here is associated with sunlight: "the sun: an electric spurt that crosses the cranium, / summer fractured with light, full of splinters, passes." The verbal effect of this sunlight recalls the visual effect of pointillist painting of the French impressionist Camille Pissaro and the American Postimpressionist Maurice Prendergast. The blazing light becomes associated with the blazing noise of the lawnmower reverberating in the brain. Fragmentation of light, sound, shadow, and water reflects fragmentation of mind which observes all the organic and inorganic elements of the scene, each distinctly and each as a part of the composition.

"La cara en el espejo / The Face in the Mirror"

In "The Face in the Mirror" Ilarregui works with reflections of faces, hers and those of passersby in the street whose images are reflected in her own face as well as in shopwindow mirrors. The images are refracted through time and space as well as through

---

coding (use of irony, ambiguity, and contradiction), multivalence (inclusive and resonant), tradition reinterpreted, new rhetorical figures (including eclectic quotation), and return to the absent center. Simon During characterizes "post Modern thought ... as that thought which refuses to turn the Other into the Same. Thus it provides a space for what postmodernity denies: otherness. Postmodern thought also recognizes, however, that the Other can never speak for itself as the Other" (p. 449). Nelly Richard points out that Latin Americans have traditionally defined themselves from the periphery as "other" in relation to the European tradition of Modernism with its dependence on rationalization and progress and the concommitant expansion of multinational capitalism and Western patriarchal culture. Richard contends that the Latin American recognition of multiple origins was a kind of Post Modernism "avant la lettre" because of the concurrent recognition of fragmentation and dispersion.

generations--the child, the adult. Isolated moments spring to mind: the fleeting image of yesterday's face in a secret landscape, a child running towards night, the future cry of the newborn who, after much pushing, finally emerges into someone's arms. The particular frame of the mirror impresses itself upon the mind as much as the faces reflected therein. In this poem the reader sees Ilarregui exemplifying the credo of the poet as sibyl in the capturing of isolated, seemingly unrelated images out of which she seeks to restore a pattern.

The particular pattern Ilarregui develops here is the Lacanian concept of the mirror image. Lacan identified the crucial psychic moment as that in which the child looks into the mirror and recognizes himself as himself, a discrete human being. The mirror may not be an actual mirror but the concept of himself that the child sees enacted upon him by his parents and other nurturing figures in his environment.[38] As an autobiographical poet Ilarregui searches back through time for her earliest memory, which she identifies here with birth and which in her earlier work *Indian Journeys* she identifies with a Jungian racial or archetypical memory of ancient tribal life. In the nightmare world Ilarregui evokes in this poem with her image of the child "that runs till he touches / the night's humidity" Ilarregui evokes the child's desire to return to the Imaginary where he or she enjoyed a pre-Oedipal identity with the mother, where the radical fissure between self and other had not yet been established. Her reference to the child and the infant not as herself but as someone else confirms the Imaginary stage before the fissure which pushes the child into sexuality, into the definition of self, into the Symbolic sphere and the use of language. Of this nightmare world Juliet Mitchell observes:

> Lacan's human subject is not a 'divided self' (Laing) that in a different society could be made whole, but a self which is only actually and necessarily created within a split--a being that can only conceptualise itself when it is mirrored back to itself from the position of another's desire. The unconscious where the subject is not itself, where the 'I' of a dream can be someone else and the object and

---

[38] See Jacques Lacan, "Le stade du miroir comme formateur de la fonction du Je," (1936) in *Ecrits* (Paris: Seuil, 1966), pp. 93-100; *Ecrits: A Selection*, translated by Alan Sheridan (London: Tavistock, 1977), pp. 1-7.

subject shift and change places, bears perpetual witness to this primordial splitting.[39]

The shifting perceptions of the self in Ilarregui's poem accord with Lacan's concept of the "I" as a 'shifting' pronoun. Jacqueline Rose explains:

> The 'I' with which we speak stands for our identity as subjects in language, but it is the least stable entity in language, since its meaning is purely a function of the moment of utterance. The 'I' can shift, and change places, because it only ever refers to whoever happens to be using it at the time.[40]

Thus, Ilarregui's poem captures both the Imaginary, with its portrayal of the desire to return to prenatal origins, and the Symbolic, with the adult's awareness of the reflection of one's own face through multiple mirrors in time and space.

"Nuevas lentes / New Lenses"

In the three remaining poems of *Roles and Persons* Ilarregui completes the transition from fragmentation to perspectivism which is initiated by "The Face in the Mirror" with its theme of the poet seeing herself, her own face, in those of others. She spoke there of the looks of others with their memory-filled eyes and expressed her desire "to travel with the eyes, to get wet / from that image of yesterday that smiled in the interior / of a secret passage." The poet wishes to enter into another person's psyche, to travel within another mind, to add another perspective to her own.

"New Lenses" opens with a quotation from Italo Calvino's *Invisible Cities*[41] in which Marco declares that traveling makes one discover what he does not possess: it reveals one's own ignorance. Calvino, who was born in Cuba in 1923 and who died in Siena, Italy in 1985, gained fame through his use of playful fantasy and shifting

---

[39] "Introduction–I" in *Feminine Sexuality: Jacques Lacan and the école freudienne*, edited by Juliet Mitchell and Jacqueline Rose (New York: W.W. Norton & Company), 1982, p. 5.

[40] "Introduction II" in *Feminine Sexuality*, p. 31.

[41] Translated by William Weaver (New York: Harcourt, Brace, Jovanovich, 1972), p. 29.

perspectives to comment on coincidence and change. In her poem Ilarregui too joins the most disparate things: (1) from the natural world "the revolutions of waves and of birds" and the light shining on the water and the rocks, underwater stars; (2) from the human world she recreates scenes of a woman threading a needle to darn socks, and of an optician supplying lenses which bring distant objects up close--from oysters in the seabottom to shell buttons on a blouse, to the distant planets--or even bring forward objects of former time--ruins of former civilizations. The fragmented images are brought together to suggest that they form a pattern if one can but gain the proper perspective. Through her poetry Ilarregui endeavors to give the reader that new perspective, to make the reader see as though for the first time. With Dante, Ilarregui and the reader might declare: "but as my sight by seeing learned to see" (*Paradise*, Canto 33, line 12).

"El sol sobre la hora del vidrio / The Sun on the Hour of Glass"

"The Sun on the Hour of Glass" captures and disperses a single moment in a fall day where a window washer is suspended in space, washing windows on the ninth floor of a skyscraper. Ilarregui adopts the point of view of the window washer with his unique perspective on the street below (where "the world appears possible" with its threads of walkways, avenues, flags on banks), on his own reflection in the insect-stained glass, and on the plane flying overhead. Dream and reality unite in the window washer's Surreal perspective, which has now become that of the poet and her readers. A keen sense of nature imbues this urban poem: the yellow of the fall day is reflected in the yellow dust on the windows and the wind whips through the city streets and against the window. The conjunction of the color yellow with the windowpane recalls T. S. Eliot's description of J. Alfred Prufrock venturing out into the London street in the early evening:

> The yellow fog that rubs its back upon the window panes,
> The yellow smoke that rubs its muzzle on the window panes.[42]

---

[42] T.S. Eliot, p. 4.

Ilarregui incorporates a sense of time as she recounts the window washer awaiting five o'clock and suggests that he is sustained "fragilely by his own predictions." The end of the shift suggests the end of life and resonates with Federico García Lorca's emphasis on five o'clock in "Llanto por Ignacio Mejías Sánchez / Lament for Ignacio Mejías Sánchez." Yet Ilarregui creates a character with all the vibrancy of life Ignacio manifested while still alive and that J. Alfred Prufrock, so timid that he could scarcely venture into the streets much less to a window washer's platform on the ninth floor of a skyscraper, never approached. The individual life at an exact moment in time and space is punctuated with the rich awareness of myriad connections to ongoing time, one's own past and future, as well as that of the species. Here Ilarregui, like Dante, seeks to read the world as a book, an effort underscored in the image of the sky's "blue pages."

"Corte de pelo / Haircut"

"Haircut," the last poem of *Roles and Persons* and the simplest and most poignant, depicts a six-year-old child having his hair cut. Ilarregui captures the effect of a haircut exactly as she describes naked ears and eyes emerging from the wealth of hair like "those of a dog / morning fresh." She describes the child's mind. He remembers pretending to be an Indian running through forests beneath a cloud-streaked sky. This poem recalls Gabriela Mistral's "Niño mexicano / Mexican Child" generally in its maternal tenderness for the child and specifically in its allusions to the child's hair and to the bow. Mistral wrote:

> Estoy en donde no estoy,
> en el Anáhuac plateado,
> y en su luz como no hay otra
> peino un niño de mis manos.
>
> En mis rodillas parece
> flecha caída del arco,
> y como flecha lo afilo
> meciéndolo y canturreando.
>
> . . .
>
> Resinas de pino-ocote

van de su nuca a sus brazos,
y es pesado y es ligero
de ser la flecha sin arco...

(I am where I am not,
in the silvered Anáhuac
and in the light as there is no other
I comb a child with my hands.

On my knees he appears
a fallen arrow from the bow,
and as an arrow I sharpen him
rocking him and humming.

. . .

Resins of ocote pine
go from his nape to his arms,
and he is heavy and he is light
from being an arrow without a bow

In Ilarregui's poem the happy memory of playing with the bow is supplanted by the recollection of a whipping by the father which left the child weeping, face down, on the earth, then alone in his room barren of any image of a loving father. Only the barber caresses his head and treats him as though he were still an innocent child. The poem admirably captures the mood of a chastened child and permits the reader to enter into the perspective of such a child, who--like the poet--gathers moments from his past and recombines them. Coming as it does at the end of a book treating the process of creating poetry through collecting fragments and placing them in new perspectives, it suggests the poet's desire to regain the innocent child's perspective, a perspective which may be lost by the tender age of six. This child retains an affinity to nature and to make-believe. His mature forests are full of "hojas potentes / potent leaves,": leaves of trees, leaves of books, the enigmatic leaves of the Cumaean Sibyl.

BOOK III: GUÍA PARA PERPLEJOS / GUIDE FOR THE PERPLEXED

Guide for the Perplexed contains 49 poems in comparison to the 15 of *Indian Journeys* and the nine of *Roles and Persons*. These 49 poems, 48 of one-page length like those of *Roles and Persons* and one four-page poem ending the volume and carrying the same title as the book, i.e. "Guide for the Perplexed," are divided into seven sections, with the first section of 15 poems containing four subsections. As Ilarregui explains in her preface, she took her title from a book of philosophy written in the twelfth century. This book was the *More nevukhim (Guide of the Perplexed)*, originally written in Arabic, then translated to Hebrew, Latin and other European languages. In this work Moses Maimonides (1135-1204), Jewish philosopher who resided in Córdoba, sought to place Judaism on a rational foundation and to forge an accommodation between science, philosophy, and religion. Ilarregui must have been profoundly moved to discover this book, so evocative of the intellectual foundations of Spanish culture, in a twelfth century Bavarian monastery--in Germany, the country which emerged as philosophical leader of the West in the nineteenth century. Here, indeed, she came face-to-face with the paternal roots of her culture. Adopting this title, Ilarregui implied that the poet serves as guide, oracle, and sibyl.[43]

The cover illustration of the original Spanish edition of the poems[44] reinforces the Cumaean Sibyl association for it contains a doll in Russian dress lying atop a pile of written-over leaves of paper, some crumpled up. A butterfly, an image Ilarregui will frequently use in this book, appears on one leaf. The doll will also figure in autobiographical poems where the poet recalls her childhood as a sickly child in Argentina, a child who sometimes felt that she herself

---

[43] Dante is frequently placed in this role; the *Commedia* is perceived as "a warning to mankind and a guide for the perplexed, and finally a prophecy of divine things to come." See Paolo Milano, *The Portable Dante* (New York: The Viking Press, 1947), p. xx.

[44] Gladys M. Ilarregui, *Oficios y personas / Guía para perplejos* (Alexandria: Los Signos del Tiempo, Editores, 1996).

was little more than a doll to be carted about and left on beds at home and in hospital. Ilarregui at least partially attributes her choice of poetic vocation to her childhood illness which prevented her from playing with other children and confined her to the sickroom where much reading and studying turned her inward to the world of imagination. Her emphasis on the fragility of life and the fragmentation of the self, especially her emphasis on breaking--the breaking of a dove--may also stem from this early experience.

"Personas perdidas / Lost Persons"

As *Roles and Persons* ended with a poem about a child, *Guide for the Perplexed* begins with such a poem, "Lost Persons," the name both of the initial poem and of the initial section of fifteen poems. The opening quotation from Heinrich Böll, German winner of the Nobel Prize for Literature in 1972, could be applied to the ten-year-old Ilarregui herself: "I am looking for a girl, ten years old, probably pale, with dark hair and very large, rather melancholic dark eyes." The placement of the poem reinforces the idea that Ilarregui wishes to recapture the wonder of the innocent child before creation in her poetry and that she has somehow lost touch with that child, hence "lost persons."

The Romantic poets popularized the concept of the child as miniature artist with imagination not yet restrained by societal conventions. Wordsworth's ode, "Intimations of Immortality from Recollections of Early Childhood," remains the best expression of the idea that "the Child is father of the Man." His lines have so permeated the English-speaking world as to have become fragments of popular film titles: "Though nothing can bring back the hour/ Of splendour in the grass, of glory in the flower."[45] The neoromantic García Lorca continued to employ the idea of the superior affinity of the child to beauty and to nature in "El niño Stanton / The Child Stanton" from *Poeta en Nueva York / Poet in New York*:

---

[45] Quoted from *An Anthology of Famous English and American Poetry*, edited by Willian Rose Benét and Conrad Aiken (New York: Random House, Inc., 1944), 200-205.

Stanton, vete al bosque con tus arpas judías,
vete para aprender celestiales palabras
que duermen en los troncos, en nubes, en tortugas,
en los perros dormidos, en el plomo, en el viento,
en lirios que no duermen, en aguas que no copian,
para que aprendas, hijo, lo que tu pueblo olvida."[46]

(Stanton, go to the forest with your Jewish harps,
go to learn celestial words
that sleep in the tree trunks, in clouds, in turtles,
in the sleeping dogs, in lead, in wind,
in lilies that do not sleep, in waters that do not copy,
so that you learn, son, what your people forget.

Vicente Aleixandre, another poet from the Generation of 1927, expresses the neoromantic conception of the child's acute perception in "El cometa / The Comet/Kite":

Así niños y hombres
pasan. El hombre duda.
El viejo sabe. Sólo el niño conoce.[47]

(Thus children and men
pass. The man doubts.
The old man knows. Only the child recognizes.)

The idea goes back to the mystics and finally to the Bible in the praise of simple, innocent faith in God before creation. Both Saint Teresa of Ávila and Saint John of the Cross used the image of the babe in its mother's arms to figure a high stage in the mystic way to illumination of the nature of Creation and Creator. In his notation for Song 27a [A 18] of the *Cántico Espiritual / Spiritual Canticle* Saint John explains the verse "Allí me dio el pecho / There he gave me his breast":

> Y así, aquí está empleado en regalar y acariciar al alma como la madre en servir y regalar a su niño, criándole a sus mismos pechos; en lo cual conoce el alma la verdad del dicho de Isaías, que dice: *A los pechos de*

---

[46] Federico García Lorca, I: 496.

[47] Aleixandre, p. 321.

Dios seréis llevados y sobre sus rodillas os holgará" (Isaías LXVI.12).[48]

(And thus, here He is employed in spoiling and caressing the soul as is the mother in serving and spoiling her child, feeding him with her own breasts; through which the soul recognizes the truth of Isaiah's saying: *then shall ye suck, ye shall be borne upon* her *sides, and be dandled upon* her *knees*" [Isaiah, 66.12]). [49]

Ilarregui's poem opens with a winter scene in which the poet looks out her window "when ice falls like a cleft dove." The striking originality of Ilarregui's simile inheres in the union of the biological and the elemental: of the pulsating life in the soft-feathered creature and the hard transparency of frozen water. She joins these images with the violence of the verb "cae / falls" and the past participle "partida / cleft." She achieves an equally felicitous union of the biological and the abstract in "a shiny snail's line between the hands of its time." Poetry and Time are both personified as the poet transfers her own struggle to create the poem to the poem itself struggling into form and life. The poem is so extremely personified that it excretes a substance leaving a viscous trace on time, almost imperceptible to the eye in its transparency but tingling the nerve endings on the skin.

The word "paloma / dove" carries heavy resonance in Spanish. The "Romance de Fonte-frida," a ballad about a faithful turtledove who rejects the nightingale's seduction in favor of fidelity to her dead mate, is part of the Hispanic poetic idiom. In Western literature the dove has traditionally been perceived as a sign of the Holy Spirit and hence of peace. Saint John of the Cross invoked such traditional symbolism in referring to the soul, bride of Christ, as a dove in the *Cántico espiritual / Spiritual Canticle*:

Vuélvete, paloma,
que el ciervo vulnerado
por el otero asoma,

---

[48] San Juan de la Cruz, *Poesía completa y comentarios en prosa*, Edición, introducción y notas de Raquel Asún, 2nd Ed. (Barcelona: Editorial Planeta, S.A., 1989), p. 280.

[49] While the translation of Saint John of the Cross is my own, the verse from Isaiah comes from the King James Version of the Holy Bible (Boston: Pathfinder Publications, Inc., n.d.).

al aire de tu vuelo, y fresco toma.

(My dove, turn back,
for now the wounded stag
is climbing up the slope,
freshened by the breeze of your flight.)[50]

In Saint John's poem the soul then defines the Beloved through a list of images taken from nature.

The vulnerability and amorous habits of doves make them symbols of fragility and love. Thus, to turn to the English tradition equally available to Ilarregui, John Keats writes of the death of the dove resulting from its need of freedom in a manner especially relevant to Ilarregui's poem:

I had a dove, and the sweet dove died;
And I have thought it died of grieving:
O, what could it grieve for? Its feet were tied
With a silken thread of my own hand's weaving.[51]

Ilarregui repeats the image "the cleft doves of snow," which she then applies directly to the self: "the depths of oneself / that mirror image where I smiled when I was ten years old." The difficulty of the Lacanian fissure of the self upon self-recognition in the mirror is beautifully rendered in the image of the "cleft dove." Also present in the poem is the concept of premature birth: that is, the poem will not be understood or noted when it first appears but will become manifest in the future, like the prophecies of the Cumaean Sibyl. Yeats' idea of time as a spiral appears in Ilarregui's image of "a shiny snail's line between the hands of its time." Transparency, fragmentation, and courage to assay expression are elements of the poetics outlined here.

Nonetheless, Heinrich Böll's essay "Missing Persons" (1971) is, unquestionably, the primary source of Ilarregui's poem. In this story

---

[50] *The Poems of Saint John of the Cross*, translated by Willis Barnstone (Bloomington: Indiana U P, 1968), p. 47.

[51] *The Poetical Works and Other Writings of John Keats*, edited by Harry Buxton Forman (London: Reeves & Turner, 1883), p. 281.

Böll recalls his search for the girl "ten years old, probably pale, with dark hair and very large, rather melancholy dark eyes,"[52] who eighty-five years ago had walked nine miles to fetch turnip tops for her impoverished family. Böll is obsessed with learning the exact details of her trek. He is not satisfied with merely imaginatively recreating the details of the child's life. He wants to know the weight of those turnip tops, the time it took the child to make her journey, the amount of money she saved her family by making the trip, how that money was spent. In the course of the essay the reader learns that the girl was named Maria and that she was the narrator's mother. The essay continues with the narrator's burning curiosity to learn similar details about the "thin, freckled, ten-year-old boy, probably red-haired,"[53] who was to become the narrator's father. Finally the narrator reveals that the exactness of knowledge that he wants about the many people he knows, indeed, even of himself at ten-years-old, will always escape him, for he wants the person herself or himself: "not as a souvenir, not as a vehicle for an anecdote, not as a fetish to keep behind glass: no, because it was there, no longer exists, and will never exist again. I want the one hair of the head that has fallen to the ground."[54] Böll cannot describe the acquisition of such knowledge, only the search for it. In his obsessive questioning, he engages the reader's imagination and allows each reader to picture for himself what that lost child must have been. In his insistence on something so ephemeral and yet so concrete as a single hair, he is choosing the unique object that symbolizes the fullness of the moment, a process that art and lyrical poetry adopt in rendering moments eternal.

Böll's choice of the single hair as portentous object recalls the exact rendition of this very detail in the hairs wafting over Venus's face in Botticelli's *Birth of Venus.* To the Hispanic reader Böll's

---

[52] Heinrich Böll, *Missing Persons and Other Essays*, translated by Leila Vennewitz (New York: McGraw-Hill Book Company, 1977), p. 3.

[53] Böll, p. 6.

[54] Böll, p. 8.

reference to the single hair would recall Garcilaso de la Vega's celebration of the beloved's hair in a sonnet on the *carpe diem* theme:

y en tanto que el cabello, que en la vena
del oro se escogió, con vuelo presto,
por el hermoso cuello blanco, enhiesto,
el viento mueve, esparce y desordena; [55]

(and so long as the hair, that in the vein
of gold was chosen, with ready flight,
over the beautiful white neck, erect,
the wind moves, spreads and disorders;).

Hispanic readers would also recall Saint John of the Cross, who insists upon the uniqueness of the single hair blowing on the bride's neck, a hair which captured the Husband's love in the "Cántico espiritual / Spiritual Canticle:"

En sólo aquel cabello
que en mi cuello volar consideraste,
mirástele en mi cuello,
y en él preso quedaste,
y en uno de mis ojos te llagaste.

You stared at that one lock
of windblown hair you saw against
My nape, and on my neck
You were a prisoner
gashing yourself in one of my eyes.[56]

Instead of the single hair, Ilarregui develops the snail's trace as the tenuous object capturing the spirit.

---

[55] In *The Oxford Book of Spanish Verse,* edited by J. B. Trend (Oxford: Clarendon Press, 1965), p. 95.

[56] Barnstone, pp. 102-103.

From the way she develops the poems of the "Lost Persons" section it is clear that Ilarregui was influenced by Böll, assimilated through the filter of earlier Spanish and English poets, especially through the mystics. She set about restoring "lost" past moments and persons to the present; she too recalls her mother, her father, her grandfather, her brother, and herself at specific moments from the past. In a private correspondence Ilarregui revealed that she took her title for this section of *Guide for the Perplexed* from Böll:

> Incluyo el cuento: "Missing Persons" que podría traducirse como "personas desaparecidas" pero yo preferí: "personas perdidas" a partir de que lo encontré con más música. (I include the story "Missing Persons" that could be translated as "personas desaparecidas" [missing persons] but I preferred "personas perdidas" [lost persons] because I found it more musical.

Her choice may also have been conditioned by the political resonance of "personas desaparecidas" in Argentina, where the term refers to persons taken as political prisioners and never seen again.

"El grado cero de la escritura / Zero Degree Writing"

In "Zero Degree Writing" Ilarregui points to her younger brother's imaginative stories and his listening for sounds of the sea in a seashell as source of her poetic impulse. Since the sea is an archetypal symbol of the unconscious and of death, Ilarregui suggests in this image of the boy listening to the seashell his unbroken access to the unconscious. As a poet she gathers together fragments of existence, *"that fusion of invisibility and moment"* like ocean-swept pieces of bottles gathered up by a rosyfooted child, who transforms them into the sun. As she had done in *Indian Journeys*, she again brings water and fire--the sea and the sun--together as symbols of the unconscious and of consciousness which must unite in poetic creation. The wind and the birds function as symbols of the spirit or of inspiration.

"mi tiempo, mi nostalgia / My Time, My Nostalgia"

The joining together of childhood moments with the present in which the adult poet looks out upon the winter landscape forms the subject of the metapoetry of "My Time, My Nostalgia." Ilarregui's description of "knitting and unknitting" words--putting them in order and erasing them--recalls the scene where Penelope wove and unraveled her tapestry as she awaited Odysseus's return, as it also recalls the Cumaean Sibyl writing messages, which were then disordered by the wind. The precise present moment must be evoked as it is joined to moments from the past: "what I wanted to be / what I am, what I dreamt / what is not dreamt now, a wind appearing / at 7 o'clock on a winter's morning." Disjointed phrases, her mother's injunctions from the past, spring to mind: "'don't get cold' 'don't catch cold' 'don't run too much.'" All these phrases and images must be combined to create on the computer a blue scarf of "afflicted sparrows" to put around the reader's neck.

A quotation from the Swedish poet Tomas Tranströmer, who was born in 1931, prefaces the poem. Known for the simplicity of his imagistic style and his appreciation of nature, Tranströmer's *17 dikter* (1954; "Seventeen Poems") bring a cosmic perspective to bear on Stockholm's archipelago, while *Hemligheter pa vägen* (1958; "Secrets on the Way") recounts his travel impressions.[57] Ilarregui's attraction to the Swedish poet is based on the similarity of her approach in both content and style, especially the nostalgic recreation of the past. The "sun's rays on the lock" which open "the doors of darkness"[58] of the Tranströmer quotation link this poem with the preceding one where she recalls her little brother telling stories to himself as a child. Here

---

[57] See the *Encyclopedia Britannica, 15th Ed.* (Chicago: U of Chicago P, 1988), ll: 900.

[58] The quotation comes from the poem "Kyrie." I have not been able to locate Ilarregui's Spanish translation, from which I have translated to English. Robert Hass, *Tomas Tranströmer: Selected Poems 1954-1986* (New York: The Ecco Press, 1987), p. 36, gives a more restrained translation than did the Spanish translator:

> Sometimes my life opened its eyes in the dark.
> A feeling as if crowds drew through the streets
> in blindness and anxiety on the way towards a miracle,
> while I invisibly remain standing.
>
> As the child falls asleep in terror
> listening to the heart's heavy tread.
> Slowly, slowly until morning puts its rays in the locks
> and the doors of darkness open.

the conscious and the unconscious aspects of the mind appear as sunlight and darkness. Ilarregui's memory strengthens her resolve to commemorate such moments in poetry, like the child who gathers pieces of bottles, glistening in the sunlight at the seashore.

The remaining poems of the "Lost Persons" section are autobiographical narratives recreating childhood, depicting family members, and touching upon feminist issues. The four poems of "A la manera de Frida Kahlo / In the Manner of Frida Kahlo" depict Ilarregui's childhood and communicate the loneliness of the invalid, suffering from kidney disease. With their emphasis on blood and organs, the poems do recall Kahlo's paintings of herself with skin laid back to reveal the circulation of blood through her body. Kahlo (1907-1954) painted the body's organs and its wounds both as a symbol of psychic states (in such pictures as *Memory, 1937*, *Remembrance of an Open Wound, 1938*, and *The Two Fridas, 1939*) and as an illustration of the real physical ailments which afflicted her, as in the depiction of her miscarriage in *Henry Ford Hospital, 1932* and of her broken spine in the Surreal *The Broken Column, 1944.*

From childhood the Mexican painter had suffered from a physical defect of a shorter and thinner right leg, the result of polio or scoliosis or spina bifida. Unlike Ilarregui, Kahlo was not isolated from other children through hospitalization, but she did become the brunt of their jokes for her "pegleg." Herrera comments that Kahlo's alienation encouraged the development of her imagination:

> Frida's differentness accentuated her loneliness. To counter it, she became purposefully different, first a tomboy and later an exotic personality. But, even though she became extroverted, she never lost the sick child's awareness of the distance between her inner and outer worlds, and she kept her inner world as a haven and a terrain for adventure.[59]

At the age of 18 Kahlo suffered an accident which left her hospitalized for months as she recuperated from two broken ribs, a broken right leg and foot, as well as a broken spine, pelvis, and

---

[59] Hayden Herrera, *Frida Kahlo: The Paintings* (New York: Harper Collins Publishers, 1991), p. 29.

collarbone and a dislocated left shoulder. These injuries plagued her the rest of her short life, which ended in a series of operations and the amputation of her right leg. During her recuperation she began to paint, much as Ilarregui would later turn to literature during her illness.

Ilarregui could also identify with the pronounced autobiographical element in Kahlo's paintings. Kahlo depicted *My Grandparents, My Parents, and I* in a painting in 1936; she also painted her father, her mother, her nurse, her sister, and her husband Diego Rivera. However, most of her paintings are of herself and provide a narrative of her psychic and physical crises. Like Kahlo, Ilarregui has also experienced the frustration of the maternal impulse. This frustration sometimes surfaces in both Kahlo's and Ilarregui's work.

En La Manera de Frida Kahlo: "La edad de las muñecas" / In the Manner of Frida Kahlo: "The Age of Dolls"

This poem begins with a quotation from Frida Kahlo in which she affirms that the wondrous if somewhat grotesque self images she offered were taken not from the dream world but from her own reality. Ilarregui found this quotation written by Kahlo on her bedroom wall in the "Blue House" she shared with Diego Rivera in Coyoacán, Mexico City.[60] Like Kahlo, Ilarregui through pain became acutely aware of her body's functions: the flow of blood through veins and arteries, the passage of electrical messages from nerves to the brain, and the rise and fall of the lungs informed her consciousness.

In the first stanza Ilarregui, projecting herself back to her childhood, recalls her identification with dolls strewn carelessly on the patio. She attributes to these dolls a desire to be awakened to life by a flash of sunlight. Kahlo's *Me and My Doll, 1937* depicts the painter sitting stiffly on a rush bed beside a naked doll whose face resembles Kahlo's own. The doll looks almost alive, as though it would need only a spark of energy to make it become a real baby. In Ilarregui's

[60] The house is now a museum. Kahlo repeated this statement in an interview with Bertram D. Wolfe, "Rise of Another Rivera," *Vogue*, Nov. 1, 1938, p. 64.

poem the spark of light did not animate the doll, but instead only awakened the child to the pain of life--to the aching of her kidneys as she lay on her back, looking at the apparatus of bottled blood and tubes to which she was connected. As the dolls seem to be speaking to a blue-black cloud, she sees part of herself--her hopes, promise, and learning--flowing with the blood out into her house.

In her dreams she joins the other girls playing with dolls, even as she is forced to lie between white hospital walls. Her deeds are only those of the imagination, which she cultivates through reading illustrated books. Ilarregui contrasts the unknown, original colors she envisions with the colors of the reduced sphere she is forced to inhabit.[61] She moves from the blue-black of the cloud, to the whiteness of the hospital walls, to the redness of blood suffusing her paralyzed body. As the dolls' eyes stare at the sky, so her open arms stare at the ceiling. Her hands do not play with dolls, nor does she laugh with other children. In a final transformation Ilarregui unites her physical and emotional pain in the image of "sangre negra / black blood," the color evoked in the "blue-black cloud" at the beginning of the poem. Ilarregui captures the grief and pain she experienced as a child as well as her youthful escape into the world of imagination where she enjoyed games, colors, reading with an intensity beyond that of healthy children. Her illness forced her to create her own world of the imagination.

En la manera de Frida Kahlo: "Ahí cuelga mi vestido" / In the Manner of Frida Kahlo: "There My Dress Hangs"

As the previous poem began with an evocation of inanimate

---

[61] Kahlo in her diary attributed emotional values to colors: "GREEN: warm and good light; REDDISH PURPLE: Aztec. Tlapali [Aztec word for "color" used for painting and drawing]. Old blood of prickly pear. The most alive and oldest; BROWN: color of *mole*, of the leaf that goes. Earth; YELLOW: madness, sickness, fear. Part of the sun and of joy; COBALT BLUE: electricity and purity. Love; BLACK: nothing is black, really *nothing*; LEAF GREEN: leaves, sadness, science. The whole of Germany is this color; GREENISH YELLOW: more madness and mystery. All the phantoms wear suits of this color . . . or at least underclothes; DARK GREEN: color of bad news and good business; NAVY BLUE: *distance*. Also tenderness can be this blue; MAGENTA: Blood? Well, who knows!" Cited by Herrera, p. 147.

dolls and then imbued them with life, "There My Dress Hangs" begins with the description of another inanimate object--a Sunday dress hanging on the clothesline on the patio. In this poem Ilarregui captures the brilliant burst of sunlight which eluded the dolls of the previous poem. The line "there my dress hangs" of the title is repeated twice, once after the description of the house, once after the detailed description of the dress. Ilarregui seeks to bring this object before the reader's eyes and before her own with all its tangibility. The landscape assumes human characteristics: the leaves have green eyes that watch the dress sway back and forth; the summer has dry lips. The dress enjoys an existence apart from herself, apart even from memory. As it hung free of the child's body, so it exists in its own time free of the poet who recalls it. Ilarregui suggests the uniqueness of each passing moment and insists upon the existence of each thing within its moment in time. In the last two lines, Ilarregui then evokes herself as a child who "set two doves free." The freeing of the doves recalls the free movement of the dress tossed by the wind and, because of the association of doves with the spirit, the freeing of the imagination. Through her imaginative recreation of the scene the poet has recaptured images of her youth. In view of the autobiographical information imparted in the previous poem, which described the child's paralysis, the reader may conclude that the poet as a child learned to observe, more carefully than a healthy child might have done, the objects of her reduced world. With such a precarious hold on life, she learned to endow with human life, to personify, not only Nature but the products of human ingenuity.

While the title of Ilarregui's poem recalls Kahlo's painting *My Dress Hangs There, 1933,* the content of the poem reflects more Kahlo's *Memory, 1937*. Ilarregui as an adult relies on memory to recall a dress and a scene from her childhood: so Kahlo depicted herself in the present in the center of her picture, full figure to the spectator. She is wearing a white dress and a brown jacket, but no hands emerge from the jacket's sleeves. To her left hangs her empty Tehuana dress, from which the right arm and hand emerge to link themselves into the jacket's left sleeve. To Kahlo's right hangs a child's dress, from which an arm and hand extend from the left sleeve and reach toward, but do not touch, Kahlo's right sleeve. Herrrera provides a description of the schematic background and narrative of the painting:

> *Memory* is as simple and direct as a valentine: torn from her body, Frida's huge heart lies at her feet pumping rivers of blood into the landscape. To create an extraordinarily accurate visualization of the sensation of pain in the chest caused by extreme sorrow, Frida pierced the hole left by her extracted heart with a steel rod and put seesawing cupids on either end. The puttis' blithe indifference to her ever-expanding wound recalls Diego's propensity to thoughtless frolic. The poetry of blood in *Memory* joins the cruelty of Aztec sacrifice with the violence of Spanish Catholic martyrdoms. The greater the pain she wished to convey--especially pain caused by rejection from Diego--the bloodier Frida's self-portraits became.[62]

Kahlo's *My Dress Hangs There, 1933* projects her Tehuana dress against the background of New York City to offer a commentary and criticism of the United States. Herrera provides an excellent description of the painting:

> Frida's Cubism went so far as to include bits of collage: fragments of newspaper photographs of breadlines, a military parade, the audience at a baseball game, and political demonstrators. The steps of Federal Hall, presided over by a statue of George Washington, are made out of a collaged graph showing "weekly sales in millions." She poked fun at American values--sports and plumbing--by setting a golf trophy and a toilet on top of classical columns. A skyscraper forms the pedestal for the almighty telephone, whose cord snakes in and out of city buildings so depersonalized they resemble tombstones. Trinity Church with a dollar sign in its window is linked by a red ribbon to Federal Hall, which in Frida's view stood for capitalism. Other false values that Frida gently remonstrates against are the commercialization of sex seen in the sex goddess Mae West (whom Diego worshiped) vamping Manhattan from a peeling billboard above buildings going up in flames, and conspicuous waste suggested in a garbage pail stuffed with detritus, including a human hand. Suspended from a blue ribbon tied with bows to the toilet and the trophy, Frida's Tehuana dress hangs empty. Disgusted with watching millionaires sip cocktails while the poor starved, she wanted to flee to Mexico, a longing hinted at by the collaged steamship chugging out of New York Harbor while the Statue of Liberty appears to wave."[63]

---

[62] Herrera, pp. 112-115.

[63] Herrera, pp. 101-105.

From this description it is evident that Ilarregui relies on Kahlo only for the image of the empty dress to create an entirely different aesthetic experience. Instead of Kahlo's public background Ilarregui depicts a personal landscape from the past, contemporaneous with the dress from childhood. As her memory reaches into the past, she touches the child who existed then.

En la manera de Frida Kahlo: "Retrato con mariposas" / In the Manner of Frida Kahlo: "Portrait with Butterflies"

In "Portrait with Butterflies" Ilarregui recurs to one of her favorite images, the butterfly. She often uses this image to communicate the ephemeral beauty and the briefness of life: as a poet she recreates in words these tenuous creatures. She begins in the present where she imagines herself putting on lipstick in front of a mirror. The vision of the person she has become triggers the memory of the child she once was, a child who was a potential person, not yet realized. A vivid image of herself in starched crinolines or dresses covered with little flowers and sporting huge collars flashes before her eyes. She then watches herself as a child who mentally collected butterflies as she quietly sat in a chair with her legs swinging. The two scenes are joined by the color yellow, which evokes both sunlight and the color of autumn leaves. She gives herself up to the union of the two moments, transfixed, until the color darkens to ocher which closes the doors and windows of her house and of her mind.

There are several subtle allusions to Kahlo in this poem. In *Self-Portrait, 1940* Kahlo depicts herself full face and shoulders towards the viewer. Such portraits were usually done by painting her own reflection in a mirror. Kahlo paints what she sees, her present image with two filigree butterfly pins atop her woven headdress. Herrera points out that the butterfly was a symbol of transcendance for Kahlo.[64] The painter adds two real animals to the portrait: her black cat sits behind her left shoulder, while her black monkey sits behind the right. Heavily symbolic objects complete the portrait.

---

[64] Op. Cit., p. 142.

Around her neck are broken sticks whose thorns cut into her neck to draw blood. Attached to them is a dead hummingbird. Masses of leaves in shades of green and yellow form the background. Herrera interprets the painting as Kahlo's representation of her anguish during her separation from Diego Rivera. Ilarregui also begins with a study of her own mirror reflection, but immediately is drawn through the mirror to her childhood image. The butterflies that child collects exist in her imagination. Ilarregui is more concerned with showing the mental processes of imagination and memory. Through the medium of words she can create a narrative to show the mind in motion; in her painted images Kahlo captures a single moment.

Ilarregui's reference to windows and doors may reflect a description Kahlo made about the working of her own memory on her childhood experience:

> I must have been 6 years old when I experienced intensely an imaginary friendship with a little girl more or less the same age as me. On the glass window of what at that time was my room, and which gave onto Allende Street, I breathed vapor onto one of the first panes. I let out a breath and with a finger I drew a "door."...
>
> Full of great joy and urgency, I went out in my imagination through this "door." I crossed the whole plain that I saw in front of me until I arrived at the dairy called "Pinzón."... I entered by the "O" of Pinzón and I went down in great haste into the *interior of the earth*, where "my imaginary friend" was always waiting for me. I do not remember her image or her color. But I do know that she was gay–she laughed a lot. Without sounds. She was agile and she danced as if she weighed nothing at all. I followed her in all her movements and while she danced I told her my secret problems. Which ones? I do not remember. But from my voice she knew everything about me. . . . Thirty-four years have passed since I experienced this magic friendship and every time that I remember it, it revives and becomes larger and larger inside of my world.[65]

Kahlo too described the loss of youthful joy and innocence when she discovered the reality of pain and the nearness of death during her accident. At the age of 18 in a letter to her sweetheart, Alejandro Gómez Arias, she wrote:

---

[65] Herrera, p. 29.

> Why do you study so much? What secret are you looking for? Life will reveal it to you soon. I already know it all, without reading or writing. A little while ago, not much more than a few days ago, I was a child who went about in a world of colors, of hard and tangible forms. Everything was mysterious and something was hidden; guessing what it was was a game for me. If you knew how terrible it is to know suddenly, as if a bolt of lightning illuminated the earth. Now I live in a painful planet, transparent as ice; but it is as if I had learned everything at once in seconds. My friends, my companions became women slowly, I became old in instants and everything today is bland and lucid. I know that nothing lies behind; if there were something I would see it.[66]

En la manera de Frida Kahlo: "A veces yo perdía los anteojos" / In the Manner of Frida Kahlo: "Sometimes I Lost My Eyeglasses"

This poem depicts the child's disorientation and her sudden sense of despair from the isolation brought about through her illness. The disorientation is akin to losing one's eyeglasses and no longer being able to focus. In moments when her illness violently asserted its presence with sudden bloodlettings, the happiness and innocence of childhood disappeared, to be replaced with the images of doves hovering in the plaza outside the window. The doves, through their association with the Holy Spirit, symbolize spiritual aspiration which depends upon a knowledge of suffering unknown to the healthy child. The poem's emphasis on blood augments the Christ-like aura the sick child assumes, as does her posture of lying on the bed with her arms facing upward in a prone crucifixion. Despite the knowledge she has gained, Ilarregui recalls that she would gladly have exchanged her sickroom, her caretakers, her solitary bookish amusements for the normal existence of the healthy child. She perceived the world through her illness: the colors of the sunset resembled those of the blood used in her transfusions; her dolls appeared as broken as she was; her caretakers seemed as cold and distant as robots. She longed for the independence and carefree existence of healthy children who played till the sun set, a sun as tired as they were when they returned to the comfort of home and mother.

Bereft of a normal childhood, Ilarregui has had to invent or

---

[66] Herrera, p. 37.

recreate a childhood for herself. In fact, she may owe her poetic vocation to her illness: her enforced passivity made her turn to books, music, and art. However, this compensatory theorizing does not conceal the essentially tragic nature of her childhood: she might have enjoyed a normal childhood and still have become a poet. Regret, more than anger, dominates her poems about childhood.

"Focusing"

In "Focusing" Ilarregui imagines her grandfather's spirit returning from some distant star to once again occupy his body and his gray suit on the streets of Buenos Aires. The world as book appears in the description: "una caligrafia en blocks perdidos/ de calles destartaladas / a calligraphy in lost blocks / of shabby streets" (Gpp, 42). Once again Ilarregui connects the person to doors as she describes her grandfather's "fidelidad de puerta vieja a tres o cuatro amigos / faithfulness of an old door to three or four friends." On the mythic level Ilarregui's grandfather functions as the "wise old man" who appears to help the hero achieve individuation. He "opens doors" to understanding the world and the self. Although he died when she was only four years old, the family kept his memory alive. Because of his warm character and his affinities for poetry and music, he exerted a major influence upon the poet's self-definition.

The three poems bearing the title "**Cool Memories**" recall happy images of Ilarregui's childhood and record three important moments in the poet's young life. In these poems as in "Corte de Pelo / Haircut" from *Roles and Persons* Ilarregui shows how imagination enables the child to enlarge reality and sometimes to escape from a harsh reality. In her peception of childhood Ilarregui thus subscribes to the ideas of such Romantic writers as Jean Jacques Rousseau, who held that the education of the child should draw upon what the child knows instinctively and should foster his native intelligence. Ilarregui spent two years working and studying in a school for special children in Buenos Aires. This school was grounded on the principles of Jean Piaget. According to Piaget the child's instruction should be accommodated to the child's developmental stage; to educate the child the adult must be aware of the child's concepts of time, world, reason, and morality.

"Cool memories: Introducción a las esperas / Cool Memories: Introduction to Delays"

This poem is a delightful recreation of the poet and her brother as children waiting in "a South American delay" for the icecream to harden within the refrigerator. Ilarregui captures the child's sense of time which seems to stretch when he is anticipating something. She also communicates the child's magical perception as the refrigerator, source of his delight, becomes a totem.

"Cool Memories: Graffiti"

In this poem Ilarregui returns to the theme of the child as artist as she recalls her brother writing upon the walls of the house with crayons. Instead of rewarding his expression, their parents punished the young "jackson pollock" with a three-day suspension from the dinner table. Again the poet emphasizes the child's creativity.

"Cool Memories: La piel de un globo / Cool Memories: The Balloon's Skin"

Ilarregui recounts her awakening to metaphysics when her uncle told her that all people end up like the balloon exploding against a branch. Overcome with the realization of death's finality, the child withdrew "as if I were leaving a frame, / as if I were disappearing from a photograph." The child thus internalizes the balloon's end by reenacting it in her own disappearance, a disappearance that foreshadows her own eventual death.

"Serie de retratos / Series of Portraits"

Ilarregui's attitude towards her mother is tinged with guilt for having monopolized her time so completely as a child. Her mother, like so many Argentine and North American women of her generation, lived through her family, in the small world of home and neighborhood. In Virginia Woolf's terms she did not have "*A Room of One's Own*,"[67] that is, a space in which to develop her own person.

---

[67] (London: The Hogarth Press, 1929).

Ilarregui's mother lived the life of the housewife that Betty Friedan describes in *The Feminine Mystique*.[68] Dispersing their time and attention upon their social and familial duties, such women retained nothing for themselves. Theirs was a life of service to others and they were not encouraged to develop a sense of self and a separate identity. Ilarregui evokes the constriction of that life and its ephemerality.

"Series of Portraits" depicts a contemporary insight into Ilarregui's mother's life compared with the poet's own. Ilarregui's mother, while in her thirties, was confined to the life of the typical homemaker, watching butterflies on the patio, as she herself became a kind of butterfly fluttering from marketplace to home. The women of her generation did not have an "image," nor did they consciously order their emotions. Ilarregui evokes the sadness of these women by describing a kind of malaise that affected them physically and spiritually. Sometimes her mother scarcely had the energy to reach day's end. Ilarregui attributes the sadness and sense of loss felt by most women of her mother's generation to living an unexamined life. Rather than asserting and establishing themselves as individuals, they subsumed themselves entirely in the role of wife and mother, servant of the family. Ilarregui's mother lived as instinctively as an insect, exhibiting the beauty of her final stage of development in a reduced circuit and leaving no record of achievement except in her daughter's poem. In "Epoca: Rostro sobre rostro / Epoch: Face on Face" Ilarregui will compare herself to a curious insect, but to one who does leave a record.

---

[68] (New York: Norton, 1963).

"Se acabaron los cuentos: Imelda Marcos, Cenicienta / The Stories Are Over; Imelda Marcos, Cinderella"

In these two poems Ilarregui examines the Cinderella fairytale that conditions the vast majority of women's dreams as Collette Dowling has demonstrated.[69] By depicting her mother's life in the previous poem, she had shown what happens to Cinderella after the marriage to her Prince Charming. The woman who defines herself only through love finds a husband and disappears into the home and market. In "Imelda Marcos" Ilarregui treats a woman who accomplished Cinderella's dream exactly by marrying a man with the status of a prince. Imelda lives the life of Cinderella at the ball but discovers that being trapped in that ambiance is no more satisfying than the life of the ordinary woman. In fact, she longs for just such an ordinary life. Ilarregui suggests that Imelda's obsessive shoe purchases resulted from an unfulfilled Cinderella fantasy. The poet humorously depicts the notorious celebrity with her 150 pairs of shoes as a woman who really wanted to be Cinderella with only one pair of shoes: sneakers to find her Prince Charming. He might have been only an ordinary man, in Central Park, but one who would have responded to her on a fundamental human level with understanding, support, and love. Implied is the fact that Imelda has lived a life less satisfying than did Ilarregui's mother and most ordinary homemakers. Imelda has frittered her life away within the lap of luxury and has failed to define herself; she continues as an unfulfilled Cinderella. Ilarregui subtly transforms the Cinderella story by making the girl the active pursuer of her Prince Charming rather than the passive damsel who awaits him. The fragile golden slippers have become athletic sneakers. Still, Ilarregui's transmutation highlights an aspect of the Cinderella fairytale that is often overlooked. Cinderella did actively pursue the opportunity to attend the ball and to interact with the prince. She purposefully dropped the shoe which provided the clue of his discovery of her.

In "Cinderella," the second poem in this section, Ilarregui again recasts the fairytale, concentrating not on Cinderella's

---

[69] *The Cinderella Complex* (New York: Simon and Schuster, 1981).

relationship with the prince but on her relationships with the other women in the story. She fleshes out the fairytale character by concentrating on her mind, and not as in the fairytale on her beauty and her sweet personality. Ilarregui retains from the fairytale the emphasis on Cinderella's virtue as an industrious female and her low economic status. In Ilarregui's version Cinderella is a woman somewhat knowledgable of philosophy, including Martin Buber's concept of "disencounters." As she cleans the house, she meditates upon the distance between members of a family. The distance separating herself from her stepmother and stepsisters is greater than that between heaven and earth. In *Ich und Du (1923; I and Thou)* Buber contrasted the I-Thou relationship with the I-It relationship and espoused the former whenever possible, both in one's relationships with other persons and with God, for it is based on the full realization of both individuals.[70] The stepmother and stepsisters are immersed in the I-It relationship in their attitude towards Cinderella. In both these poems, as in life, the Cinderellas awaiting their charming princes are looking not only for economic security but for someone with whom they can engage in an "I and thou" relationship, i.e. for love. She awaits her prince in the form of the writer who will end "this female litigation." In the fairytale the prince affords the only means of escape from an unhappy home life and for the woman to establish her own, presumably happier, home. Hence the competition for the male's attention throughout the story. In Ilarregui's account the prince has been transformed into the writer, which suggests that he or she would have control over the story and the power to change its ending. On an autobiographical level the two Cinderella poems indicate that Ilarregui herself lived for a period caught up in this myth--awaiting her Prince Charming--as most young girls do. In Ilarregui's case the awareness of the writer's vocation competed with Romantic illusions. The poet suggests that a writer could remake the Cinderella tale. Perhaps

---

[70] Buber explains: "The *It* is the eternal chrysalis, the *Thou* the eternal butterfly--except that situations do not always follow one another in clear succession, but often there is a happening profoundly twofold, confusedly entangled. In the beginning is relation." In Martin Buber, *I and Thou,* translated by Ronald Gregor Smith (Edinburgh: T. & T. Clark, 1937), pp. 17-18.

Cinderella herself could become that writer. In the "**Indigo**" poems Ilarregui will show the work required to become such a writer.

"Cambio de palabras: Final de juego / Exchange of Words: Game's End"

Disputes about women's roles yields to an awareness of what is most important in this last poem of the "Lost Persons" section of *Guide for the Perplexed.* Here the poet's "I and thou" relationship with her father contrasts with the "I and it" relationship of Cinderella with her stepsisters and stepmother in the previous poem. The title of this poem recalls Luisa Valenzuela's *Cambio de armas (Exchange of Arms),*[71] a work dealing with conflicted modern sexual roles in Argentinian society. In Ilarregui's poem her father, convinced that they shall never see each other again, insists that they treasure their last moments together. Affection is more important than disputes and one must treasure people "before they go out like stars." Beneath the roles of father and daughter which Time imposed upon them is his continuing vision of her as a child, "the girl with dark eyes, Marcelita." The father's sense of irreparable loss, that the present moment is passing never to return, is communicated through the image of the keys which we keep despite the fact that we no longer remember which doors they may open. Such a situation constitutes a dilemma more serious than the loss of a key, for one could somehow gain entrance through the door by forging another key or by breaking the door down. To have lost the door symbolizes loss of an opening to experience, to life, and to death. Variations on the images of keys and doors appear throughout these two books of poetry and become the refrain and last line of the very last poem in *Guide for the Perplexed.* There Ilarregui expresses her faith that "sometime keys will find doors."

Ilarregui's reversal of the loss of the door instead of the loss of the key rejuvenates traditional door/key symbolism. Virgil had described the Cumaean Sibyl as one whose lips must be "unlocked" and one whose messages are scattered when the door to the cave turns upon its hinge. Ilarregui's fear of not finding the door may signal

---

[71](Hanover, N.H.: Ediciones del Norte, 1982).

her fear of being locked within the cave or within her own mind with no opportunity to communicate to those outside. In this context the reader may recall "Little by Little," the opening poem of *Roles and Persons,* where the poet described "the heart beating so hard against the doors of oneself."

Knowledge as a body of material kept under lock and key, perhaps because books were so guarded in ancient times, is a traditional metaphor in Western literature. In Goethe's *Faust* that paradigmatic seeker after knowledge, Faust, must descend to the realm of the terrible mothers, another variation on the cave of the Cumaean Sibyl, to gain access to Helen of Troy, eternal beauty. Mephistopheles gives him a magic key which will make the Mothers accede to his request.[72] Ilarregui uses "keys" in her poetry to communicate access to knowledge. Her image becomes even more striking when her poetry is translated into English, for in the latter language not only "llaves" but the "teclas" of the typewriter and computer to which she sometimes refers are translated as "keys."

"Índigo: Poema con los ojos lejos / Indigo: Poem with Eyes in the Distance"

The "**Indigo**" section of *Guide for the Perplexed* returns to the metapoetic themes typical of Ilarregui's poetry. The entire section evokes the ambiance of Picasso's blue period. "Poem with Eyes in the Distance" with its moonlit ambiance recalls García Lorca, especially the "Romance de la luna, luna / Ballad of the Moon, Moon." At the same time the poet's keen awareness of her body, of the "blanket of blood" covering her bones and brain and of the passage of messages from one neuron to another, returns again to the artistic representations of Frida Kahlo. In the act of poetic creation Ilarregui is conscious of the brain, "the heart heavy as an iron bell," and of her nerves. While in the earlier "Transparencies" she sought the transparency of rain, here she seeks a "bello texto nocturno / a beautiful nocturnal text," the clarity of the house's image against the moonlight. The joining of the significant image to the present moment

---

[72] Johann Wolfgang Von Goethe, *Faust: Part II*, translated by David Luke (Oxford: Oxford U P, 1994), pp. 49-54, Part II, Act 1, lines 6173-6306.

yields poetic ecstasy: life opens up "like a cask of birds / of southern birds, straying, secret."

"Indigo: Cabellos sueltos / Indigo: Loose Hair"

"Loose Hair" illustrates Ilarregui's poetic method. As she stands before a Degas painting in St. Petersburg, she feels herself entering into the painting of the woman brushing her hair. She climbs up its waves to experience the thought of the woman in the picture. At the same time an image of herself undressing on a fall day occurs to her. The falling hair of the woman in the painting triggers the association of a previous afternoon, personified also as a woman casting her hair over the poet and now recounted in the immediate present, when "*between the windows and the doors is an intimacy of known days.*" She studied then her own hair under the lamplight as the museumgoers study the hair of Degas' model in the painting. Outside the museum life continues in the fall day, as it had continued in her remembrance of the fall day at home. Ilarregui seeks to recreate the texture of the combination of the present moment (afternoon in fall), with the past moment which resurges, and with the similar emotions and thoughts which struck her on both occasions.

"Indigo: Magma rising"

In "Magma Rising" Ilarregui posits an equivalence among a geological phenomenon and her psychosomatic responses to a sunset, to initial lovemaking, and to "female" depression. Magma, the phenomenon to which the poet refers, is molten rock beneath the earth's surface which builds up pressure over time and eventually flows out as lava or erupts; this movement cannot be stopped and it is unpredictable. She compares the effect of the sunset to the primal innocence of lovers' first touches. In the last two stanzas the poet ties the "occult forces" of magma to poetic inspiration which visits her before dawn when everyone is asleep and dreaming. The forces bring "voices of / destroyed dreams, little pieces, fragments of that thing which / was going to be life, potential life, not private life." Here Ilarregui has returned to the overriding conception of the fragmentation of the psyche. On the physical plane Ilarregui may be referring to the feelings women often feel at the onset of menstruation where they feel a certain sadness for the lack of conception. This explanation would seem to harmonize with the distinction she makes between generic attitudes of women and private life where she describes her writing as "another form of failure, an inverse sign / a rebellion, a way of falling on the page / my imperfect summer, my revolutions." This poem would seem to indicate some conflict between woman's biological role and the poet's vocation. Nevertheless, the poem does imply that the urgency for creating poetry is as much the product of "occult forces" as biological reproduction.

"Índigo: Tiempo del objeto / Indigo: Time of the Object"

"Time of the Object" opens with a quotation from the Russian artist Wassily Kandinsky (1866-1944), who observed that "Cezanne made a living thing out of a teacup, or rather in a teacup he realized the existence of something alive."[73] Within her poem Ilarregui begins by showing how people can deaden things, like the dawn and time, instead of letting them open up and manifest themselves until people themselves become objectified. The morning cup of coffee becomes part of a routine in a wintry day. The poem centers on a startling image in which Ilarregui compares reality to "a ripping apart of doves to take their flight away." As a child I once tried to see how baby chicks fly by holding a chick up by its wings' tips until the unfortunate creature died. Hence, Ilarregui's image of ripping up the dove to take away its flight struck home. The image reveals an ambiguous attitude toward the scientific method that verifies truths only by killing the object under investigation. Language in this method becomes "ghostlike, sure, monologic" as though people were perfect machines. Removing the barrier between the animate and the inanimate, Ilarregui then proceeds to accomplish in words what Cezanne did in paint: she suggests that "you" are not a living person but a hot cup of coffee. However the cup of coffee takes on an aura of life when she describes

[73] *Concerning the Spiritual in Art*, translated by M. T. H. Sadler (New York: Dover Publications, 1977), p. 17.

it as "an object wet with moonlight." Instead of taking life away from animate objects, Ilarregui prefers to endow inanimate objects with life. Ilarregui appears to be transposing to poetry the method that Kandinsky, pioneer of abstract, non-figurative painting, applied to art. She wants to make the meaning of the object, including the person as object, manifest, to reveal its inner rational and emotional significance.

"Índigo: Partes del discurso de la lluvia / Indigo: Parts of the Rain's Discourse"

Like "Zero Degree Writing," "Parts of the Rain's Discourse" appears entirely in italics. The poet adopts an objective attitude, situating herself within a large framework of the universe and time and her own life: adolescence recalled from the perspective of the present young adulthood. This deliberate situating of the narrative persona and the large issues considered recalls T.S. Eliot's "Gerontion." While Eliot writes as an old man "in a dry season," where people are "waiting for a sign," Ilarregui (here recapitulating Neruda's biography) writes in youth in a wet season where people believe they have seen a sign. Children close their eyes and make wishes upon two or three stars which have fallen from a galactic spiral. Personifying the earth by attributing a throat to the nocturnal ocean and eyes to the hemisphere, Ilarregui shows the reflection of the macrocosm in the microcosm of her own body. The galactic dust, upon falling into the ocean's throat and spreading, caused a change in the Southern hemisphere's eyes, a change reflected in her own "transparent body." She began to sprout wings ("and in my / shoulder blades a sign of 'something is going to grow'"). In the decalcomania, or decal-like impression of the cosmos on her psyche, she was changed completely. She experienced a new way of seeing the rain, a new way of tracing and smelling the day. Using an image she had previously used to describe her poetry in "Magma rising," ("a way of falling on the page"), she declares "that way of falling upon the world, something cosmic, like the surging / forth of a poem...." Poetry involves a new way of seeing and venturing to speak. As one throws oneself into the abyss, or dares to test the ice, so the poet attempts expression of the connections he has been privileged to experience. That step is both unusual and commonplace:

it partakes both of the astronaut's first step on the moon and of the trace of the child's sneakers on wet earth, as it also partakes of the abandonment of allowing oneself to fall in love. Ilarregui associates the process with rain on windows. Dante associates it with the sun's immense light in *Paradise*, "Canto XXIII," where he turns from Beatrice to the Virgin Mary. Both poets speak of the conjunction with the abyss and with love. Dante writes:

> So, in its picturing of Paradise,
> My sacred song a leaping-place must find,
> As when obstruction in the highway lies.[74]

In "Gerontion" Eliot claims to have lost his passion as he has lost the use of his senses of "sight, smell, hearing, taste and touch."[75] He, like Dante before him and Ilarregui after him, "surrendered completely / physically, emotionally, to the hands of emptiness."

In the description of the "sprouting of wings" Ilarregui's poem echoes a famous short story for children by Gabriel García Márquez: "Un señor muy viejo con unas alas enormes / A Very Old Man with Enormous Wings." In this story a fleabitten angel falls to the earth where his arrival is perceived as sign by the more devout but as a nuisance by the materialistic couple who exploit him as a sideshow for the curious. He survives a hard winter and with the coming of summer gathers the strength to fly away, buoyed by a strong seabreeze and inspired by "the sea chanteys that he sometimes sang under the stars."[76]

In the description of the change a first great love effects in the psyche--in the contrast of the before and after of this experience--the poem reverberates with the melody of Ezra Pound's "The River-Merchant's Wife: A Letter." Ilarregui's poem also has the tone of a

---

[74] Translated by Dorothy Sayers, p. 259.

[75] Eliot, p. 23.

[76] In *Collected Stories*, translated by Gregory Rabassa (New York: Harper & Row, Publishers, 1984), p. 210.

letter addressed to a particular person. The recollection of distant youth is equally poignant in Ilarregui's "then I was many years younger, so many years younger" and in Pound's "while my hair was still cut straight across my forehead."[77]

"Índigo: Ella va a irse de esta página / Indigo: She Is Going To Go Away from This Page"

"Ella va a irse de esta página" expresses an Eliot-like disenchantment or despair with the youthful faith expressed in "Parts of the Rain's Discourse." Ilarregui compares the difficulty of expressing her depression with a burst of blue light through the window which soaks into a wicker chair and to the feeling one has about things that have been lost. She also compares it to a convolution in one's life when one changes friends and becomes alienated from one's own image in the mirror. The physical response to anguish is compared to a toboggan in the throat. She has relinquished "worlds that freely shall never be." As things mature and change, she becomes involved with other things. She depicts poignant scenes of the abandoned youthful self: she recalls earnest discussions of young people talking with their hands in their pockets or running through their hair. The present hour distances her from her companion to whom she listens, abstracted. Her images for the present sadness evoke loneliness and emptiness: the glass's ring left on a napkin, chairbacks resting against tables in an empty cafe.

"Índigo: Celeste maduro / Indigo: Mature Sky Blue"

"Mature Sky Blue" records a more optimistic attitude towards present and past. Now instead of herself falling on the page or on the world, "this sky will fall on me." The feeling of connection between microcosm and macrocosm has reasserted itself. She repents her rejection in "She Is Going To Go Away from This Page" of her adolescent self and of her loss of faith in finding connections. The first verses are evocative of Vicente Aleixandre. As he would use violent

---

[77] William Rose Benét and Conrad Aiken, editors, *An Anthology of Famous English and American Poetry* (New York: Random House, 1944), p. 793.

images to describe nature as in "Mar y noche / Sea and Night" where he attributes mouth, horrid fauces, and teeth of foam to the sea, or as in "La selva y el mar / The Forest and the Sea" he would characterize the sunset as full of tigers, lions, hyenas where wild beasts "muestran sus espadas o dientes (show their swords or teeth"),[78] Ilarregui declares that the sky "will wound me tomorrow with its celestial teeth." Instead of a fierce beast, the sky for Ilarregui is "a tender animal / that doesn't know how to bite." Yet it does bite her hands. The distance between herself and the sky becomes a pleat where she writes her memories.

She picks up again the image of the unraveling used in "My Time, My Nostalgia." Here she describes the poem unraveling and brings it close to herself by describing herself as wearing an old pullover (subject also to unraveling) and then incorporates nature by associating the thread with the day. Finally she assimilates language into this intimate association of self, nature, and poetry by speaking of her "branch of preterits." Illustrating her use of preterits through her memories of her adolescent self, she declares that she cursed that younger, ecstatic self so sure of accessing "modes of seeing behind the window," a hope that she briefly lost. Nevertheless, she once again longed that "a literature of fragments, as of cups and old plates, / might fill the page, would be a scene where others, my Others / might leave a trace." These lines reaffirm her concept of poetry as gathering together of fragments ("retazos") of past memories, present and past selves, and leaving an imprint on time. The lines also recall Dante's description of the loss of the trace of the Cumaean Sibyl's verses on leaves tossed by the wind, messages that disappeared as "the sun melts the imprint on the snow."[79] Dante struggled to regain from memory a glimmer of what he had seen as Ilarregui too struggles to reach back through memory for a vision of conjunction. Between the sky and herself, she is confident that through the continuing pages she writes, a door will open.

---

[78] *Mis poemas mejores* (Madrid: Editorial Gredos, 1961), p. 59.

[79] *Paradise*, Canto XXXIII, line 64, p. 345.

"Época / Epoch"

The next section "Epoch" consists of four poems and is dedicated to Michel Foucault, a philosopher/historian famous for questioning past interpretations and for studying the minutiae of history to arrive at new ones. A structuralist, Foucault showed how we define the other by isolating a part of ourselves and setting it outside the limits. He especially worked with the concept of the body to show its lack of immediacy in modern times. Foucault's major works include: *Madness and Civilization* (1961), *The Birth of the Clinic* (1965), *The Order of Things* (1966), *I, Pierre Rivière, having slaughtered my mother, my sister, and my brother* . . . (1975), *Discipline and Punish* (1977), and *The History of Sexuality* in three volumes (1978-1984). Speaking of Foucault and the "young conservatives" who follow him and other Post Modern thinkers, Jürgen Habermas declares: "they remove into the sphere of the faraway and the archaic the spontaneous powers of imagination, self-experience and emotion."[80] As a poet Ilarregui keeps alive this "archaic" and childlike awareness of the body.

"Época: Si me rompo / Epoch: If I Break"

"If I Break" brings the idea expressed in earlier poems of the poet falling on the page and falling on the world to an immediate harsher reality of falling on her mouth onto the street. Fear of failure in adulthood and in modern urban life has increased and the images Ilarregui uses have become degraded. The dove now has become "a yellow dove" and the moon is the fall moon of ocher, ranging from pale orangish to reddish yellow. One thinks of T. S. Eliot's use of yellow to describe the London fog in "The Love Song of J. Alfred Prufrock."

Scattered images from various stages of her life are recollected in the poem: a "fragmented ABC book," remains of "open hands" and "swallowed words." The devouring imagery of fauces eating her nightgown, "releasing my body full of wonders" recalls "She Is Going

---

[80] "Modernity--An Incomplete Project," in *Post Modernism: A Reader* (New York: Columbia U P, 1993), p. 107.

To Go Away From This Page." From the affirmation of the "marvellous body" the imagery again rises as the poet recalls her youth with its antique objects and heart "made of epiphanies." She appeals to the reader to fix his eyes on her poetry which she again associates with a rebellion against modern, rationalistic attitudes. The reader must turn himself/herself into a "nocturnal insect" to appreciate the poet's rebellion; he must participate in it as she, the poet, confronts her own history and that of the reader (though he/she may yet be unaware of it) and, by remaking it through memory, reactivates it in her poetry. Ilarregui as poet sees herself as a representative but especially intuitive person. She perceives poetry as an interactive process between poet and reader. She must fall onto the page, even if she breaks herself in the process.

The final line of the poem "If I Break" recalls Federico García Lorca, towards whom Ilarregui has moved in the course of her poetry from the tranquillity of earlier verses to a recognition of the suffering poetry may bring in her later life. An impending sense of destruction fills this poem, but there is not yet the absolute certainty of mortality that Lorca implied in "Memento," a poem whose refrain echoes through Ilarregui's "If I Break." Lorca used "cuando / when" as opposed to Ilarregui's "si / if" in the prophecy of his death: "¡Cuando yo me muera! / When I die."[81]

"Época: El poema en mangas de camisa / Epoch: The Poem in Shirt Sleeves"

In "The Poem in Shirt Sleeves" Ilarregui turns to her own native tradition of magic realism to portray her younger self in the throes of poetic creation. In *Cien años de soledad / One Hundred Years of Solitude* Gabriel García Márquez describes the death of the second José Arcadio. A thread of blood made its way from his body, beneath doors, through rooms, into the street, around corners, under the chair of Amaranta, who was giving an arithmetic lesson to Aureliano José, to appear in Úrsula's kitchen, and finally to return to its point of origin. Seeing the thread of blood, José's mother Ursula

---

[81] "Memento" from *Poema del cante jondo, Obras completas* II: 208.

recognized her son's death with the words "¡Ave María Purísima!"[82] In her poem Ilarregui describes the sound of her typing on her old manual German typewriter. The sound travels from the paper, to her neighbor's house, to the bakery, through the tails of cats, through bicycles, to arrive finally at her mother's ear. Ilarregui imagines the history of that typewriter which had known the destruction of street corners and buildings in war, but yet shamelessly hammered on as though it were entering upon a new war. She compares the typewriter's transition from death and destruction in war to a new kind of death in the writing of poetry, which records the passing and dying of each day. The sound of the noisy typewriter becomes associated with the sounds of poetry, which attack the ears of the listener. Her mother's reaction is to weep, blow her nose, and stare at the grass where the insects smile back upon her. Ilarregui depicts her mother as one who regarded the daughter's writing poetry as a rebellion or as an abnormal development, much to be lamented. Nevertheless, the daughter continued like a crazy person writing her leaves of paper. The narrator's similarity to the Cumaean Sibyl is striking in this poem. Like the Sibyl Ilarregui is compelled to keep on writing on innumerable leaves. She too takes on the aspect of a kind of instinctive insect with four hands whose periods perforate the page "like a summer prick." Like the Sibyl, Ilarregui wishes to aid other people and to create something for their use, though her poems may only be enigmatic discourse which reflects the rubbish and fragments of the texts of other lives. Ilarregui adopts the obsessive character of the Sibyl as her own, as she does her manner of composition and her effect upon others.

"Época: Rostro sobre rostro (la construcción de una experiencia) / Epoch: Face on Face (The Construction of an Experience)"

"Face on Face" carries the subtitle "(The Construction of an Experience)." The parentheses around the subtitle indicate the effect of constructing a poetic experience: the poem sets that experience off from the flow of history. Poetry memoralizes a particular poet's

---

[82] (Buenos Aires: Editorial Sudamericana, 1967), p. 121.

particular reactions to all things both outside and within the psyche; both outside and within the body. Ilarregui's poetry consciously analzyes the poetic process and thus can be labeled "metapoetry." As "The Poem in Shirt Sleeves" described her relation to the outer world, to the society of neighbors and parents, this poem describes Ilarregui's internal psychic organization. Ilarregui imagines a more profound, archetypical face--the overriding face of herself as poet--superimposing itself upon the particular faces she has shown to the world at different times of her life. The eyes of the archetypical poet have remained constant throughout her life; they have observed her during youthful efforts to decipher the world as they observe her now as an adult woman holding her face in her hands. Ilarregui attributes to this archetypical face "the surprise of a curious insect, illuminated by the rain;" both are elements she has associated with poetry in earlier poems. In the course of the poem the archetypical face becomes dominant and displaces the particular, historical face Ilarregui had been holding in her hands at the moment the poem began.

Returning to her theme of the fragmentation of the poet's perspective, Ilarregui describes the poet's face as one knowing the developments and exiles of her own autobiography, as it also knows the outer world: It "is a piece of eye looking at the fall of a day of history / is a piece of hand caressing the morbid page of a newspaper." The superimposition of one image on top of another as peculiar to poetry also recalls Dante, who described his supreme insight as the superimposition of three spheres upon one another. While Ilarregui's insight is "de los techos abajo" or "from the roofs down," that is confined to the human sphere, Dante's is a religious insight, a mystic awareness of the significance of the trinity. Repetition of the word "pedazo / piece" emphasizes the fragmentation which becomes a dominant motif in the remainder of Ilarregui's poem. Like the Cumaean Sibyl, Ilarregui anticipates a future time when she no longer exists and when "writing and belonging to myself will not be the same thing." Then her words will remain without her as a remembrance:

the north / the south: the bones of my desires and my shoots.

"Brotes" means both shoots or buds, the promise of new life, and in common speech "crumbs" or "fragments." Her poetry exists both as a skeletal remains of her thoughts and as a prophecy for the future.

"Época: Época / Epoch: Epoch"

"Epoch," repeating the title of this section, recasts succinctly its themes. Now Ilarregui concentrates on the poet's instruments, her words, through which she affirms herself. She joins the adjectives "eléctricos / eclectric" and "azules / blue" to her words, while at the same time insisting on their own essence as words: "words splendidly / words." "Electric" suggests both their power and the means through which she produces them on her computer; "blue" is also associated with means for she refers elsewhere to the computer's "blue scarf" but is more profoundly tied to "indigo" and the poems of that section where the color blue was associated with emotion. Words become not a sign but the things themselves: they are full of creation--trees, universe, stones. She savors them in her mouth from whence they issue. The phrase "palabras partidas / words cleft" recalls the "paloma partida / cleft dove" of "Personas perdidas / Lost Persons," the very first poem of *Guía para perplejos / Guide for the Perplexed.* The affirmation of the self in poetry is again presented as a rebellion as it was in the first poem of this section, "Si me rompo / If I Break" and earlier in "Magma Rising." As she had described the sky "splashed with stars" in "Celeste maduro / Mature Sky Blue," here the words are "splashing the page with occult powers."

The definition of her own vocabulary reinforces Ilarregui's movement between microcosm and macrocosm and the transference of that movement into poetry. The "occult power" she attributes to poetry reinforces her conception of the poet as Cumaean Sibyl whose words were so portentous for those who consulted her. As in "La cara en el espejo / The Face in the Mirror" from *Personas y oficios / Persons and Roles*, she can see "in the / eyes of the windowpanes" the faces of others. The transfer of eyes from herself to the glass animates this transparent medium. The animation of the exterior world continues in the description of her keyboard with its "encías / gums." The transposition suggested here is that the words which issue from her mouth with its gums also issue physically from the typewriter. She, who out of her own feeling of impotence ("como si el hastío de sentirme impotente / as if being fed up with feeling impotent") in "El poema en mangas de camisa / The Poem in Shirt Sleeves," threw herself into the abyss by creating poetry, has discovered that words "*son mis potencias / are my power.*" This use of "potencias" recalls the "hojas potentes / potent leaves" of the forests which fill the child's imagination in "Corte de pelo / Haircut," final poem of *Oficios y personas / Persons and Roles*. In this poem too the imagination is associated with power. The glass between herself and the world, the mirror, is identified with history itself. To use a hackneyed metaphor that Ilarregui does not use but which may, nonetheless, help to illuminate her concept, history flows like a river dragging all its episodes and the constant revolutions of the day in its wake. The very thickness of these events in movement becomes clear as glass because nothing is remarked about the particular event. Each event of each particular individual is simply carried along on the current.

Through poetry Ilarregui seeks to reestablish the particularity of her self and of her own "epoch." Thus she hurls herself against this glass, against windows and doors, and is aware that she rather than the glass may break in her effort to break history's transparency. The final words of this poem align so well with my perception of Ilarregui as Cumaean Sibyl, that they must be quoted in their entirety:

> they are my words, I repeat against the table, hitting the gums
> of the keys, they are my power. My bits of shattered mirror
> my living organs like my own cells.
>
> Pieces of time, illuminated rebellion,
> my words are the only ones that can
> break the transparency of history.

Here in her movement between microcosm and macrocosm Ilarregui establishes the inseparableness of her awareness and the things that fill that awareness: poetry, history, body, and time. Fragments of all fill her fragmented consciousness.

"Una mujer con la mano en la frente: Una mujer con la mano en la frente / A Woman with Her Hand on Her Forehead: A Woman with Her Hand on Her Forehead"

In this section Ilarregui illustrates the credo of "Epoch" by celebrating moments of her particular time as a mature woman. The title poem is the first poem of this section. The poet lists the disparate things that fill her consciousness from telephone calls to an awareness of the planet and its revolution around the sun, to newspapers. From the external world that fills her consciousness Ilarregui moves to the storing of these images in the mind and to her emotional reaction to such images. To describe the potential of external things to strike a chord in the psyche she uses the images of "sleeping doves breathing," of dying stars, and of "black holes." Into these black holes fall all the things that once existed but which exist no longer. She has the power to recreate these things through thinking them as she thinks of "you." The "you" referred to here seems to be to her first reader, her husband Carlos María, but can also be taken by all readers of the poems as a generic allusion to her readers. The poem closes with the awareness of time. The poet expresses past time with a description of "yesterday's moon" which still lingers on her sheets and present time with "this morning's sun."

"Aquí adentro / Here within," a thrice repeated phrase joins the sections of the poem together as she speaks first of worlds within, then of sleeping and breathing doves, then of a person, herself. The use of the capital on *Aquí / Here*, because the use of capital letters is rare in Ilarregui's poetry, gives special importance to the immediacy of the place evoked.

"Una mujer con la mano en la frente: Transparencias / A Woman with Her Hand on Her Forehead: Transparencies"

In "Transparencies" Ilarregui joins two moments in time. In the present moment she gazes out a window and is traversed by a ray of sunlight, which like an X-Ray reveals her vertebral column and part of her cranium. Within her brain she keeps "butterflies" or memories of the past summer. The strength of her memory yields a "moment of truth" which leaves her weak and trembling, not because of the fall season nor because of the clarity of the moment itself, but rather because of her acute recollection of the beloved's particular way of speaking, a murmuring of words. Repeating the "nobody expected" in an anaphora which begins each stanza of this poem, Ilarregui declares that no one expected that the beloved would settle into her very bones nor that his image waving goodbye, "as if he were saying goodbye / to death" would appear before her eyes. In its description of present astonishment to a past event and in its recreation of the gestures of the beloved this poem parallels John Crowe Ransom's "Bells for John Whiteside's Daughter."[83] Ransom memoralizes a dead child by exactly recalling over five stanzas her play with farm animals; he contrasts that energy with the child's strange stillness in death. Ilarregui recalls a gesture of the beloved, so full of vitality that he seemed to be challenging death. Both poems demonstrate the power that images of beloved people wield in one's consciousness and how they become part of one's bone and marrow.

Ilarregui's poem is a secular counterpart to Saint Teresa's transfixation when the angel appeared to her and seemed to burn her entrails with his sword. The exact description of psychosomatic effects of the mystical experience, the solitude of its subject, the unexpectedness of the experience, the conviction of having been selected for the experience through no particular merit of one's own, and the joy the experience brings are present both in Ilarregui's poem and in Saint Teresa's description in her *Vida* (end of Chapter 29):

> Veíale en las manos un dardo de oro largo, y al fin del hierro me parecía tener un poco de fuego. Éste me parecía meter con el corazón algunas veces, y que me llegaba a las entrañas: al sacarle me parecía las llevaba consigo, y me dejaba toda abrasada en amor grande de Dios. ...
>
> Antes en comienzando esta pena, de que ahora hablo, parece arrebata el Señor el alma y la pone en éstasi, y ansí no hay lugar de tener pena, ni de padecer, porque viene luego el gozar. Sea bendito por siempre, que tantas mercedes hace a quien tan mal responde a tan grandes beneficios.[84]

---

[83] *Poems and Essays* (New York: Random House, Inc., 1955), p. 10.

[84] Santa Teresa de Jesus, *Las moradas; Libro de su vida* (Mexico City: Editorial Porrúa, S.A., 1975), p. 238.

> (I saw in his hands a long golden dart, and at the end of the iron it seemed to me to have a little fire. This he seemed to me to thrust into my heart a few times, and it reached my entrails: upon removing it he seemed to me to be taking them with it, and he left me burning in great love of God. ...
>
> Before as this pain was beginning, of which I speak now, it appears that the Lord snatches the soul away and puts it in ecstasy, and thus there is no place for feeling pain, nor of suffering, because enjoyment soon comes. May He be blessed forever, who gives so many mercies to the one who responds so poorly to such great benefits.)

Ilarregui may owe something to Saint Teresa also for her use of the image of the butterfly. In the *Moradas* (Book 5, Chapter 2) Saint Teresa describes the soul as a worm that makes its cocoon from the love of God and finally emerges as "una mariposita blanca / a little white butterfly."[85]

The title of the poem, "Transparencies," repeats that of the fourth poem of *Oficios y personas / Roles and Persons* and fulfills that poem with a concrete example of the process described there. We find the poet caught in the same situation, gazing out a window. She commented there more generally on the people receding into the distance as they were viewed through the window. The window itself collected "esa forma de decir para adentro, secretamente / this way of saying from within, secretly" and said goodbye. There also Ilarregui spoke of "el brillo de deseos escondidos / the lustre of hidden desires," a line which allows the reader to link her epiphany with those of Saint Teresa and of Gabriela Mistral. While Saint Teresa relates her epiphany directly to Christ, and Mistral perceives herself filling the office of poet as a Christo-imites, Ilarregui remains on the secular plane where the beloved who triggers her keen insight into time and memory is another human being. Once again Ilarregui speaks about herself in the third person, while both Saint Teresa and Gabriela Mistral used the first person in describing their experiences.

---

[85] *Ibid.*, p. 44.

"Una mujer con la mano en la frente: Schmetterling (Conversaciones de mujeres / A Woman with Her Hand on Her Forehead: Schmetterling (Women's Conversations)"

"Schmetterling" is the first of four poems within this section of eight poems to bear the subtitle "Women's Conversations." The poem translates to a female context the form of Neruda's "Arte poética / Poetic Art" and the content of his "Walking Around." Like the former Ilarregui uses a series of similes all introduced by "como / like." Neruda declares:

como si llegaran ladrones o fantasmas,
y en una cáscara de extensión fija y profunda,
como un camarero humillado, como una campana un poco ronca,
como un espejo viejo, como un olor de casa sola
en la que los huéspedes entran de noche perdidamente ebrios,[86]

(as if thieves or ghosts were arriving,
and in a shell of fixed and deep extension
like a humiliated waiter, like a bell a little hoarse
like an old mirror, like the smell of a lonely house
in which wildly drunk guests enter at night)

The rhythm of Ilarregui's lines tolls the same bell in the initial repetition "como una mariposa atrapada," ("like a butterfly trapped") followed by "como si fueran," ("as if they were,") then "como una casa prestada / como una mariposa" ("like a borrowed house / like a butterfly") and the return to "como si no fuera" ("as if I were not"). A similar sonambulist ambiance impregnates the three poems; life has become a nightmare existence. In Ilarregui's poem the butterfly, signified by the German "Schmetterling" and repeated hypnotically in its Spanish form "mariposa" thrice, does not evoke the happy image of a creature in flight at the end of its transformations from egg, larva, chrysalis, to adult flitting from flower to flower sucking nectar. Such was the construction Saint Teresa imposed on the butterfly image when she recounted her transformation in Christ in *Moradas* 5.2. Ilarregui's butterfly is an instinctual insect trapped in glass in the

[86] Neruda, p. 39.

entymologist's speciman table or hovering over and trying to escape from the artificial light cast by a lamp. Here Ilarregui develops the image of the butterfly somewhat in the manner of Tomas Tranströmer in his poem "Secrets on the Way." There he records a dream where "I stood in a room that contained every moment-- / a butterfly museum."[87]

While Neruda's narrator in "Walking Around" feels entrapped by life's routine, there is yet a sense of his being able to control or change that routine. He can at least meditate breaking out of it by "asustar a un notario con un lirio cortado / o dar muerte a una monja con un golpe de oreja" ("frightening a notary with a cut lily / or killing a nun with a blow on the ear").[88] Ilarregui shows her narrator entrapped within a typical woman's life which is circumscribed within other lives of people who do not communicate, within the bodies of other people to whom she must minister. She lives "entre puertas" / "between doors" and keeps her smiling mask pasted firmly upon her face. The woman has a sense of her own impotence. Within the honeyed atmosphere of her small patio the petals of orange and fig trees become petals of the woman herself, who is forced to contemplate things without affecting or changing them.

The writer's block that this state seems to indicate is revealed in the image of cold wind soaking leaves and swirling papers in the middle of the street. Those images relate to the image of the poet as Cumaean Sibyl. When the wind tossed the leaves on which the Sibyl wrote her messages, she too could not communicate with others. In this poem Ilarregui shows herself participating in the female condition that had entirely absorbed her mother, compared to an entrapped butterfly in "Serie de retratos" / "Series of Portraits." Ilarregui, the child who mentally collected butterflies in a world full of possibility in "A la manera de Frida Kahlo: Retrato con mariposas" / "In the Manner of Frida Kahlo: Portrait with Butterflies" has herself become another butterfly entrapped in the female condition.

---

[87] In Robert Hass's translation, op.cit., p. 34.

[88] Neruda, p. 85.

Remade in a poem which recreates the particularity of the female poet's condition, the poem develops the ancient comparison of persons and leaves. Thomas M. Greene points out that Horace and Dante in his wake used leaves to figure the mutability of language and of life itself. Both words and their speakers are subject to time like the leaves which fall each year. Horace expressed this thought in the *Ars poetica*, lines 60-63 and 70-72, here in Greene's translation:

> As forests change their leaves with each year's decline, and the earliest drop off: so with words, the old race dies, and like the young of human kind, the newborn bloom and thrive. We are doomed to death--we and all things ours. . . . Many terms that have fallen out of use shall be born again, and those shall fall that are now in repute, if Usage so will it, in whose hands lie the judgment, the right and rule of speech.[89]

Dante repeated this insight in *Paradise* 26: 137-38 where he commented "for the usage of mortals is like a leaf on / a branch, which goes and another comes."[90] Ilarregui too is keenly aware of the solitude of the individual poet in time and that his/her words may be understood differently from their meaning when they left the poet's mouth. One sees this especially in her poem "4 de julio" / "4th of July" where she views her poems as orphans once they are published and "beyond" her control.

"Una mujer con la mano en la frente: Her/Story (Women's Conversations) / A Woman with Her Hand on Her Forehead: Her/Story (Women's Conversations)"

"Her/Story: Conversaciones de mujeres" illustrates the courage of women who would overcome their political impotence in a totalitarian society anywhere on earth. The mothers who protested the "disappearance" of their children by holding vigils every Sunday in the Plaza de Mayo in Buenos Aires during the 1970s years of military dictatorship and who never gave up the search for those

---

[89] *The Light in Troy: Imitation and Discovery in Renaissance Poetry* (New Haven and London: Yale University Press, 1982), p. 14.

[90] *Ibid.*, p. 5.

children are celebrated in this powerful poem. After reading the stricken eyes of these women, the poet affirms her solidarity with them. If she were to lose a child to the government, she too would never give up her search. Insisting on the horror of the missing young persons' fate, Ilarregui orders her adjectives in a series of increasing violence: "detenido, secuestrado, desnudo, maltratado" / "detained, sequestered, naked, mistreated." The reality of their fate is again emphasized in a series of nouns as the narrator describes the method of her search. Here she insists on identifying the particular parts of the tortured bodies: "archivos de rastros,/ de pies húmedos, de caras fracturadas, de trozos de recuerdo" / "archives of vestiges / of wet feet, of fractured faces, of pieces of memory." Counterbalancing the lists of horrors enacted on the sons and daughters is the depiction of the resolution of the mothers which Ilarregui evokes with a list of their actions. She repeats "yo saldría / I would leave" or simply "saldría / [I] would leave" five times and "buscarlo / to find him" four times within the compass of this short poem. At the end she contrasts the wild "unbuttoned" look of herself as mother, searching for her child with the instinct of a frantic motherbird, with her arming herself by buttoning the very world against herself in unrelenting search. The title of the poem emphasizes the invisibility of women's experience in official history.

This poem recalls "Los antepasados / Ancestors" of *Indian Journeys* in its images of containers for memories or body parts and in its image of "caras fracturadas / fractured faces." The use of identical imagery reveals the impact of Argentina's political situation on Ilarregui's psyche, the fear in which she lived, as it also reveals the violence she felt upon having to uproot herself to emigrate to another country.

"Una mujer con la mano en la frente: Fotografía de verano / A Woman with Her Hand on Her Forehead: Summer Photograph"

In its whimsical evocation of a woman enjoying a day at the beach "Summer Photograph" offers a welcome contrast to the two darker poems preceding it. Ilarregui reminds the reader that she too can take joy in the simple pleasures of being at one with nature and with her fellow creatures--children playing, vagabonds searching the sand for treasures, a young woman chasing a dog (or life), and insects. She is comfortable in her own body and within nature and her immediate society. Poetry remains present: it is her study even here where she looks for treasures in dialogues and letters which themselves resemble "animales raros / rare animals." She sees nature making poetry in the unique footprints left on the sand. Ilarregui mixes categories in this poem as in others. Her fingers are "mariposas efimeras, / ephemeral butterflies" which "miran / look" at a glass; the sand has "frases / phrases" and the ocean "labios...corriendo / lips running." Despite the happy mood of this poem, Ilarregui still describes her eyes as "tristes / sad" and thus recalls the first poem of *Guía para perplejos / Guide for the Perplexed* with Heinrich Böll's search for a girl with "melancholic dark eyes."

"Una mujer con la mano en la frente: Leyendo cartas / A Woman with Her Hand on Her Forehead: Reading Letters"

"Leyendo Cartas" continues making transpositions between the "real" and the verbal world. As she reads her letters, the poet is interrupted by the stars, by time, by the calligraphy of her correspondent, and by the cold. In the night outside her window cars pass and the wind raises a cloud of fall leaves. She thinks of her correspondent sleeping on a pillow in another hemisphere; the two exchange signs like animals or themselves are embodied in the signs of their letters. The poet attempts to decipher the "lizards" of her correspondent's calligraphy as though it were an ancient text. Ilarregui's textualization of the world can work in the opposite direction and become an "animation" or "animalization" of textual things. Thus the letters look like lizards. In this poem Ilarregui follows her typical course of establishing connections between the present moment, exactly evoked, and people in a distant time or place. The allusion to the leaves and the effort for deciphering letters again bring to mind the image of the poet as Cumaean Sibyl.

"Una mujer con la mano en la frente: Textos del atardecer / A Woman with Her Hand on Her Forehead: Twilight Texts (Women's Conversations)"

In "Twilight Texts (Women's Conversations)" Ilarregui observes that the significance of events in a life, like the significance of some texts, only becomes clear in the future. Thus, the Jews could not foresee the meaning of the prophecy of their deliverance from bondage until they had witnessed the parting of the waters and walked through the Red Sea. Ilarregui accepts the lapse of time between the poet's writing her poem and her reader's comprehension of it (though it may be forty years) as necessary for the maturation of both poet and reader through suffering. Here Ilarregui seems to accept her role as servant to her readers as her mother accepted the role as servant to her family.

The poet discusses coming to terms with the possible. She accepts the closing of the uterus with the foreclosure of children, as she accepts the opening towards literary creation, and as she accepts the changes in her life brought about by moves from one place to another. She evokes the nature of the move with the description of "a sky of goodbyes" beneath which "landscapes fade away." Then she lists the concrete things that must be given up in such moves: houses, furniture given away or exchanged, family pictures. Beneath all this persists her comforting awareness of the flowers which continue year after year to grow and bloom. Thus, she affirms her identification with nature.

The second stanza applies this awareness of the possible to writing. As a young writer, one dreams of success although one's words may deny such hopes. Both dreams and words are squeezed through the final destiny of an idea which the poet attempts to communicate not to gain reknown but to express his or her own individual consciousness, union of soul and body.

Considering her own ambiance with its books and dirty coffeecups, the poet admits that one can see the pattern of one's existence only in hindsight, when one has gained a higher perspective on one's world and one's own suffering. She would "exchange glory for a minute of comprehension." Again Ilarregui situates that minute of comprehension within a concrete ambiance--her own home with its beloved objects, her kingdom which "is balanced softly, in a line opened through and by others."

"Una mujer con la mano en la frente: Estando sola / A Woman with Her Hand on Her Forehead: Being Alone (Women's Conversations)"

"Being Alone: Women's Conversations" evokes the poet's fear upon finding herself alone in her home, a fear so many women and no doubt more than a few men have shared. Ilarregui emphasizes the fragility and the insecurity of such a time with references to furniture pieces that seem about to change places and the fall "with elongated eyes" changing its clouds. Clocks and mirrors suddenly adopt a Surreal, threatening aspect. She is aware that no neighbor could hear her cries for help. She then contrasts this Surreal ambiance with the security she would feel were her beloved present: she would curl up beside him, let down her hair, slip her arm beneath his pillow, and enter into his very skin. In other words she would exchange the present nightmare world for one of a pleasant dream. Reinforcing the present fear she feels, Ilarregui alludes to the color blue, so often used to indicate high emotion: "Blue would not come / out of my throat."

"Cerrando los ojos: Baseball / Closing My Eyes: Baseball"

The section "Closing My Eyes" contains only three poems: "Baseball," "Butterfly Games," and "4th of July." The setting of a professional baseball game becomes the occasion for a meditation on values, a transposition to a modern idiom of Fray Luis de León's "Noche serena / Serene Night." In that poem the priest/poet viewed the starry firmament to realize how few people, caught up in daily cares, in "getting and keeping," ever lift their eyes heavenward to appreciate the wonder of creation. Speaking in the language of the earthly creation, he suggested that true beauty can be found in the heavenly creation:

"¡O campos verdaderos!
¡O prados con verdad dulces y amenos!
¡Riquísimos mineros!
¡O deleitosos senos!
¡Repuestos valles de mil bienes llenos!

(O meadows! O sweet field
of truth, fresh, redolent with pleasure! Springs
from deepest veins revealed!
O swollen hills and rings
of hidden valleys filled with all good things!")[91]

In her poem Ilarregui observes that like baseball players, who, fascinated by the brilliant lights of the field, never look beyond them to the stars, you and I pursue the less beautiful, the immediate triumph, the immediate realization of low goals. We lose the awareness "of where we are," as we lose the awareness of the suffering of fellow creatures and of the lack of hope in many lives. Most of all we lose the awareness of the present moment, the sacredness of holding the beloved's hand in one's own. While Luis de León, writing in the sixteenth century, criticized the pursuit of worldly ambition because its rewards did not survive time and death, Ilarregui criticizes them because they prevent the full enjoyment of the present moment. As the poem began with an appreciation of the brilliance of the stars, it ends with an appreciation of the brilliance of the tiniest earthbound creatures, the fireflies. Ilarregui locates their brilliance in their eyes, rather than in their phosphorescent bodies, a reminder to the reader not to forget to use his/her eyes.

"Cerrando los ojos: Juegos de mariposas / Closing My Eyes: Butterfly Games"

"Butterfly Games" casts an ironic, but ultimately sympathetic, glance at women's dependence upon social intercourse. The poet depicts her own chattering at parties and on the telephone at home, the delight in making small or large plans, the delight in trips and clothes, the delight in appreciating the details of men's clothing. Now the ephemeral aspect of life is perceived as a joy rather than as slavery within a narrow world as it was in "Schmetterling" or in "Series of Portraits." The difference lies in the implication that the woman's life in "Butterfly Games" is not limited only to socializing. The poet declares that nearly all women need other women and men. She then

---

[91] *The Unknown Light: The Poems of Fray Luis de León*, Translated by Willis Barnstone (Albany: S U of New York Press, 1979), pp. 62-63.

uses a metaphor taken from literature to describe the effect of socializing with men who "like commas in paragraphs / may mark a pause--soft, firm, brief-- / and may stop death's text." The passage recalls Gracián's description of people in terms of marks of punctuation in *El criticón*, Part III, Crisi IV. There the seventeenth-century writer reduced men to mixed dipthongs, useless parentheses, unworthy etceteras, vain ellipses, petty diminutives, hypocritical *alterutrums*, affected *qutildeques*, finally to unimportant accent marks and tildas.[92] Ilarregui's comparison reveals her textualization of life with the perception of social life as a book. However her intention is the opposite of Gracián's: while he derides certain men as useless, she affirms the necessity of men and women with the comparison to essential marks of punctuation.

A humorous but illuminating digression may illustrate this essentiality. The ten-year-old daughter of a friend of mine was once undergoing the rigors of instruction in grammar and in human sexuality at school. One day she came home and asked her mother with perfect seriousness: "If girls have periods, what do boys have? Commas?" To me the episode offers a proof that Ilarregui, as a poet, maintains a link with the child's perception for she too identifies men with commas.

"Cerrando los ojos: 4th of July / Closing My Eyes: 4th of July"

"4th of July" establishes parallels between the national holiday where the United States declared its independence of England, the personal declaration of independence of the poet who arrived alone from Argentina to a new country, and the literary declaration of independence of her poems which, upon being published, lose the nurturing of the mother-poet to find themselves alone in the world as adults subject to the acceptance or rejection of readers. The first stanza sets the scene of the particular 4th of July when the poet as a young woman, alone and frightened, had to guide her own steps in her travel within the United States. The second stanza describes the recollection of the fear that still fills the poet as she recalls that

---

[92] Baltasar Gracián, *Obras completas* (Madrid: Aguilar, 1960), pp. 879-883.

previous moment in her life, her introduction to life in the United States. She describes the lonely American night as "pedacitos de hielo, / little pieces of ice" in another allusion to her conception of the fragmentation of life. Again, her poetic method relies on joining together portentous moments--combining a moment from the past with one from the present. In the final stanza the poems themselves take on a human aspect as she attributes to them the very emotions she felt upon finding herself alone and responsible for her own destiny. Butterflies are again associated with emotion as she describes the "millones de mariposas en el estómago / millions of butterflies in the stomach" which overwhelmed her and will overwhelm the poems.

"Fuerza blanca: Morning manuscript / White Force: Morning Manuscript"

The section "White Force" elicits primarily the poet's feelings before the white sheet of paper upon which she records her poems and the oblivion, or white blankness, into which she fears her poems may fall. "Morning Manuscript" reveals a faith in connections achieved through thought and memory. Ilarregui elucidates the process through which she sometimes forges the connections used in her poetry. Here she creates a scene inside a lighted room with the curtains closed, a scene which takes on a generic quality: the room could be anywhere. Suddenly, the dog from a storyteller--whether Chekhov or a LatinAmerican or an English writer--appears to be present. In the second stanza the poet connects her present morning meditation upon her mother in Argentina with the latter's similar meditation upon her daughter in the United States. As the poet visualizes her mother arising and dressing, perhaps her mother is also thinking of her daughter. Ilarregui particularizes the two women by describing the different kinds of clothing each would be putting on. In the final stanza the poet extends these connections to nature itself, suggesting that blooming flowers may also remember other flowers in bloom. As she opens the door to leave the room, the poet imagines that she may be stepping into the sigh which her mother emits upon looking at photos of her daughter. Most interesting in this poem is the net of connections Ilarregui establishes between different kinds of reality: thought, memory, fiction, and history (the photograph).

"Fuerza blanca: Estado de luz / White Force: State of Light"

The use of italics in "State of Light" signals a special attention to the process of creation in the keen experience of a prophetic moment--as it did in "Zero Degree Writing" and in sections of "Fragments of the Future," "The Face in the Mirror," "New Lenses," **"In the Manner of Frida Kahlo:** Sometimes I Lost My Glasses," "Loose Hair," and in the entire poem, "Parts of the Rain's Discourse." Ilarregui begins by evoking the presentiment of a change in the weather which she connects with the awareness of antennae seeking voices in the galaxy ("that spiral disk"), sounds to which people are oblivious in their daily routine. This planetary awareness has always been a part of the poet's consciousness as she moves "from the edge of a cloud" through "rings of wind" until her solid house becomes simply a mental construct: "doors and windows." Inspiration for a poem comes to the poet in the same way as the consciousness of a change in the weather and of galactic realities. In a series of similes Ilarregui compares the moment of poetic conception to an abstract picture which arouses curiosity without supplying answers and to a church which is paradoxically "empty of expectation" but "full of desires." The description of the church reflects the state of mind of many twentieth-century Christians whose faith in the literal fulfillment of a the promise of the afterlife has been shaken. They still hope, but they no longer expect eternal bliss. She also compares it to a brilliant blue thread, not of yarn but of time which suddenly is transposed to weather ("splashing windows, the fresh water on my face / on your face: the poem that I feel still has not been born / it is an omen, it is a nostalgia upon looking at photos of galaxies." Here Ilarregui affirms the poet's oracular power: her ability to draw together past, present, and future. She also affirms the poet's special sense of place which can be easily displaced from the concrete to the abstract and the emotive. Finally Ilarregui affirms that the poem is greater than the poet: it has a reality and existence apart from the woman who becomes the instrument through which it becomes manifest. This conception of poetry as oracular utterance ties Ilarregui to the image of the Cumaean Sibyl, an image which becomes even more pronounced in the remaining poems of this section.

"Fuerza blanca: Hemisferio blanco / White Force: White Hemisphere"

In "White Hemisphere" Ilarregui describes the physical act of writing and the physical conditions that obtain as she writes during a brilliantly sunlit morning. She attributes to the the sun the power to draw from her very womb the words that her hands type onto the seductive white paper. The sun, the house, the paper, the periods and commas of her text, and her metaphors become as alive through personification as the poet creating the text. Ilarregui details the physical aspect of writing: the neurons through which intellectual messages pass, the hands which move like female birds over the computer and the paper, the eyes which are filled with dreams, the throat which becomes an avenue through which the power of the sun passes, the saliva which partakes of the qualities of the stars. In this last image Ilarregui associates desire with saliva because of the salivating which occurs when one anticipates and/or smells food cooking. As the body desires food, so the poet desires the stars, the comprehension of the universe. All the senses are involved in the act of writing. The sun enters through her ears in the first verse; her fingers touch the keys and the paper; her eyes see dreams; her throat and mouth salivate. What she sees, as in previous poems, is associated with fragments and the ability to bring a new perspective upon things through the use of special lenses: "Pedacitos de vidrio iluminado, anteojos / Little pieces of illuminated glass, eyeglasses."

"Fuerza blanca: Creando/viviendo / White Force: Creating/Living"

In "Creating/Living" Ilarregui affirms that poetry has become so entrenched in her being that it is an inseparable part of living. She communicates this idea by showing how poetry fills her consciousness at all times of the day and night: during the fullness of day, in the afternoons "that passed / segments of yellow" in the night when "these poems descend / night phosphorescence." Using paradox, the poet suggests that the poems may dream during "the day's solar cavity" as they may be awake during the night. Poetry evokes what is not present: cups without the human hands which hold them; days without their shadow; fingers without rings. As in previous poems, she associates poetry with potentiality: "power that went away, I feel, I think, I tremble like the leaves / these poems are no more than parts of myself, incomplete, / complex, silent." The association of the poems with leaves and with petals as well as the emphasis on fragments ("segments of yellow" or sun and the incomplete cups and hands) ally this poem very closely with the theme of the Cumaean Sibyl.

"Fuerza blanca: Alaska / White Force: Alaska"

"Alaska" opens and closes with a resonance of Alejo Carpentier's *Los pasos perdidos (The Lost Steps),* 1953. As he had penetrated the Amazonian jungle to return in time and space to the Spanish conquerors and finally to prehistoric man, so Ilarregui travels through Alaska's glaciers beneath the twenty-four hour summer sun to return to the white colonists, who once traveled Alaskan waterways, and finally beyond them to the Eskimos, who had only an oral history which celebrated the seals with their eyes lifted to the boreal skies. Ilarregui evokes the power of Alaskan sunlight; her comparison of it to an evening gown covered with sequins at once captures the sun's glitter and its continuance into the summer night. This sun makes objects stand out; it reveals their essence. At the same time it obliterates detail in an overpowering whiteness.

In the second stanza Ilarregui returns to the macrocosm-microcosm theme to communicate her own place within this landscape: "yo enuncio la palabra Yo partida en hielo / I enunciate the word I split in ice." The image recalls the first verse of "Personas perdidas / Lost Persons": "Cuando el hielo cae como una paloma partida, como una lengua transparente/ en mi ventana el mundo avanza con formas de invierno" / "When ice falls like a cleft dove, like a transparent tongue / in my window the world advances with winter forms." There she had defined the split dove as "el fondo de uno mismo / the depths of oneself." She reflected and participated in the macrocosm. Here she becomes the conscious voice of the tribal memory as she travels over the frosty water and remembers the animals so important to earlier peoples: the yellow eyes of the husky and the mulberry wings of the crow. In "Lost Persons" she had developed the idea of a poem passing though the world like a comet. Here the landscape and all the creatures in it participate in the vast poem of creation. In her desire to communicate that sacred mystery, she puts her hand on the window to touch the morning and finds herself becoming lost in the macrocosm of place and time. The whiteness of Alaska is reflected in the white page upon which she writes and in which she is lost. She is moving back into the zone of history's transparency and silence.

"Fuerza blanca: Resplandores y ausencias / White Force: Splendors and Absences"

"Splendors and Absences" continues the theme of macrocosm-microcosm as the poet describes the voices she hears in space and within her own bones. Among these voices are those of children and newborn things, those of the native Indian women Ilarregui celebrated in *Indian Journeys*, those of male philosophers, and that of her grandfather, who hopes she will meet with greater success than he did. Ilarregui repeats the transposition from the physical to the mental plane that we have seen assayed in other poems, indeed in "Alaska," the poem immediately preceding this one. The landscape becomes a literary one: "where my vegetation is a thicket of books, and leaves / fallen on the earth that give me white paper, / and mountains of periods and of commas like fleeting spiders." The fallen leaves, which are here directly related to paper, are the most striking incidence of the Cumaean Sibyl motif in all of the poems. The association receives reinforcement in Ilarregui's depiction of herself as a poet or wild prophetess, the comunal voice of her people:

> And I lose my shoes, I untie my hair, I move
> into the sacred zone where we all make the poem
> where because I was born others died, and yet my grandfather--
> sad, long, thin--speaks to himself in a low voice
> of his well-known failures in life,
>
> And expects that I may be able to triumph
> looking at the stars, greeting him with my hand on high.

In the last five verses of this quotation Ilarregui joins the communal poet with the concept of the particular, individual poet, tied to her personal family history.

In her depiction of the comunal poet or oracle, Ilarregui approaches the attitude of Rosario Castellanos, the Mexican poet who also assumed the role of tribal spokeswoman and who developed Indian themes in some of her poetry and novels like *Balún Canán* (1957) and *Oficio de tinieblas / Role of Darkness* (1962). In the latter novel the Indian seer Catalina sacrifices family to gain tribal power. Ilarregui does not follow this division of family and tribe but instead joins the two. Her image of the poet as oracle recalls, in a more restrained and intellectualized and less tormented formulation, Castellanos' verses in "Toma de conciencia / Examination of the Conscience":

En medio de este corro de presencias
soy lo que soy: materia
que arde, que difunde calor y luz. Crepito
la respuesta gozosa: ¡viven todos![93]

(In the midst of this circle of presences
I am what I am: material
that burns, that gives off heat and light. I crackle
the joyous response: all are living!)

"Fuerza blanca: Palabras del camino / White Force: Words on the Road"

"Words on the Road" begins with a quotation from the German philosopher Martin Heidegger (1889-1976): "To think is to confine yourself to a single thought that one day stands still like a star in the world's sky."[94] The single thought most closely identified with Heidegger's philosophy is that behind the many uses of the verb "to be" there is a basic ontological concept. In *Sein und Zeit (1927, Being and Time*, 1962) and in *Was ist Metaphysik (1929, What Is Metaphysics, 1949)* he questioned the nature of being; the important question was not so much "what it is to be" but "how it is to be." Technology has led Western man into inauthentic ways of being or

---

[93] Rosario Castellanos, *Materia memorable* (Mexico City: Universidad Nacional Autónoma de México, 1969), p. 30.

[94] *Letter on Humanism* in *Martin Heidegger: Basic Writings*, Edited by J. Glenn Gray (New York: Harper and Row Publishers, Inc., 1977), p. 189.

alienation, but the existential potentiality for more authentic being exists. Man exists in relation to things but should not be submerged in them as is *das Man ("the they")* of "nobody in particular." To experience anxiety (*Angst*) is to confront nothingness and to "face the potentiality of authentic being;" this experience may open the door to joy by giving the individual the potentiality "for being joyfully active." Ultimately, then, "being is associated with 'light' and with 'the joyful.'"[95] The impact of Heidegger's ideas on Ilarregui can be seen in much of her poetry where she endeavors to relate to things in a meaningful way. The danger of being subsumed by things, by daily ephemeral socializing, can be seen in "Baseball" and "Butterfly Games."

Heidegger was himself an example of a philosopher who clung to a single idea whose importance was realized in the English-speaking world only late in his life. The major theme of "Words on the Road" is the obscurity that many poets suffer during their lifetimes and the fame that may come later. Many poets do not mirror their own age, but instead forecast the future. During their lives they are condemned to seeing their works pass silently "from one drawer to another drawer / from one winter to another." Winter is a negative image signifying a cold reception in these verses. Earlier in the poem Ilarregui uses a winter landscape in a positive way. One day, she declares, the verses that cost the poet such effort will be valued for their easy lucidity by future readers. The words that "break" the poet's lips will slide from those of the future readers with the ease of skiing downhill. The poet's words will have the transparent clarity of the tracks left by the skier: white hieroglyphics. The light of the poet's verses may be too brilliant for the indifference of present readers but will be regarded as prophetic by future readers. Ilarregui again associates poetry with rebellion, "rebel pages," and identifies her major theme as "listening to the thread of the universe," a verse which recalls the "hilos de agua / threads of water" of "Alaska" and the "hilo azul brillante / brilliant blue thread" of "Estado de luz / State of

---

[95] Quotations are taken from the article "Martin Heidegger" in the *Encyclopedia Britannica*, op. cit., 5:801.

Light."

"Las formas del espejo que regresa / The Forms of the Mirror That Returns"

The final section of *Guía para perplejos / Guide for the Perplexed* includes five poems; it is entitled "The Forms of the Mirror That Returns" and carries an opening quotation from René Char: "La luz me dure para siempre. / Let the light last for me forever."[96] This French poet, born in Provence in 1907, is famous for his concise, diamond-like expression; he is master of the "heraclitic" phrase in which opposites are brought together. The title of one of his works, in its stress on doors and windows, may have influenced Ilarregui who frequently incorporates these objects into her poems: *Fenêtres dormantes et porte sur le toit* (1974; "Fixed Windows and Door on the Roof"). Ilarregui's aesthetic follows that of René Char in some aspects and diverges in others. In "La biblioteque est un feu / The Library Is Afire" Char defines his aesthetic philosophy of the *poème pulvérisé / pulverized poem*. He associates being with poetry:

> Pourquoi *poème pulvérisé*? Parce qu'au terme de son voyage vers le Pays, après l'obscurité pré-natale et la dureté terrestre, la finitude du poème est lumiére, apport de l'être à la vie.
>
> Why the *pulverized poem*? Because during his voyage towards the Country, after prenatal obscurity and terrestrial hardness the finitude of the poem is light, it brings being to life.[97]

Unlike Char, Ilarregui does not reject the prenatal, but rather seeks to establish contact with buried memories of that period.

---

[96] Ilarregui has indicated to me that she took this quotation from a Spanish translation of Char's *Fureur et mystère*: *Furor y misterio* (Madrid: Colección Visor de Poesía, 1979), unidentified translator. A similar verse appears in "La bibliothèque est en feu [The Library Is Afire]" from the collection *La parole en archipel [The Word in Archipelago]* where Char writes the verse "L'éclair me dure." In René Char, *Commune présence [Common Presence]* (Paris: Gallimard, 1964), p. 212.

[97] Char, p. 213.

"Las formas del espejo que regresa: Esferas de poder / The Forms of the Mirror That Returns: Spheres of Power"

In "Spheres of Power" the poet projects herself against the rain that has figured prominently in early poems as a symbol of transparency. The desire to know herself and the universe fully lies behind the description of her face which lifts "an invisible cape of universe." She then specifies some of the things that would be entailed in such knowledge: her age, her vocabulary, and her adornments. More abstractly she looks for the significance of time, history and emotion. The images of "time, its divisions, the road's stones" suggest suffering, difficulty and fragmentation. In the second stanza Ilarregui describes the physical means of knowing as messages pass from neuron to neuron, sent from the left and right hemispheres of the brain. As these two hemispheres control contradictory impulses, so we are all made up of contradictory aspects; we contain the north and the south, the spring and the fall, the adult and the child, experience and innocence.

The poet tells herself that if she were to go away, to die to herself as an individual and to remain as a bare intelligence, she would be able to understand both her physical and intellectual self. The humanistic and scientific approaches to knowledge would remain. But the poet refuses to bury her individuality for her essence is comprised precisely of the combination, contradictory though it may be, of the individual self and the abstract intelligence. This combination allows her to travel from the adult to the child to the uterus. It helps her to appreciate the light from lamps as well as the splendor of glass, the bonding with others, and the failure to bond. At last she recognizes that her individuality is sacred. Transposing this metaphysical insight to a literary context, as is her wont, Ilarregui declares: "someone sacred like the interior of a page." Thus, the reader perceives again the extreme textualization of self and universe that informs Ilarregui's poetry.

"Las formas del espejo que regresa: Sky Mirror / The Forms of the Mirror that Returns: Sky Mirror"

In "Sky Mirror" Ilarregui reiterates her faith that her poems, her children, will communicate her inner being. As astronauts see the world whole from their distant perspective, so these poems will give a complete picture of herself, the inside of herself. They will achieve the transparency of water, here of a tear which is both impotent and hard in its inability to overcome the suffering of the individual and the world. Clarity or transparency may not ameliorate the human condition, but it does provide the satisfaction of knowledge. The poet addresses herself to her future reader who called her with a cosmic awareness. The verse "(in my ear there were loose fish, wet sand, buckles)" conjoins primeval and technological elements of creation, while at the same time suggesting the union of the poet and reader in the "buckle." Reader and poet have become the two ends of a belt; they form a circle as they meet in the buckle. The fragmentation that has so often figured in Ilarregui's poetry resurfaces here. Now the poet suggests not only that she must bring together scattered moments of the past, scattered aspects of the self, but that she must break herself apart in poetic creation; such breaking apart constitutes experience. The "splinters" of her face reflect pieces of sky and from this mirror image thought is born. The recognition of the microcosm in the macrocosm elicits reverence, a recognition of the sacred. This poem transposes to a cosmic realm the earthbound rebellion of "If I Break."

The degree to which Ilarregui views her poems as her children, a motif also developed in "4th of July," is evident in her use of the astronaut image to figure her poems. In "Retrato de una mujer con un mensaje / Portrait of a Woman with a Message" from *Indian Journeys* Illarregui predicted that the pregnant Indian woman would bear a child who would become an astronaut of his tribe.

"Las formas del espejo que regresa: La fiesta/metáfora privada / The Forms of the Mirror That Returns: La Fiesta/Private Metaphor"

"La fiesta / Private Metaphor" opens and closes with an identical quotation from Tomas Tranströmer. Ilarregui's poem is an expansion and personal application of Tranströmer's line: "Sometimes my life opened its eyes in the dark."[98] The first line of Ilarregui's poem joins contradictory images: "and timidly, subtly, metaphors appeared like radiographs of / a time of pain: photocopies of sad eyes, of fallen shoulders." In actuality "radiografías," whether interpreted as X-Rays of the body's illness or as radio-transmitted telegrams reporting painful news, give precise, scientifically-clear messages to the person trained in deciphering them. Thus, Ilarregui implies that both the poet and later her reader must undergo some training to understand her metaphors. The weight of the poet's burden in attempting to extract life's meaning, as well as her humility, is suggested by the "fallen shoulders."

This image of the sadness of the message and its depressive effect on the poet contradict the title of "La fiesta," the party. The rest of the poem suggests that Ilarregui received this insight into the nature of her poetry during a party of celebration with fireworks during which she had to conceal her poetic persona beneath a social mask so that "no one sees me lifting a drink to a fresh moon, / that falls like congealed water on the world." Her communication with nature, her awareness of the reflection of the microcosm of self within the macrocosm of the universe, must be hidden. Once again she underscores the transparency of that insight by associating it with water and she joins the water figuring the unconscious to the consciousness suggested by the fire of the fireworks. The festivity of the social scene then imposes itself on the epiphany experienced through poetry. Insight into the nature of life becomes a "stretch of bubbles that lets fly comets or kites." The fireworks reflect fallen stars. The party itself, possibly another 4th of July celebration, heralds the passing of time.

Ilarregui's meditation on the *fiesta* bears certain similarities to René Char's prose poem "Grège." Char writes:

> La Fête, c'est le ciel d'un bleu belliqueux et à la même seconde le temps au précipité orageux. C'est un risque dont le regard nous suit et nous maintient, soit qu'il nous interpelle, soit qu'il se ravise.

---

[98] From "Kyrie," in Robert Hass's translation, op. cit., p. 36.

> C'est le grand emportement contre un ordre avantageux pour en faire jaillir un amour... Et sortir vainqueur de la Fête, c'est, lorsque cette main sur notre épaule nous murmure: 'Pas si vite...', cette main dont l'équivoque s'efforce de retarder le retour à la mort, de se jeter dans l'irréalisable de la Fête.[99]
>
> (The Party, it is the bellicose blue sky that at the same second the weather hurries to storm. It is a risk whose glance follows us and holds us, either that it questions us, or that it changes its mind. It is the great anger against the advantageous order to make love burst forth. And to leave victorious from the Party, it is when the hand on our shoulder murmurs to us: "not so quick...," this hand whose equivocation forces itself to slow down the return of death, to throw itself into the unrealizable of the Party.)

In both poems the heavens are described as an eternal backdrop for an "ephemeral" social celebration which yet shows people bonding with one another in an affirmation of themselves and human life against death. In both poems the poet is ambivalent about his participation in that party and withdraws into meditation in the midst of celebration. In both poems metaphysical questions occur to the poet.

Ilarregui's perception of the *fiesta* corresponds with the ideas developed in Octavio Paz's popular *El laberinto de la soledad / The Labyrinth of Solitude*, which first appeared in 1950. Paz theorized that Mexicans alternate between being withdrawn and private to the dropping of inhibitions to join in wild communal celebration. These two aspects of the self are present in Ilarregui's poem where she seems to be withdrawn from the group celebrating but is enjoying a purely interior celebration. She describes the partying as a a kind of rebellion against death while admitting its inexorable approach. As a poet she experiences the party with the people, yet as their conscience and voice, apart from them in her private world. Paz perceived the *fiesta* as a liberation from society's usual norms, a return to chaos, the mixture of the good and the bad, the saintly and the damned:

> La Fiesta es una operación cósmica: la experiencia del Desorden, la

---

[99] Char, p. 262.

> reunión de los elementos y principios contrarios para provocar el renacimiento de la vida....la Fiesta niega a la sociedad en tanto que conjunto orgánico de formas y principios diferciados, pero la afirma en cuanto fuente de energía y creación.[100]
>
> (The *Fiesta* is a cosmic operation: the experience of Disorder, the meeting of contrary elements and principles to provoke the rebirth of life. the *Fiesta* denies society as an organic joining of differentiated forms and principles but it affirms it as a source of energy and creation.")

Bakhtin depicted a carnivalesque aesthetic in European culture in his study *Rabelais and His World*, which:

> celebrates the anarchic, body-based and grotesque elements of popular culture, and seeks to mobilise them against the humourless seriousness of official culture....This attitude is to be traced to what Bakhtin calls 'the collective ancestral body of all the people,' that is to the epochally prepared ground of carnival images and festive forms which is no less than the material and bodily continuity of human life.[101]

In the second stanza Ilarregui personifies life as having come to her "with a dress of shining pleats." This image recalls Jiménez's famous personification of poetry in "Vino, primero, pura":

> Vino, primero, pura,
> vestida de inocencia;
> y la amé como un niño.
>
> Luego se fue vistiendo
> de no sé qué ropajes;
> y la fui odiando, sin saberlo.
>
> Llegó a ser una reina,
> fastuosa de tesoros...
> ¡Qué iracundia de yel y sin sentido!
>
> ...Mas se fue desnudando.
> yo le sonreía.

---

[100] (Mexico City: Fondo de Cultura Económica, 1989), p. 46.

[101] Simon Dentith, *Bakhtinian Thought: An Introductory Reader* (London: Routledge, 1995), pp. 66-67.

Se quedó con la túnica
de su inocencia antigua.
Creí de nuevo en ella.

Y se quitó la túnica,
y apareció desnuda toda...
¡Oh pasión de mi vida, poesía
desnuda, mía para siempre![102]

(At first she came to me pure,
dressed only in her innocence;
and I loved her as we love a child.

Then she began putting on
clothes she picked up somewhere;
and I hated her, without knowing it.

She gradually became a queen,
the jewelry was blinding...
What bitterness and rage!

...She started going back toward nakedness.
And I smiled.

Soon she was back to the single shift
of her old innocence.
I believed in her a second time.

Then she took off the cloth
and was entirely naked...
Naked poetry, always mine,
that I have loved my whole life!)[103]

Although she keeps the image of Life and Poetry personified as a woman in a pleated dress, Ilarregui places it in a social context missing in Jiménez's absolutely private setting. At the end of the poem Ilarregui transmutes the image of the girl in pleated dress to the abstract plane and the dress becomes one "full of questions." Once again she joins contradictory images: the doubt yields a final splendor

---

[102] Jiménez, pp. 130-131.

[103] Juan Ramón Jiménez, *Forty Poems*, Translated by Robert Bly (Madison, Minnesota: The Sixties Press, 1967), p. 89.

even though her questions remain unanswered for life wears a dress "lleno de preguntas / full of questions" when it bids her adieu. Ilarregui suggests that a comprehension of the mystery of life, of the things that cannot be known, is an essential aspect of her epiphany as she draws the reader into her experience. The theme of the poem fits in well with the title of the book in its emphasis on perplexity. In the course of the poetry in these two books Ilarregui has moved from the effort to break up the transparency of history by breaking herself to the effort to make herself and her poetry transparent. This theme becomes manifest in the next poem.

"Las formas del espejo que regresa: Tiempos paralelos / The Forms of the Mirror That Returns: Parallel Times"

Instead of lamenting that previous moments of time are irretrievably lost as Böll had suggested (only to prove the contrary) in "Missing Persons," Ilarregui in "Parallel Times" celebrates the ability of poetry to restore those moments. The creative work of Böll, of Tranströmer, of Ilarregui--indeed, that of most great poets--overcomes the restrictions of time. The sacredness of insight into time is evoked in Ilarregui's comparison of the circle formed by her arms around her knees to a church both now and in the past. She insists on the specific places where she has assumed this stance: the sidewalk to her home which is her sidewalk to the world. Each person looks out upon the world from the vantage point of his particular situation. In assuming this posture, Ilarregui's body formed the image of the Shri-Yantra mandala, her knees making a triangle within the circle of her arms, and her back and legs forming a square around the circle. The mandala symbolizes "the desire for spiritual unity and psychic integration."[104]

She is watching the leaves fall now, as she did in the past. She repeats the word "hojas / leaves" or "hoja / leaf" five times, mentioning it once in stanzas one, three and four, and twice in stanza two, so that the word becomes the dominant leitmotif of the poem. The falling of leaves from trees is perceived both by the eye in stanza

---

[104] Guerin, et al., p. 151.

one and by the ear in stanza two, where they are associated with "la paloma escapada / the escaped dove," the image for the poet's spirit used in earlier poems. The falling leaves whisper her name. In the third stanza the leaves recall the sheet of glass behind which people make gestures in a well-lit airport from which she is flying. The interchange between herself and the falling leaves continues in the last stanza where she declares that time both embraces and destroys her as it does the leaves. The poet becomes one with time and nature as her atoms are mixed with those of the leaves and both are blown by the wind, till only golden dust and the sound of sighs remain. The association of Ilarregui with the archetype of the Cumaean Sibyl as oracular poet enriches the comprehension of this poem for the leaves are then intimately associated with the means and the method of the poet's transmission of her messages. She accepts dissolution into the universe in a mystic union recalling Aleixandre's "La destrucción o el amor" more than Horace who, as previously mentioned, used leaves to show the mutability of poetry and the poet:

> As forests change their leaves with each year's decline, and the earliest drop off: so with words, the old race dies, and like the young of human kind, the newborn bloom and thrive.[105]

"Las formas del espejo que regresa: Guía para perplejos / The Forms of the Mirror That Returns: Guide for the Perplexed"

The final poem of this volume carries the same title as the book: "Guide for the Perplexed." It is Ilarregui's most ambitious poem, extending to four pages and divided into seven sections in contrast to the one-page poems in the rest of the book. It is also one of her most accessible poems for the length allows a development which reduces the enigmatic quality of some of the earlier poems. The poem gathers together the dominant images and themes from throughout *Oficios y personas / Roles and Persons* and *Guía para perplejos / Guide for the Perplexed*: magma, the face in the mirror, childhood illness, travel, hieroglyphics, hands with rings, buckles,

---

[105] Translated by Thomas M. Greene, p. 14.

butterflies, the celestial blue, sacredness of the self, keys, windows, doors, photographs, and the wind. In the fourth section Ilarregui alludes to René Char's theme of "cultivating one's own strangeness."[106] The reader is reminded that this last group of poems was entitled "The Forms of the Mirror that Returns" and that the poet had included a quotation from René Char on the subtitle page: "La luz me dure para siempre. / Let the light last for me forever." This injunction expresses the poet's faith, her affirmation, that, like Dante and Goethe, in the last moment of life she too may be able to say: "Light, more light."

Nevertheless, in this final poem, Ilarregui only cites herself in italics. Part VI begins with "*alguna vez las llaves encontrarán las puertas / sometime keys will find doors;*" the line is repeated at the beginning of Part VII and again, with a significant variation, at the end of this section and of the entire poem: "*sí, yo sé que un día, alguien,/ alguna vez encontrará las puertas (yes, I know that one day, someone / sometime will find the doors).*" An appreciation of Ilarregui's variation may be enhanced by recalling Gertrude Stein's famous question and response as she lay on her deathbed. She asked Alice B. Toklas: "What is the answer? I was silent. In that case, she said, what is the question?"[107] Ilarregui too suggests that in the difficult search for significance, the crucial step is to define the questions even if one cannot obtain the answers. Still, Ilarregui is confident that the answer can be found and that it exists in the poetic expression of the human condition. The reliance on a citation of herself reveals the poet's triumphant acquisition of her own poetic voice. That voice, whose timbre is thickened with the reminiscences of a myriad body of poets from her own and from other languages, rings clearly and truly with its own unique chords.

---

[106] In "La bibliothéque est en feu" Char declares: "Semons les roseaux et cultivons la vigne sur les coteaux, au bord des plaies de notre esprit. Doigts cruels, mains précautionneuses, ce lieu facétieux est propice. [We plant reeds and cultivate the vine on the slopes, on the edge of the wounds of our spirit. Cruel fingers, precautionary hands, this facetious place is propitious.]" In *Commune présence*, op.cit., pp. 215-216.

[107] Renate Stendhal, editor, *Gertrude Stein in Words and Pictures* (Chapel Hill, N.C.: Algonquin Books of Chapel Hill, 1994), p. 262.

The poem was written from Benediktbeuren, a German town containing a medieval monastery, in 1993. There Ilarregui viewed a twelfth century manuscript which supplied the title for this volume of verse: Moses Maimonides' *Guide of the Perplexed.* The fortuitous discovery of this manuscript provides the climax of Ilarregui's reconciliation with paternal roots in these two books of poems. Maimonides' text encapsulates Spanish culture--with its Jewish, Arabic, Roman and Iberian elements--for the text was written by a Jew originally in Arabic, and then translated to Latin and other European languages. Furthermore, by attempting to reconcile reason and faith, Maimonides emblemizes Western man and the desire to subject nature to rational control. As Louis Farmer from *Indian Journeys* represents the Wise Old Man of the rural indigenous culture, which affirms its unity with Mother Earth and the cosmos, Maimonides represents the Wise Old Man of the urban, European paternal culture, which seeks to master nature and remake it according to man's will.

Adopting this title for her own poetry, Ilarregui implies the affirmation of the poet as prophet and legislator for his or her community. Yet, in the way she refashions the image it becomes evident that she perceives herself more as a priestess who instructs by recalling her devotees to their integral role within, not apart from, creation and to the ultimate mystery of life to which even reason must at last bow. She guides her readers not by supplying a set of moral laws but by sensitizing them affectively to nature, society, history, memory, and self and their interrelationships. This title offers the poet as a guide to questioning readers, the same role that the Cumaean Sibyl played before her petitioners.

In the first section Ilarregui sets the scene of her visit to the monastery. In the first verse magma is transposed from subterranean zones to the sky, which reminds the poet of the quality of the sky on her visit to the monastery. The sky exerts an irresistible pull upon the poet's consciousness. Just as her mind is filled with past memories, the monastery is filled with signs from many epochs. Ilarregui evokes exactly her first reaction to the monastery: her awe upon seeing it emerge before the car's windows on a quiet afternoon. Her own appearance as a contemporary woman sporting a backpack contrasts with the antiquity of the sacred place. She was aware of the history of the place as she touched the white walls so many others over the centuries had touched. Here white walls become symbolic of light, peace, and tranquility restored after experience in the world. These white walls transform the white hospital walls of Ilarregui's childhood, which symbolized deprivation and the inability to experience a normal life. The silence of the monastery is transposed to the quality of light, the "thread of light," supplied by candles. In the muted epiphany of this poem, Ilarregui combines the darkness within the sacred monastery, whose gloomy interior is made visible only with candles, with the brilliance of the sun in the blue heavens outside. The monastery functions as an equivalent to the Cumaean Sibyl's cave, anther sacred place, as it also reminds the reader of Plato's cave.

In Part II the whiteness of the monastery's walls triggers the poet's memory of the white walls of the hospital where she stayed as a four-year-old child. There, confined to inactivity, she felt not only that her time was being stolen from her--the time that should have been spent in childhood pastimes--but that it was actually consuming her. This section of the poem resonates with the topos of Time as the Destroyer of Everything, developed most poignantly by the seventeenth-century poet Francisco de Quevedo:

> ¡Fue sueño ayer; mañana será tierra!
> Antes, nada; y poco después humo!
> ¡Y destino ambiciones, y presumo
> apenas punto al cerco que me cierra!
>
> Breve combate de importuna guerra,
> en mi defensa, soy peligro sumo;
> y mientras con mis armas me consumo,
> menos me hospeda el cuerpo, que me entierra.
>
> Ya no es ayer; mañana no ha llegado;
> hoy pasa, y es, y fue, con movimiento
> que a la muerte me lleva despeñado.
>
> Azadas son la hora y el momento
> que, a jornal de mi pena y mi cuidado,

Cavan en mi vivir mi monumento.[108]

(It [Life] was a dream yesterday; tomorrow it will be earth!
A little before, nothing, a little later smoke!
And I make ambitious plans, and I presume
scarcely a point on the fence that encloses me!

Brief combat of inopportune war
in my defense, I am the greatest danger;
and while with my own arms I consume myself,
even less my body, that buries me, welcomes me.

Now it is not yesterday; tomorrow has not arrived;
today passes, and is, and was, with movement
that to death carries me over the cliff.

The hour and the moment are hoes
that, for the daily wage of my pain and my care,
in my living dig my monument.)

This view of time contrasts with that developed in "Tiempos paralelos / Parallel Times." In the latter poem Ilarregui embraced time's destruction of the individual configuration of her atoms as a return to, or a mixing of those atoms with, the universe in a pantheistic merging of self and world. She perceived the spirit as an "escaped dove" returning to the world spirit and was confident that both matter and spirit at least momentarily affirmed her individual existence. She made a Quevedo-like progression from the material, now reduced to dust, to the evanescence of sound: "dust, dry noise, cloak of sighs." She then reaffirmed the union of matter with color and spirit: "Trajectories of atoms / Golden / gold / yellow / wind."

In "Guide for the Perplexed" Ilarregui reveals that the tragic sense of Time's destruction overwhelmed her not in adulthood, as it did Quevedo and as it does those who lead "normal" healthy existences, but in childhood. Furthermore, Ilarregui's sense of time was not just the awareness that death awaits all of us at some point, probably at the end of fifty or sixty years, but that it threatened her,

---

[108] Francisco de Quevedo, *Poesía metafísica y amorosa,* edited by José Manuel Blecua (Madrid: Cupsa Editorial, 1976), p. 5.

immediately and tangibly, in childhood, a period normally devoted to carefree enjoyment of life.

From her present vantage point in this final poem Ilarregui adds the moral observation that many people are confined within the constraints of their own social and economic condition to a life as unrewarding as that passed within the walls of a hospital. In the hospital too she viewed the world through the glass. Recalling Frida Kahlo's paintings of the circulation of blood through the body, Ilarregui describes her blood running through her body and into the tubes of the transfusion machine. Following her typical trajectory, Ilarregui transfers the images of the body onto a literary plane: her blood carried "pedacitos / de libros ilustrados, bocas de crayon azul (little pieces / of illustrated books, mouths of blue crayon." Illness forced the poet into the development of intellect and imagination.

Section III continues the vocational theme. Blood has become transposed into a "river of ink" in which the poet composes her "letters, papers, poems." She reads the world like a text: thus the city lights seen through an airplane window become a "hieroglyph of light." The solitude of the immigrant who divides her life between continents and whose work involves travel to unknown cities is multiplied by that of the strangers she encounters and by the goodbyes which fill her life. The periods of ellipses become a symbol of that solitude and its unspoken expectation. The magnetic pull of the sky in Part I of the poem is now associated with the urge towards poetic expression which searchs for the poet as the needle searchs for a vein from which to extract blood. Thus, the poet returns to the image from Part II of her lifeblood and its inextricability from her poetic vocation. Ilarregui shares this intimate moment with the reader by using the pronouns "we" and "us." She indicates that the world of the imagination is open to all of us, if we enter the world of dream to regain the child's joy in the magic of the sun's rays, which can be enumerated one by one.

The line "Bajando por la noche a aeropuertos / donde uno sabe que nadie lo espera (Coming down at night to airports / where you know that nobody is waiting for you)" echoes a line of Dulce María Loynaz, a Cuban poet who, like Ilarregui, spent much of her life traveling outside her native land. Using the topos of a trip as a metaphor for life, Loynaz, as Janet Pérez has pointed out, expressed the existential themes of solitude and incommunication in "Viajero":

> Yo soy como el viajero
> que llega a un puerto y no lo espera nadie;
> Soy el viajero tímido que pasa
> entre abrazos ajenos y sonrisas
> que no son para él . . .[109]
>
> (I am like the traveler
> who arrives at a port and nobody is waiting for him;
> I am the timid traveler who passes
> between another's hugs and smiles
> that are not for him.)

In Part IV Ilarregui returns to the present where she is conscious both of her body (face, hands, rings) and of her connection with what is outside her body: the Other. Through memory and verbal communication the world has become smaller. Ilarregui shifts Einstein's theory of relativity to a social dimension, declaring that we ourselves disperse ourselves to reunite, like particles in a mass. The movement of magma from beneath the earth to the sky in Part I indicates the impact of Einstein's theory that gravity is not a force but "a curved field in the space-time continuum, created by the presence of mass."[110] Einstein's theory of relativity holds that "if, for all frames of reference, the speed of light is constant and if all natural laws are the same, then both time and motion are found to be relative to the observer."[111] Ilarregui's constant emphasis on perspectivism throughout these poems stems from a cosmic awareness of Einstein's time and space. For her, Einstein's theory empowers human beings: we control our own destiny and can define ourselves "not as what we

---

[109] Cited by Janet Pérez in "Vida, poesía y existencia de Dulce María Loynaz, Premio Cervantes 1992," *Letras femeninas* 21, Números 1-2 (1995), p. 14.

[110] "Einstein" in *The New Encyclopaedia Britannica*, 18: 197.

[111] *Ibid.*, 18: 197.

have to be but / but rather what we are, for nothing more than ourselves." In accordance with René Char's philosophy, each of us must cultivate his or her own individuality.

Ilarregui's triumphant self-assertion contrasts with the depression evident in some of her earlier poems, notably those in the "Conversations with Women" section. There her attitude was more like that of Cecilia, a young journalist in Rosario Castellanos's short story "Álbum de familia." That character regrets not being able to be her boyfriend, able to travel to a foreign country to develop his career. She lamented to herself:

> Pero Cecilia no era él, era nada más ella, no sería jamás nadie más que ella y esta certidumbre le produjo una tristeza que no acertó a ocultar ante Susana.[112]
>
> (But Cecilia wasn't he, she was not more than she, nor would she ever be anything more than she and this certitude produced a sadness that she could not succeed in hiding in front of Susana.)

In this last poem Ilarregui, as a modern woman who has made a place for herself in the world, need not envy the male; her discovery of her "centro de gravitación (center of gravity)" is no longer a depressing recognition of limitations.

Part V returns to the personal, intimate note of the first line of Part IV. Ilarregui associates her most personal items of clothing--brassieres, buckles, petticoats--with her poetry. As she washes and hangs them on the line to dry, so she creates her poetry. Light and water are still associated with poetry, but now on the most intimate level. The sunbeams are "distributed" throughout her house and her petticoat is rinsed in water. The butterfly that was used as both a positive and a negative symbol in earlier poems now assumes a positive value: "a butterfly of West and East," associated with sunset and sunrise. The poet no longer feels destroyed by time, but rather feels that she can stop its flight: her days remain in sight ("debajo de los ojos") because she can evoke present, past and future days through

---

[112] Rosario Castellanos, *Álbum de familia,* 4th Ed. (Mexico City: Joaquín Mortiz, 1979), p. 154.

poetry. Finally the poet has become intimately identified with her products. The leaves on which she writes her poems are now part of her own body and psyche as her poems too have assumed bodies: "deshojarme social e individualmente en la mano frágil de / mi poema próximo (to defoliate myself socially and individually in the fragile hand of / my next poem." The climax of the poem, occurring two-thirds of the way through its development, inextricably ties Ilarregui to the concept of the poet as Cumaean Sibyl on both the social and the individual levels.

Part VI opens with the phrase in italics, the affirmation of the poet's faith: "*alguna vez las llaves encontrarán las puertas* / sometime keys will find doors." The poet returns to the scene of the monastery sidewalk where her joy in being alive, "caressed by the pale afternoon," becomes a rebirth, a repetition of her entry into the world. She is profoundly aware of being, of existing in the present. The association of memories, the awareness of the sacredness of each of our actions and expressions, the legacy of civilization's achievements establish communion with other human beings through time. The poet affirms the interconnection of people; we are blessed by others and we participate in each other's dreams. This concept, of course, recalls a touchstone of Spanish literature--Calderón's *La vida es sueño / Life Is a Dream*. Calderón developed the moral theme of the necessity of acting well since this life, whether it is a dream or a reality, is a trial for the next:

> If it [life] is but vainglory and a dream,
> Who for mere human vainglory would love
> True glory? What past blessing is not merely
> A dream? Who has known heroic glories
> That deep within himself, as he recalls them,
> Has never doubted that they might be dreams?
> But if this all should end in disenchantment,
> Seeing that pleasure is a lovely flame
> That's soon converted into dust and ashes
> By any wind that blows, then let us seek
> that which endures in thrifty, lasting fame

In which no pleasures sleep, nor grandeurs dream.[113]

Ilarregui makes no allusion to an afterlife; for her, good action in this life affirms the sacredness of life. The fully-conscious participation in life achieved through the opening of the senses and the exercise of the intellect in poetry is its own reward. Reaffirming her transposition of "magma" from beneath the earth to the heavens, Ilarregui declares that we are "bony material converted / into stars." This part ends with a return to ideas presented in "Hemisferio blanco / White Hemisphere," where the whiteness of snow was transposed into the whiteness of the page and punctuation marks became indicators of emotion. Here the period signals a scene of goodbyes.

Part VII recapitulates the poem's themes, referring to her poetry as an "archeology" of flashes of insight. Admitting the inevitability of death, the poet with Quevedo would suggest that we are born dying. Quevedo affirms:

En el hoy y mañana y ayer, junto
pañales y mortaja, y he quedado
presentes sucesiones de difunto.[114]

(In the today and tomorrow and yesterday, I join
diapers and a winding cloth and I have become
present successions of a dead man.)

Ilarregui also has left part of her very body--"broken teeth, wings of my lungs" in her work--as well as her personal experience with her family, with nature, and with art. Here Ilarregui uses italics to transform "*some time the keys will find their doors*" into *"yes, I know that one day, someone, / some time will find the doors*."

---

[113] Act III, lines 528-545, in *Life is a Dream*, translated by Roy Campbell in *Literature of the Western World*, Vol. I, edited by Brian Wilkie and James Hurt (New York: Macmillan Publishing Co., Inc., 1984), p. 2159.

[114] Quevedo, p. 4.

CONCLUSION

In presenting herself, the poet, as a Cumaean Sibyl Ilarregui is both archaic and modern. The fragmentation of knowledge, that appears to have occurred simultaneously with its discovery, leads to the conclusion that we possess the necessary knowledge, the keys to opening the doors, to understand the world if we could but properly order the fragments of knowledge which we possess. Modern physics with its discoveries of ever smaller particles of matter has increased our awareness of fragmentation. Einstein's theories have increased the awareness that time/space and movement depend upon the perspective of the viewer. Ilarregui's poetry orders fragments of myth, philosophy, science, personal experience, and literature to recreate the experience of the late twentieth-century. As the scenes of her poetry move easily over the Western world from the Americas to Europe, her allusions range over the wide spectrum of ancient and modern art, science and literature. The ancient ideas of the microcosm/macrocosm and of the four elements are as crucial as the modern idea of particles and perspectivism. The joining together of such diverse phenomena into a distinctly individual framework places Ilarregui in the forefront of Post Modern poets.

* * *

Considering the three books of poetry contained herein as the poet's autobiography, one can see the poet confronting first her maternal heritage in the evocation of Indian culture in *Indian Journeys*, then confronting the paternal European culture in the cosmopolitan settings and literary allusions of *Roles and Persons* and *Guide for the Perplexed.* Throughout these poems she never renounces the oracular view of the poet, but identifies ever more firmly with the Cumaean Sibyl, in an affirmation of the power of the mythic, the unconscious, and the femenine. Her uniqueness can be appreciated by casting a retrospective glance at "Calendarios / Calendars," the final poem of *Indian Journeys* and by comparing that poem with René Char's poem of the same title: "Calendrier." René Char is the poet to whom Ilarregui refers most often towards the end of *Guía para perplejos*. Yet note the attitude Char adopts towards the Sibyl in this poem:

Calendrier

> J'ai lié les unes aux autres mes convictions et agrandi ta présence. J'ai octroyé un cours nouveau à mes jours en les adossant à cette force spacieuse. J'ai congédié la violence qui limitait mon ascendant. J'ai pris sans éclat le poignet de l'équinoxe. L'oracle ne me vassalise plus. J'entre: j'éprouve ou non la grâce.
>
> La menace s'est polie. La plage qui chaque hiver s'encombrait de régressives légendes, de sibylles aux bras lourds d'orties, se prépare aux êtres à secourir. Je sais que la conscience qui se risque n'a rien à redouter de la plane.[115]
>
> (I have bound my convictions together and enlarged your Presence. I have bestowed a new heart to my days in leaning them back against this spacious force. I have dismissed the violence which limited my ascendence. I have seized the equinox's wrist without thunder peal or lightning ray. The oracle no longer subjects me. I enter: I do or do not experience grace.
>
> The menace is polite. The clime that saddled each winter with regressive legends, with sibyls in the clumsy arms of nettles, prepares itself to help others. I know that the conscience that takes risks has nothing to dread from the drawknife.)

Char's poem is an abjuration of the oracular and a celebration of his escape from its power. He associates it with the plague, with winter, with obfuscation and "regressive legends." He perceives himself as the lover or the enemy of the sibyl and adopts an aggressive attitude towards her. She is the one he must confront, to wrest away her secrets, whether through love or through trickery. Both the sibyl and Nature belong to the Other, against which he defines himself. He has lost both reverence and fear of the cosmic in his daring affirmation that he has grasped "the equinox's wrist" and done so without suffering punishment. The poem celebrates modern scientific man confronting the universe and affirms him as a triumphant Prometheus, who defies the gods unscathed.

Ilarregui, on the other hand, identifies with the Sibyl and as a poet becomes her modern embodiment. She has a much more intimate

---

[115] Char, p. 253.

participation in nature, with which she continues to identify as did her Indian ancestors. Male writers tend to use the muse and the oracle simply as a means to assert themselves. Dante used both Beatrice and the Virgin Mary as instruments to bring himself closer to God. Even Saint John of the Cross, who identified so completely with the feminine as he presented both the Soul and Nature as the bride of God, subjected both of these feminine aspects to the male creator. Ilarregui affirms the mystery of nature and her participation in it; this Sibyl still retains the connection between tree leaves and leaves of paper as she writes her messages. Her reverent treatment of Nature and the body denies the separation of mind and matter, the abstract and the concrete.

I shall conclude with a brief survey of Ilarregui's vocabulary most frequently used in the themes I have concentrated on in this essay. The extent and variety of vocabulary dealing with the body and nature demonstrate that this cerebral, Post Modern poet has maintained contact with the concrete. She has made these words her own: they "look like her." Thus, she has realized the goal set in her introduction: "el proyecto de crecer con un lenguaje, y dentro de ese lenguaje hacer vibrar mi tiempo / the project of growing with a language, and within that language making my time vibrate."

El Cuerpo / The Body: cuerpo (body), cabeza (head), piel (skin), cara (face), rostro (face), ojos (eyes), retina (retina), labios (lips), orejas (ears), garganta (throat), voz (voice), manos (hands), dedos (fingers), pelo (hair), cabellos (hair), cabellera (head of hair), trenzas (braids), boca (mouth), encías (gums), dientes (teeth), dentadura (set of teeth), lengua (tongue), la frente (forehead), cuello (neck), espalda (back), hombros (shoulders), brazos (arms), piernas (legs), rodillas (knees), pies (feet), neuronas (neurons), sangre (blood), células (cells), huesos (bones), columna vertebral (vertebral column), estructura ósea (bone structure), costillas (ribs), cráneo (cranium), sangre (blood), corazón (heart), cerebro (brain), hemisferio cerebral derecho/izquierdo (right and left cerebral hemispheres); útero (womb), cordón (birthcord), riñones (kidneys), vientre (belly/bowels/womb), estómago (stomach), pulmones (lungs).

La Ropa y Los Adornos (Clothing and Jewelry): vestido (dress), vestido de domingo (Sunday dress), traje (suit), traje de frenela gris (grey flannel suit), corbatas (ties), traje de noche (evening gown), traje polar (polar suit), túnicas (tunics), sombrero (hat), camisa (shirt), mangas (sleeves), capa (cape), cinturón (belt), hebillas (buckles), crinolinas (petticoats), enaguas (slips), enagua simple (half-slip), corpiño (brassiere), medias (stockings), zapatos (shoes), sandalias (sandals), ojotas (sandals), pullover (sweater), bufanda (scarf), anteojos (glasses), manta (poncho), collar (necklace), pulseras (bracelets), dedal (thimble), anillo (ring), trapo (rag), tiritas (bandages).

La Casa (The House): ático (attic), puertas (doors), ventanas (windows), cerraduras (locks), llaves (keys), muebles (furniture), cómodo (dresser), cajón (drawer), baúl (trunk), espejo (mirror), vidrio (glass/window), persianas (Venetian blinds), cortinas (curtains), cocina (kitchen), patio (patio), cama (bed), almohada (pillow), sábana (sheet), manta (blanket), cuna (cradle), lámparas (lamps), televisión (television), escoba (broom).

Los Animales (Animals): animales raros (strange animals), búfalo (buffalo), oso polar (polar bear), venado (deer), coyote (coyote), palomas (doves), mariposas (butterflies), peces (fish), ostra (oyster), pájaros (birds), gaviotas (seagulls), alas (wings), insectos (insects), luciérnagas (fireflies), gato (cat), perro (dog), escarabajos (beetles), abejas a rayas (striped bees), moscas (flies), largartijas (lizards), arañas (spiders), ardillas (squirrels).

Colores (Colors): ochre (ocher), amarillo (yellow), índigo (indigo), azul (blue), azul-negro (blue-black), blanco (white), negro (black), rojo (red), rosa (pink/rose), morado (mulberry), guinda (cherry).

La Naturaleza (Nature): universo (universe), espacio (space), planeta (planet), órbitas (orbits), mundo (world), sol (sun), tierra (earth), astros (stars), estrella (star), magma (magma), cielo (sky), viento (wind), aire (air), tormenta (storm), nieve (snow), lluvia (rain), hielo (ice), arena (sand), polvo (dust), arroyo (stream), cósmico (cosmic), galáctico (galactic), disco espiral (spiral disk), montaña (mountain), agua (water), fuego (fire), destellos (sparks), rayos (lighting bolts), arco iris (rainbow), nubes (clouds), piedras (stones), rocas (rocks), hojas (leaves), árboles (trees), flores (flowers), pétalos (petals), semillas (seeds), óvulo (ovule), naranjas (oranges), higueras (figs), manzanas (apples), maraña (thicket), nuez (nut), nervadura (nervure), primavera (spring), verano (summer), otoño (fall), invierno (winter), día (day), mañana (morning/tomorrow), noche (night), madrugada (dawn), anochecer (twilight).

Fragmentación y pérdida (Fragmentation and Loss): brotes (shoots/ fragments), fragmentos (fragments), trozos (pieces), trocitos (little pieces), parte (part), piezas (pieces), retazos (scraps/fragments), pedacitos (little pieces), pedazo (piece), astillas (splinters), fracturada (fractured), deconstruirse (to deconstruct oneself), romperme (break myself), partida (cleft), caer (fall), descoser (to rip apart),destejer (unravel), deshojarme (to defoliate myself), desparramarse (to spill myself out), deslizarse (to slide/slip), salpicar (to splash), coger (to gather/collect), recoger (to gather together), perder (to lose), hastío (to be fed up), máscara (mask), impotente (impotent), la muerte (death), morirse (to die), hundirse (to sink), olvidarse (to forget), dolor (pain/grief), nadie (nobody), solo (alone), soledad (solitude), tristezas (sadnesses), lágrima (tear), impermanencia (impermanence).

Cohesión/integridad (Cohesion and wholeness): encontrarse (to find oneself), entregarse (to commit oneself, surrender), manifestarse (to manifest oneself), abrirse (to open oneself up to),reconocerse (to recognize oneself), persona privada (private person), extraneza (strangeness/uniqueness), crecer (to grow), la vida entera (whole life), imágen (image), potencias (powers), transparencia (transparency), epifanía (epiphany), rebelión (rebellion), destraída (distracted, abstracted), adentro (within), coherente (coherent), comprender (understand), vivir (to live), anciano/a (old person), antepasados (ancestors), familia (family), madre (mother), padre (father), tío (uncle), abuelo (grandfather), abuela (grandmother), hermano (brother), mujeres (women), hombres (men), niño/a (child), tribu (tribe), luminosidad (luminosity), espejos (mirrors), camino (road), wisdomkeepers, líder espiritual (spiritual leader), alegría (happiness), parloteo (chatting), conversación (conversation), planes (plans), ronda de personas queridas (ring of beloved persons), danzar (to dance), círculo (circle), sagrado (sacred), resplandor (splendor).

Poesía (Poetry): poema (poem), textos (texts), historia (history/story), cuentos (stories), verbos (verbs/words), palabras (words), punto final (period), coma (comma), página (page), libro (book), hojas (leaves), línea (line), tinta (ink), hilo (thread), deshojarme (to defoliate myself), desparramarse (to spill oneself out), crear (to create), escribir (to write), memoria (memory), recordar (to remember), inventar (to invent), sueño (dream), espejo (mirror), caligrafía (calligraphy), jeroglífico (hieroglyphic), papel (paper), máquina de escribir (typewriter), computadora (computer), teclas (keys), llaves (keys), metáforas (metaphors), máscaras (masks), materia profética (prophetic matter), puertas (doors), preguntas (questions).

BIBLIOGRAPHY

Aleixandre, Vicente. *Mis poemas mejores*. Madrid: Editorial Gredos, 1976.

-----. *Mis poemas mejores*. Madrid: Editorial Gredos, 1961.

Benét, William Rose and Conrad Aiken, Editors. *An Anthology of Famous English and American Poetry*. New York: Random House, Inc., 1944.

Bible, Holy: King James Version of 1611. Boston: Pathfinder Publications, Inc., n. d.

Biblia de Jerusalén. Bilbao: Desclee de Brouwer, 1975.

Böll, Heinrich. *Missing Persons and Other Essays*. Translated by Leila Vennewitz. New York: McGraw-Hill Book Company, 1977.

Borch-Jacobsen, Mikkel. "The alibis of the subject: Lacan and Philosophy." In *Speculations after Freud: Psychoanalysis,Philosophy and Culture*. Edited by Sonu Shamdasani and Michael Münchow. London: Routledge, 1994.

Bray, Warwick. *Everyday Life of the Aztecs*. New York: Dorset Press, 1968.

Buber, Martin. *I and Thou*. Translated by Ronald Gregor Smith. Edinburgh: T. & T. Clark, 1937.

Calderón de la Barca, Pedro. *Life Is a Dream*. Translated by Roy Campbell. In *Literature of the Western World*. Vol. 1. Edited by Brian Wilkie and James Hurt. New York: Macmillan Publishing Co., Inc., 1984.

Calvino, Italo. *Invisible Cities*. Translated by William Weaver. New York: Harcourt, Brace, Jovanovich, 1972.

Castellanos, Rosario. *Álbum de familia*. 4th Edition. México, D.F.: Joaquín Mortiz, 1979.

-----. *Materia memorable*. México, D.F.: Universidad Nacional Autónoma de México, 1969.

Char, René. *Commune présence*. Paris: Gallimard, 1964.

-----. *Fureur et mystère*. Paris: Gallimard, 1948.

-----. *Fureur et mystère: Furor y misterio*. Unknown translator. Madrid: Colección Visor de Poesía, 1979.

Cruz, San Juan de la. *Poesía completa y comentarios en prosa*. Edited by Raquel Asún. 2nd Edition. Barcelona: Editorial Planeta, S.A., 1989.

-----. *The Poems of Saint John of the Cross*. Translated by Willis Barnstone. Bloomington: Indiana U P, 1968.

Dante. *The Divine Comedy 3: Paradise*. Translated by Dorothy Sayers and Barbara Reynolds. Baltimore: Penguin Books, 1962.

Dentith, Simon. *Bakhtinian Thought: An Introductory Reader*. London: Routledge, 1995.

Derrida, Jacques. *Writing and Difference*. Translated by Alan Bass. Chicago: U of Chicago P, 1978.

Dowling, Collette. *The Cinderella Complex*. New York: Simon and Schuster, 1981.
Eliot, T.S. *The Complete Poems and Plays*. New York: Harcourt, Brace & World, Inc., 1962.
Encyclopedia Britannica. 15th Edition. Chicago: U of Chicago P, 1988.
Friedan, Betty. *The Feminine Mystique*. New York: Norton, 1963.
García Lorca, Federico. *Obras completas*. 3 volumes. Edited by Arturo del Hoyo. Madrid: Aguilar, 1988.
García Márquez, Gabriel. *Collected Stories*. Translated by Gregory Rabassa. New York: Harper & Row, Publishers, 1984.
-----. *Cien años de soledad*. Buenos Aires: Editorial Sudamericana, 1967.
Glancy, Diane. *Claiming Breath*. Lincoln: U of Nebraska P, 1992.
Goethe, Johann Wolfgang Von. *Faust: Part II*. Translated by David Luke. Oxford: Oxford U P, 1994.
Gracián, Baltasar. *Obras completas*. Madrid: Aguilar, 1960.
Greene, Thomas M. *The Light in Troy: Imitation and Discovery in Renaissance Poetry*. New Haven and London: Yale University Press, 1982.
Guerin, Wilfred L., et. al. *A Handbook of Critical Approaches to Literature*. Oxford: Oxford U P, 1992.
Habermas, Jürgen. "Modernity--An Incomplete Project." In *Post Modernism: A Reader*. New York: Columbia U P, 1993.
Heidegger, Martin. *Martin Heidegger: Basic Writings*. Edited by J. Glenn Gray. New York: Harper and Row Publishers, Inc., 1977.
Herrera, Hayden. *Frida Kahlo: The Paintings*. New York: Harper Collins Publishers, 1991.
Ilarregui, Gladys M. "Discursos contra el silencio: Los textiles mexicas y Frida Kahlo." *Letras femeninas* 22:1-2 (Spring-Fall, 1996), 9-18.
-----. *Indian Journeys*. In *Plural: Revista Cultural de Excelsior*. Vol. 270 (Marzo de 1994), 4-15.
-----. "La metáfora del mercado: el intercambio prehispánico en los poemas de Marjorie Agosín." *MACLAS: Latin American Essays* 9 (1995), 18-35.
-----. *Oficios y personas / Guia para perplejos*. Alexandria: Los Signos del Tiempo, Editores, 1996.
Jiménez, Juan Ramón. *Forty Poems*. Translated by Robert Bly. Madison, Minnesota: The Sixties Press, 1967.
-----. *Selección de poemas*. Edited by Gilbert Azam. Madrid: Editorial Castalia, 1987.
Jung, C. G. *The Archetypes and the Collective Unconscious*. Translated by R. F. C. Hull. 2nd Edition. Princeton: Princeton U P, 1968.
-----.*The Psychology of Dementia Praecox*. Translated by R. F. C. Hull. Princeton: Princeton U P, 1974.
Kandinsky, Wassily. *Concerning the Spiritual in Art*. Translated by M. T. H. Sadler. New York: Dover Publications, 1977.
Keats, John. *The Poetical Works and Other Writings of John Keats*. Edited by Harry

Buxton Forman. London: Reeves & Turner, 1883.
Lacan, Jacques. *Ecrits: A Selection*. Translated by Alan Sheridan. London: Tavistock, 1977.
León, Luis de. *The Unknown Light: The Poems of Fray Luis de León*. Translated by Willis Barnstone. Albany: S U of New York P, 1979.
Lévi-Strauss, Claude. *Structural Anthropology*. New York: Basic Books, 1963.
Mistral, Gabriela. *Tala*. Buenos Aires: Editorial Losada, S. A., 1946.
Mitchell, Juliet and Jacqueline Rose, Editors. *Feminine Sexuality: Jacques Lacan and the école freudienne*. New York: W. W. Norton & Company, 1982.
Molloy, Sylvia. *At Face Value: Autobiographical Writings in Spanish America*. Cambridge: Cambridge U P, 1991.
Neruda, Pablo. *Residencia en la tierra (1925-1935)*. Sexta Edición. Buenos Aires: Editorial Losada, S.A., 1958.
Paz, Octavio. *El laberinto de la soledad*. México, D.F.: Fondo de Cultura Económica, 1989.
-----. *Selected Poems of Octavio Paz: A Bilingual Edition with Translations by Muriel Rukeyser*. Bloomington: Indiana U P, 1963.
Pérez, Janet. "Vida, poesía y existencia de Dulce María Loynaz, Premio Cervantes 1992." In *Letras femeninas* 21: 1-2 (1995), 9-19.
Pyle, Michael Robert. *Audubon Society Handbook for Butterfly Watchers*. New York: Scribners, c. 1984.
-----. *The Audubon Society Field Guide to North American Butterflies*. New York: Knopf, c. 1981.
-----. *The Thunder Tree: Lessons from an Urban Wildland*. Boston: Houghton Mifflin, 1993.
Quevedo, Francisco de. *Poesía metafísica y amorosa*. Edited by José Manuel Blecua. Madrid: Cupsa Editorial, 1976.
Ransom, John Crowe. *Poems and Essays*. New York: Random House, Inc., 1955.
Sahagún, Fray Bernardino de. Selections from *Historia general de las cosas de Nueva España*. In *Literatura del México antiguo: los textos en lengua náhuatl*. Edited by Miguel León-Portilla. Caracas: Biblioteca Ayacucho, 1978.
Sáinz de Medrano, Luis. *Historia de la literatura hispanoamericana (Desde el Modernismo)*. Madrid: Taurus, 1989.
Stein, Gertrude. *Bee Time Vine and Other Pieces [1913-1927] by Gertrude Stein*. Edited by Virgil Thomson. New Haven: Yale U P, 1953.
-----. *Syntax and Elucidation*. In *A Primer for the Gradual Understanding of Gertrude Stein*. Edited by Robert Bartlett Haas. Los Angeles: Black Sparrow Press, 1971.
Stendhal, Renate. *Gertrude Stein in Words and Pictures*. Chapel Hill, N. C.: Algonquin Books of Chapel Hill, 1994.
Teresa de Jesús, Santa. *Las moradas; Libro de su vida*. Mexico City: Editorial Porrúa, S.A., 1975.

Tranströmer, Tomas: *Tomas Tranströmer: Selected Poems 1954-1986.* Translated by Robert Hass. New York: The Ecco Press, 1987.

Trend, J. B. *The Oxford Book of Spanish Verse*. Oxford: Clarendon Press, 1965.

Valenzuela, Luisa. *Cambio de armas*. Hanover, N.H.: Ediciones del Norte, 1982.

Virgil. *The Aeneid of Virgil.* Translated by Allen Mandelbaum. New York: Bantam, 1972.

Woolf, Virginia. *A Room of One's Own*. London: The Hogarth Press, 1929.

La Respuesta de la Poeta

The Response of the Poet

LA POETA RESPONDE

[Me gustaba tanto ver la conjunción de tres poems "Poco a poco", "Fragmentos de futuro" y "Fotos viejas" juntos y analizados como "fragmentos", porque ¡es tan verdadero! Judy, el análisis de "Oficios" es abrumador.] Tengo que seguir en español, pues temo que mi inglés no es nada bueno, para asegurar que desde el punto de vista de mis objetivos, yo quería presentar "oficios" muy modestos que sin embargo mostraran qué cerca están de la poesía. O al revés, como una situación por pobre que sea, conlleva siempre momentos de absoluta comunión con algo supremo: la vida, la poesía e indudablemente una realidad superior. Pero es correcto que siempre hay fragmentos, no son totalidades como la felicidad no es una totalidad, me parece.

El proyecto de "Guía" presentado aquí poema por poema en un extraordinario trabajo crítico tuyo, Judy, nació--como la habláramos por teléfono, de ese cuento de Böll: "Missing Persons" que podría haberse llamada "Personas desaparecidas", pero yo traduje como "Personas Perdidas" puesto que me pareció más adecuado. Él dice que vuelve a buscar a la niña que era su madre, en un pueblo alemán antes de la guerra, y el hecho de que lleve el hilo de la narración hacia el pasado, que busque en sus padres los niños que fueron, me pareció un proyecto único. Además hay un elemento de tristeza que yo siento que involucra volver a la niñez. En primer lugar, porque la mía fue muy triste, con una enfermedad tan grave, y luego porque creo que descubrí muy pronto las pequeñas infelicidades de mi madre, que siendo sumamente inteligente no había podido acceder a una educación superior (¡como tantas mujeres latinoamericanas!), y ella deseaba tanto conocer y saber más y más... y esto, me producía también dolor, puesto que yo pensaba que mi madre merecía una vida más libre, incluso de mí y mis problemas físicos en aquel momento. Pero en ambos, mis dos padres, descubrí una cualidad muy rara: eran personas terriblemente bondadosas, con un gran sentido social.

THE POET RESPONDS

I liked so much to see the conjunction of three poems "Poco a poco" ("Little by little"), "Fragmentos de futuro" ("Fragments of the Future") and "Fotos viejas" ("Old Photos") together and analyzed as "fragments," because it is so true! And I have not realized it! . . . Judy, the analysis of *Oficios* (*Roles*) is overwhelming. I have to continue in Spanish, for I fear that my English is not good enough to communicate the assurance that from the point of view of my objectives, I wanted to present very modest "oficios" ("roles" or "tasks") that nevertheless would show how close they are to poetry. Or the reverse, how a situation however poor it may be, always carries with it moments of absolute communion with something supreme: life, poetry and undoubtedly a superior reality. But it is correct that there are always fragments, which are not totalities as happiness is not a totality, it seems to me.

The project of *Guía* (*Guide*) presented here poem by poem in your extraordinary critical work, Judy, was born--as we spoke of it on the telephone--from that story of Böll's: "Missing Persons" that could have been called "Disappeared Persons," but that I translated as "Lost Persons" since that seemed more adequate to me. He says that he looks again for the child that his mother was, in a German town before the war, and the fact that he takes the narrative thread towards the past, that he may search in his parents for the children that they were, seemed to me to be a unique project. Besides there is an element of sadness that I feel is involved in returning to childhood. In the first place, because mine was so sad, with such a serious illness, and then because I believe that I discovered very soon the small infelicities of my mother, who being highly intelligent had not been able to pursue higher education (as so many Latin American women had not!), and she wished so much to become acquainted with and know more and more . . . and this, produced so much pain in me, since I thought that my mother deserved a freer life, free even of me and my physical problems in that moment. But in both, my two parents, I discovered a very rare quality: they were terribly kind persons, with a great sense of social responsibility.

Mi padre traía bolsas de galletitas partidas a la casa, porque una fábrica cerca de donde él trabajaba vendía galletitas partidas a menos precio, y mi madre siempre hacía paquetes para otra gente, o abría la puerta de la casa para que entraran a comer. Y yo no comprendía esto en medio de tantos problemas tan difíciles como todos teníamos en aquel momento, pero supongo y sé, que esa base ética los ha ayudado a vivir toda la vida. De modo que el mencionar a Böll, en este trabajo me parece un acto de justicia.

El libro, como lo has notado, Judy, tiene una progresión entre el universo infantil aunque trastocado, y una sucesión de hechos que van desarrollándome como persona. Por ejemplo época, donde toda "mi época" está nuevamente en un ciclo de revoluciones, solamente imaginar que la mitad de las lecturas estaban prohibidas, y las películas de los cines cortadas y la gente no podía leer o escuchar casi nada "real". Este estado de censura, de cualidades siniestras, produjo en mí una persona rebelde, aunque confieso que nunca tomó la rebeldía de otras mujeres, porque mi rebeldía siempre estuvo cerca del arte, de las cosas que podían plantearse creativamente. Pero las mujeres de "conversaciones" existieron, y tenían estas confesiones tan particulares, como sentir que uno no se puede mover en "Schmmeterling" / "Mariposa", o como todavía estar "traspasado" por alguien querido, en "Transparencias", o como esa "Mujer con la mano en la frente" que piensa y piensa su mundo, organizándolo, otra vez, entre fragmentos.

Luego viene, este paso al más acá que sucede en un exilio elegido hacia Estados Unidos, y una comunicación de nieves y nostalgias pero también de gran admiración por esta cultura. En poemas como "Alaska" (cuya traducción que conservo me parece impresionante, gracias), quiero rendir homenaje a las fuerzas que sostienen este país, a las grandes fuerzas glaciales, indígenas, llenas de cielo y de pradera que están en el corazón de un país que acepta y absorbe diferencias. "Alaska" es un poema entre nosotros dos: la

My father brought bags of broken cookies home, because a factory near his workplace sold broken cookies at a reduced price, and my mother always made packages for other people, or opened the door of her home so that they could come in to eat. And I did not comprehend this in the midst of so many and such difficult problems that we had in that moment, but I suppose and I know, that that ethical base has helped them to live all of life. So that mentioning Böll in this work seems to me to be an act of justice.

The book, as you have noted, Judy, has a progression between the infantile although emotionally disturbed universe and a succession of facts that continue making me develop as a person. For example "epoch," where all "my epoch" [youth] was again in a cycle of revolutions, only imagining that half of the books were prohibited, and the cinema films cut and the people could not read or listen to almost anything "real." This state of censorship, of sinister qualities, turned me into a rebellious person, although I confess that I never assumed the rebellion of other women [women's liberation], because my rebellion was always related to art, to the things that could be set forth creatively. But the women of "conversations" existed, and they had these very particular confessions like feeling that one cannot move in "Schmmeterling" ("Butterfly"), or like being still "transfixed" by some beloved person, in "Transparencies" or like that "Woman with Her Hand on Her Forehead" who conceptualizes and conceptualizes her world, organizing it, again, among fragments.

Then comes that step towards more recent time that happened in a voluntary exile towards the United States, and a communication of snows and nostalgias but also of great admiration for this culture. In poems like "Alaska" (whose translation which I keep seems impressive to me, thanks), I want to render homage to the forces that sustain this country, to the great glacial forces, the indigenous ones full of sky and meadow that are at the heart of a country that accepts and absorbs differences. "Alaska" is a poem between us two:

tierra y yo, esta geografía y yo. Y es un poema mucho más importante porque jamás toleré la nieve, y sin embargo la acepto como parte de esta reunión con Estados Unidos. Pero también en Alaska hay fragmentos, no totalidades.

No puedo decir el impresionante caleidoscopio de referencias maravillosas que aparecen en este estudio, Judy, puesto que me asombra ver la flexibilidad para integrar poetas y filósofos a mi intento. Pienso que todas las referencias y el estudio en general son de una calidad indiscutible y quizás ponen estos poemas en un plano mucho más alto del que realmente están. También estoy de acuerdo con el posmodernismo de mi poesía en el sentido de que los centros, los principios de autoridad se pierden, si una cosa vuelve siempre es la página, la ansiedad de escribir, el deseo de comprender la vida, pero no hay espacio para nada conclusivo o cerrado. Son fragmentos que surgen de momentos, de incertidumbres, y hasta de convicciones. Esas partes me parecen mucho más iluminadoras, porque significan que cada uno de nosotros en este planeta, inventaremos la vida, el espacio, el tiempo, con los elementos internos que tenemos. Eso para mí, es la verdadera derrota del fascismo que sufrí durante diez años de mi vida, en un país autoritario y dictatorial.

Cuando yo estaba en el aeropuerto antes de venirme a este país, mi madre que nunca había dicho una palabra negativa o me había dicho nada sobre nuestra partida, comenzó a llorar diez minutos antes de salir el avión, pero ella en un gesto de gran madurez se acercó y me dijo: "Estoy llorando pero no te confundas, es de alegría. Por que vas a ser libre, y esto es lo que siempre querías". Y cuando las puertas de vidrio que nos separaban se cerraron, yo comprendí que ella me dejaba volver a nacer, sin angustias, sin culpas. Yo he pensado esto muchas veces, la forma como nos separamos en aquel momento. Y he pensado que esta fragmentación me ha dado un poco más de humildad y tal vez humanidad para mirarlo todo, para tratar de incorporarlo todo. Y además, como me siento atraída por seres extraterrestres, gente con neurosis, locura, depresión, euforia, papeles de la calle,

the earth and myself, this geography and myself. And it is a poem all the more important because I could never tolerate snow, and nonetheless I accept it as part of this meeting with the United States. But also in Alaska there are fragments, not totalities.

I shall not address the impressive kaleidoscope of marvellous references that appear in this study, Judy, since it astonishes me to see such flexibility for integrating poets and philosophers to my intention. I think that all the references and the study in general are of an indisputable quality and perhaps put these poems on a much higher plane than they really are. Also I agree with the Post Modernism of my poetry in the sense that the centers, the principles of authority are lost; if something always returns, it is the page, the anxiety of writing, the desire of comprehending life, but there is no room for anything conclusive or closed. They are fragments that surge forth from moments, from incertitudes, and even from convictions. Those parts seem to me much more illuminating, because they mean that each of of us on this planet invents life, space, time, with the internal elements that we have. That for me, is the true defeat of fascism that I endured for ten years of my life, in an authoritarian and dictatorial country.

When I was at the airport before coming to this country, my mother who never had said a negative word or had said anything about our departure, began to cry ten minutes before the plane's leaving, but she in a gesture of great maturity approached me and said: "I am crying but don't get mixed up, it is from happiness. Because you are going to be free, and this is what you always wanted." And when the glass doors that separated us closed, I understood that she was allowing me to be born again, without anguish, without guilt. I have thought about this many times, the way that we were separated in that moment And I have thought that this fragmentation has given me a little more humility and perhaps humanity for looking at everything, for trying to incorporate everything. And besides, as I feel attracted by extraterrestrial beings, people with neurosis, madness, depression,

países exóticos, modos de mirar por las ventanas, puede ser que todo eso sea lo que viene a buscar. Y como la poesía es tan rica pero tan ardua, me lo entrega en fragmentos.

Judy, desde el punto de vista crítico y de las aportaciones poéticas nada hay que yo pueda agregar a una persona que sabe tanto.

Gladys

euphoria, papers blown about on the street, exotic countries, ways of looking through windows, it may be that everything may be that which remains to be searched for. And as poetry is so rich but so arduous it is given to me in fragments.

Judy, from the critical point of view and from the poetical additions there is nothing that I can add to a person who knows so much.

Gladys

INDIAN JOURNEYS

(VIAJES INDIOS)

INDIAN JOURNEYS

CONTENIDO

CONTENTS

Para Rayén y Ayelén, por un atardecer mapuche que recordaré toda la vida.

Para los mexicanos que me regalaron un destino.

El principio de un viaje
(Introducción)

Cuando abro la ventana, hace frío y por la ventanilla del tren anticipo las montañas que llegarán con colores azules y mágicos. Estoy portando el viejo diario en donde inscribo a las personas y a las cosas, trasmutaciones de los días. Olores, formas. Al descender, el territorio que me espera es un lugar auténtico, lejos del progreso, un sitio donde el arcoiris se levanta dejando brillar puntas de oxidiana hundidas contra las rocas. Entre los papeles viejos las cartas de mi amiga me dicen que en Bajada del Agrio hay una gran necesidad de apoyo. En otras cartas leo formas de nubes. Personas. Lejos estoy de anticipar el destino de estas poblaciones, envueltas en un frío pristino, cuando entro a
las entrañas de estas montañas, a los perfumes de la cocina, me parece que he estado aquí mucho tiempo antes, que aquí me quedaré mucho tiempo después.

Cuando abro la ventana es verano, y me sumergo desde el ómnibus a la boca verde de Palenque, a las geografías blancas de las piedras cuyas voces puedo escuchar, en una comunicación íntima que siempre he tenido con las piedras, austeras y solas, resistentes como pocas, maravillosas en sus diferencias.

Al tocar con mis manos las mariposas del Templo del Sol, pienso en la fuerza de esta vida que me toca vivir, pienso en los sueños soñados por otras mujeres, niñas, mirándose desde los

For Rayén and Ayelén, for a late Mapuche afternoon that I shall remember all my life.

For the Mexicans, who bestowed a destiny upon me.

The beginning of a journey
(Introduction)

When I open the window, it is cold and through the train's small window I anticipate the mountains that will arrive with blue and magic colors. I am carrying the old diary in which I inscribe persons and things, the days' transmutations. Scents, forms. Upon descending, the territory that awaits me is an authentic place, far from progress, a site where the rainbow rises letting sunken points of rust shine against the rocks. Among old papers my girlfriend's letters tell me that Bajada del Agrio really needs help. In other letters I read cloud forms. Persons. I am far from anticipating the destiny of these villages, wrapped in a pristine cold, when I enter these mountains' bowels, the perfumes of the kitchen, it seems to me that I have been here a long time ago, that here I shall remain for a long time.

When I open the window it is summer, and I sink from the omnibus into the green mouth of Palenque, into the white geographies of the stones whose voices I can listen to, in an intimate communication that I have always had with the stones, autere and alone, more resistent than any others, marvelous in their differences.

Upon touching the butterflies of the Sun Temple with my hands, I think about the force of this life that was dealt to me, I think about the dreams dreamt by other women, girls, looking at themselves from the water's mirrors, between bunches of wild

espejos de agua, entre racimos de flores silvestres y amarillas, en comunicación con dioses que me parecen más fabulosos que los dioses del presente.

En estos viajes algunas personas encontradas, otras imaginadas, mi vida se enriquece de abecedarios desconocidos y diccionarios exóticos. Un símbolo de sobrevivencia se abre desde Acoma a Neuquén en los peces secos contra las piedras, en las hojas apretadas contra cartuchos de hojas, descompuestas, convertidas en polvo dorado.

Los rituales del paraíso que vendrá no los comprendo, pero comprendo más y más el dolor de dejar esta tierra, el principio de este viaje cósmico, entre otras mentes y fuerzas, que como poeta me enriquecen y como mujer me hacen reflexionar, con sacos pesados, o sombreros contra el sol, en líneas de un block que posiblemente nadie lea, solamente mi sentido de "yo" contra este calendario que me ha sido entregado.

Puedan mis días en la tierra ser fecundos, ricos como las cabelleras azules y negras, como los ojos agigantados, de esas niñas Rayén y Ayelén, que lloraban largamente cuando nos despedíamos en la ventanilla del tren, porque querían seguir aprendiendo a leer y escribir, y porque no tenían nada para pagarme, solamente: dos manos llenas de alas de mariposas muertas.

yellow flowers, in communication with gods that seem more fabulous to me than the present gods.

In these journeys some persons encountered, others imagined, my life is enriched with unknown ABC books and exotic dictionaries. A symbol of survival opens up from Acoma to Neuquén, in the dry fish against the stones, in the leaves pressed against cones of leaves, decomposed, converted into golden dust.

The rituals of the paradise that is to come I do not understand, but I understand more and more the pain of leaving this earth, the beginning of this cosmic journey, among other minds and forces, that as a poet enrich me and as a woman make me reflect, with heavy sacks, or hats against the sun, in lines of a block that posibly nobody may read, only my feeling of "I" against this calendar that has been handed over to me.

May my days on the earth be fecund, rich like the blue and black heads of hair, like the hugh eyes, of those children Rayén and Ayelén, who wept for a long time when we said goodby from the train's small window, because they wanted to continue learning to read and write, and because they had nothing with which to pay me, only: two hands full of the wings of dead butterflies.

LOS ANTEPASADOS

(el principio de un viaje)

como un baúl de espejos de caras fracturadas
aparezco buscando mis caras anteriores, y en la montaña
de miradas, de un espejo a otro, saco la cara de la niña
que mira pasar la lluvia

entre tantos espejos está también mi cara con dolor,
con ojos largos, mi cara adolescente, mi primera arruga
caras de mis caras en estos espejos, en el ático
donde otros guardan muñecas yo guardo gestos,

una luz de atardecer se filtra por la casa mágicamente
una luz que al tocar las cortinas las pone pálidas

de rodillas busco mis otras caras, mis pertenencias:
sonrisas, lágrimas, astucias inocentes, es que llega
una edad donde la literatura

es un deconstruírse y encontrarse a uno mismo:
los verbos sueltos, el pelo suelto, los lazos, las hebillas
desde una persona potencial a una privada
haciendo versos: buscando mis caras.

ANCESTORS

(journey's beginning)

like a trunk of mirrors of fractured faces
I appear searching for my earlier faces, and in the mountain
of glances, from one mirror to another, I take out the face of the girl
who watches the rain passing

among so many mirrors there is also my griefstricken face
with long eyes, my adolescent face, my first wrinkle
faces of my faces in these mirrors, in the attic
where others keep dolls I keep gestures,

an afternoon light filters magically through the house
a light which touching the curtains turns them pale

on my knees I search for my other faces, my belongings:
smiles, tears, innocent tricks, so one reaches
an age where literature

is a deconstructing to find oneself:
loose words, loose hair, ties, belts
from a potential person to a private one
making verses: searching for my faces.

ME DISTRAJE

y perdí la noción del tiempo y el espacio
avancé por la calle empapada de lluvia o era un camino indio

seguí la línea invisible de una mañana repartida en casas
o fue una línea de agua, la vena transparente de un arroyo

me perdí con las piedras de ojos ocres, las miradas fugaces
de las piedras, que al rodar bajan cantando como niñas

se estampan en el camino, reacomodan su propia permanencia
botas llenas de polvo, imágenes de polvo rosa tocando

los objetos como mi mano, mi cara cuando pasa un auto
cuando de tanto en tanto pasa un auto y levanta una capa

de tarde y de universo. Me distraje y fui a parar al fin
del mundo, iba de la mañana caminando hasta encontrar

el sol sobre las rocas, palabras partidas en ausencia
palabras que empujaban como niños que empujan desde un vientre

palabras que querían ser posibles terminaron heridas
por el atardecer, en mis oídos un pájaro pasó como una onda

eléctrica, una onda de luz del espacio a mi cuerpo: sentí
la vibración de otro ser vivo: mis palabras, mi tiempo

crear es distraerse, perturbarse, morirse en el camino
nunca quedarse quieto caminando, desarrollando formas como

I GREW DISTRACTED

and I lost the sense of time and space
rainsoaked I came down the street or was it an Indian road

I followed the invisible line of a morning divided into houses
or was it a line of water, the transparent vein of a brook

I got lost amongst the stones of ocher eyes, the fleeting glances
of the stones, which roll down singing like girls

they sink in the road, reaccommodating their own permanence
boots full of dust, images of rose dust touching

objects like my hand, my face when a car passes
when from time to time a car passes and raises a cloak

of afternoon and of universe. I grew distracted and came to a stop
at the end
of the world, I would go away in the morning walking 'til reaching

the sun on the rocks, words divided in absence
words that would push like children that push from a womb

words that wanted to be possible ended up wounded
by the afternoon, in my ears a bird passed like a slingshot

electric, a wave of light from space to my body: I felt
the vibration of another living being: my words my time

to create is to grow distracted, to become perturbed, to die in the
road
never to be quiet walking, developing forms like

espacios donde poner secretos, y formas de morir y de vencer
experimentan con nosotros, en besos prohibidos y sus
cuerpos

en el camino, con el camino me distraje y no sé si me
preguntaron
por una calle o el borde un arroyo, o si al dar vuelta

la página, el esplendor del sol dictó el poema.

spaces to put secrets into, and forms of dying and of conquering
experiment with us, in forbidden kisses and their bodies

in the road, with the road I grew distracted and I do not know if
they asked me
about a street or the edge of a brook, or if upon turning

the page, the sun's splendor dictated the poem.

CONVERSACIONES

"ask me questions from your heart,
and I'll give you answers from my heart"
Big Cypress Indian Reservation. *

este verbo: crecer, es un búfalo,
un búfalo rebelde corriendo en la pradera de la página
la primavera crece y desparrama insectos invisibles a la luna
la sensibilidad de las semillas es tanta, que apretados
los pétalos dan besos sin saber cómo darlos, se aprietan
y se besan las bocas de los pétalos

este verbo: crecer, lleva la vida entera
no tiene tiempo pero vive en el tiempo, se desparrama azul
entre palabras, toma la forma de casas y puertas, ingresa
a las personas que perdimos, a los que querremos,
quién sabe mañana...

un búfalo que pasa cargado de noche sobre
las teclas de mi máquina. Conversación con un anciano,
la boca de la luna, aquella noche/ esta madrugada,

los búfalos: mi tiempo.

**"hazme preguntas de tu corazón,
y to te daré respuestas de mi corazón"
Reserva India de Çiprés Grande.**

CONVERSATIONS

ask me questions from your heart
and I'll give you answers from my heart
Heard on the Big Cypress Indian Reservation

this verb: to grow, is a buffalo,
a rebellious buffalo running in the page's meadow
spring grows and spills out invisible insects to the moon
the seeds' sensibility is such, that when pressed
the petals give kisses without knowing how to give them, they press against each other
and the petals' mouths kiss each other

this verb: to grow, carries all of life
it does not have time, but it lives in time, it spills out blue
between words, it takes the form of houses and doors, it enters
the persons that we lose, those that we shall love,
who knows tomorrow

a buffalo weighed down with night that passes over
the keys of the typewriter. Conversation with an old man,
the moon's mouth, that night / this dawn

buffalos: my time.

AUTUMN PRAYER

"pero si nosotros hemos estado aquí durante tantos siglos,
duraremos, seremos siempre jóvenes como el ojo de un animal
que recién se despierta".
Rocogido en Puebo de Acoma, Nuevo México, 1990

uno junta las manos y hace un hueco para recoger agua
de un arroyo, al reclinarse uno se ve los ojos en el agua,

encuentra las hojas secas que cayeron y viajan mirando
por última vez hacia arriba, la cabellera de los árboles
repletos de universo

es un minuto donde uno escucha dentro de sus pulmones
el cielo y en un suspiro el aire que cruza la mañana
vuelve impecable, nítido hacia las manos juntas

hay tantas lunas y tantos planetas, esto que vemos es
una parte de tantas otras partes, fragmentos

una hoja amarilla cruza el agua, una señal del ocre
que se lo lleva todo, fugacidad de esta cara, estos ojos

con estos pensamientos que son líneas de mí, yo te recuerdo.

AUTUMN PRAYER

But if we have been here for so many centuries,
we shall last, we shall always be young like the eye of the animal
that recently awakened.

Collected in Pueblo de Acoma, New Mexico, 1990

one joins one's hands to make a hollow to hold water
from a stream, upon leaning over one sees one's own eyes in the water,

one finds dry leaves that fall and travel looking
up for the last time, the hair of the trees
full of universe

it is a minute when one hears within one's own lungs
the sky and in a sigh the air that crosses the morning
returns impeccable, clear towards one's joined hands

there are so many moons and so many planets, this that we see is
a part of so many other parts, fragments

a yellow leaf skims the water, a sign of ocher
that carries everything away, the fleetingness of this face, these eyes

with these thoughts that are lines of myself, I remember you.

CRIAR ESPEJOS

aunque uno reconozca su cara al mirar un espejo
siempre existe una zona de vacío,
es casi prodigioso el ejercicio de reconocerse
cada vez que nos miramos, como si fuéramos los mismos

pero con las palabras de boca en boca de cultura
en cultura, una palabra va cambiando de manos y de ojos
inclusive hay palabras que cambian de sentido
si digo lluvia en otra parte puede ser tan buena

pero lluvia aquí adentro con trozos de lamento,
lluvia encendida de fuego, de potencia, o lluvia que
al borrar todos los rostros, inventa nuevamente un
camino, leyendo las pisadas de animales antiguos

o un desparramarse: este crecer de un texto,
de una vida, fragmentos de luminosidad, criar espejos,
escribir páginas que solo se parecerán a ellas mismas.

BREEDING MIRRORS

although one may recognize one's face upon looking in a mirror
a zone of emptiness always exists,
it's almost prodigious this exercise of recognizing oneself
each time that we look at ourselves, as if we were the same

but with words from mouth to mouth from culture
to culture, a word changes its hands and its eyes
there are even words that change meaning
if I say rain somewhere else it may be so good

but rain here within with bits of lamentation,
rain lit up with fire, with power, or rain which
upon erasing all the faces, invents anew a
road, reading the steps of old animals

or a spilling out: this growing of a text,
of a life, fragments of luminosity, nurturing mirrors,
writing pages that will only look like themselves.

RETRATO DE UNA MUJER CON UN MENSAJE

ula-ula
ulalala
todas las cunas silenciosamente guardan fuerzas preciosas
cuando mi madre descorre la sábana me encuentra sin potencias
con los ojos cerrados y el mundo cósmico que conocí en su vientre
se enmudece, duerme callado sobre una neurona,

(recordaré después cómo rompí la bolsa del agua
invirtiendo los mensajes sagrados)

nadie sabe que duermo sin dormirme, que con los años al
crecer las palabras, imprimiré con rasgos nuevos la primera
órbita azul que en el útero ven por primera vez los niños

ahora una mujer que está cansada se apoya en una silla
con su vasija ocre, una mujer de trenzas largas, de ojos
indios
que lleva el vientre repleto de mensajes,

ese niño es un astronauta de su tribu, esa mujer está
sintiendo un niño que prendido a su cordón viaja por el
universo
códices, fogatas, destrucciones, y ahora este cansancio:

la miro, sonreímos.

PORTRAIT OF A WOMAN WITH A MESSAGE

hush-hush
hush, baby, hush
all the cradles silently keep precious forces
when my mother pulls the sheet back she finds me powerless
with closed eyes and the cosmic world that I knew in her womb
hushes up, it sleeps upon a neuron

(I shall remember later how I broke the waterbag
spilling sacred messages)

nobody knows that I sleep without falling asleep, that with
the years' passage,
and the words' maturation, I shall imprint with new features the
first blue orbit that children see in the uterus for the first time

now a woman who is tired rests in a chair
with her ocher vessel, a woman with long braids, with Indian eyes
who carries a womb full of messages,

that child is an astronaut of his tribe, that woman is
feeling a child that fastened to his cord travels through the
universe
codices, bonfires, destructions, and now this weariness:

I look at her, we smile.

WISDOMKEEPERS

Mi madre era una mujer buena. Yo pensaba que era la persona más sabia del mundo. Así que un día - cuando yo era pequeño, probablemente de seis o siete años - le pregunté cómo podía ser sabio como ella. Y ella se rió y se rió y me dijo: pero si eres tan joven para preguntar esto ..."
Uncle Frank, líder espiritual.

Decía mi madre: hay que perder algo para poder hablar,
hay que perder un sueño muy grande entonces lo perdido
se recupera de otro modo, uno crece como las habitaciones vacías
extraña los abrazos, se mete para adentro igual que los pulóveres
cierra las puertas porque tiene frío.

hay un tiempo para cada palabra, viejas lámparas usan viejos ojos
e iluminan pedazos de silencio que caen como la lluvia
mojando sobre el patio el frágil recorrido de las hojas

como una mujer india que teje con las sílabas de un hilo
el texto de su propio pensamiento y al pasar de los años
esa manta está llena de voces que surgen como en cuentos

decía mi madre: que al perder algo podemos comenzar
a comprendernos, como cerrar los ojos e imaginar el patio
con los abuelos vivos/ los abuelos muertos: esos guerreros,
esos antepasados que lo perdieron todo

y lo ganaron en trozos de sueño: esparcidos, desparramados
entre otras generaciones: para todo hay un tiempo.

WISDOMKEEPERS

"My mother was a good woman. I thought that she was the wisest person in the world. So that one day--when I was small, probably six or seven years old--I asked her how I could be as wise as she.
And she laughed and told me: but aren't you very young to be asking this . . . ."

UNCLE FRANK, spiritual leader

my mother used to say: you have to lose something in order to be
able to speak,
you have to lose a very big dream then the lost thing
is recuperated in another way, you grow like old rooms
you miss the hugs, you turn yourself inside out the same as
pullovers
you close the doors because you are cold.

there is a time for each word, old lamps use old eyes
and illuminate pieces of silence that fall like rain
wetting the fragile flurry of leaves on the patio

like an Indian woman who knits with syllables of a thread
the thought of her own text and with the passage of years
this cloth is full of voices that surge forth as in stories

my mother would say: that upon losing something we may begin
to understand ourselves, like closing your eyes and imagining the
patio with living grandparents / the dead grandparents: those
warriors, those ancestors who lost everything

and won it in bits of dream: scattered, overflowing
among other generations: for everything there is a season.

CONTANDO CUENTOS

"Oral tradition carries the fire, the spirit of the people.
It's an invisible library. A personal and tribal identity."

*Claiming Breath - Diane Glancy**

vivir: desparramarse en otros
esta forma de fuego es la alegría, saber que alguien
alguna vez nos espera: en la vida así como en la muerte
y una ronda de personas queridas emigran del silencio
hasta los cuentos, ponernos sus vestidos: sus dolores,
avanzar por la tierra intactos como el agua que lloraron
volver a repetir con ellos viejos hábitos
mirar la luna, escuchar el coyote, ser tan sensible
como para entender el bostezo de un gato

"de niña fui un venado" - dijo ella corriendo hasta
donde estaba la abuela con sus cuentos y toda la familia
se transformó a mi lado, imitando sonidos y lamentos

no hay mujeres que escriben como yo con las manos,
y sin embargo la memoria está llena de textos, que van sobreviviendo
de casa en casa -pensé- de generación en generación

imponiéndose al olvido, a la cinta grabada, al silencio.

---

*"La tradición oral lleva el fuego, el espíritu del pueblo.
Es una biblioteca invisible. Una identidad personal y tribal."
Reclamando respiración, Diane Glancy

TELLING STORIES

"Oral tradition carries the fire, the spirit of the people.
It's an invisible library. A personal and a tribal identity."

DIANE GLANCY, Claiming Breath

to live: to spill joyously over onto others
this form of fire is happiness, to know that someone
some time awaits us: in life as in death
and a round of beloved persons emigrates from silence
to stories, to put their clothes on us: their sorrows,
to advance through the earth intact like the water that they wept
to repeat again with them old habits
to look at the moon, to listen to the coyote, to be as sensitive
as to understand a cat's yawn

"as a girl I was a deer"--she said running
to where the grandmother sat with her stories and the whole
family
was transformed at my side; imitating sounds and laments

there are no women who write as I do with my hands,
and nevertheless their memory is full of texts, that continue
surviving
from house to house--I thought--from generation to generation

imposing themselves upon forgetfulness, upon the recorded
tape, upon silence.

LAS CUENTAS DE UN COLLAR

este collar que llevo puesto
una marca de luna sobre el cuello
una marca de dentadura blanca de astros, osos polares
cósmicos dedos que hicieron el universo
este collar
mi cuello, mi forma de apoyar la cabeza en la mano
un lugar donde encontrar el tiempo: mi cara, mi silencio

vuelo de mariposas detrás de las ventanas
un mundo blanco por el anochecer, mis cuentas

mis secretos.

A NECKLACE'S BEADS

this necklace that I have on
a moon mark upon my neck
a mark of the stars' white dentures, polar bears
cosmic fingers that made the universe
this necklace
my own neck, my way of resting my head on my hand
a place to encounter time: my own face, my silence

the flight of butterflies behind the windows
a white world as night falls, my beads

my secrets.

MIS TRISTEZAS

Relato de una informante de Tlatelolco
*no recogido por fray Bernardino de Sahagún**
entre 1550 y 1555.

igual que los cometas viajando en Tlatelolco
diez años antes una lluvia de fuego, igual que esos cometas
presagiando la muerte, ahí viaja mi tristeza
me humedece los ojos
resplandece mientras pierdo miradas en la noche
y toco con suavidad la almohada, las lámparas me conocen
me responden y cuando se iluminan calcan sombras

viejos álbumes, viejas fotos: desparramadas sobre
*mis cobijas, pulseras, bolsos, blocks** de poesía*

igual que esos cometas siento signos de angustia
manifestándose y rompiéndose entre la noche y los árboles,
mis dijes, mis tristezas.

---

* Fra Bernardino de Sahagún hizo entrevistas con los indios para aprender más sobre sus lenguas y sus mitos; transcribió esta materia en español en su *Historia general de las cosas de la Nueva España,*, que terminó en 1569 y revisó en 1585. Este volumen fue redescubierto por Juan Bautista Muñoz a fines del siglo diez y ocho.

** bloques

MY SADNESSES

Tlatelolco female informant's statement
*not collected by Fra Bernardino de Sahagún**
between 1550-1555.

like the comets traveling in Tlatelolco
ten years before a rain of fire, like those comets
presaging death, there my sadness travels
it moistens my eyes
it shines while I lose glances in the night
and I touch the pillow softly, the lamps know me
they answer me and when they light up they trace shadows

old albums, old photos: spilled out over
my bedclothes, bracelets, purses, blocks of poetry

like those comets I feel signs of anguish
manifesting themselves and breaking out between the night and the trees,
my amulets, my sadnesses.

---

* Fra Bernardino de Sahagún interviewed the Indians to learn more about their languages and myths; he transcribed this material into Spanish in his *Historia general de las cosas de la Nueva España,* which was finished in 1569 and revised in 1585. This volume was rediscovered by Juan Bautista Muñoz in the late eighteenth century.

PINTURAS INDIAS

con la arena formo esta flor que dejará de hundirse
en el olvido
la arena vive para morir, para pasar como un suspiro
pero en este lienzo se quedará dormida y cuando
se despierte habrá una nueva forma de contener
la impermanencia de la historia,
esos minutos de la arena que se despiden siempre
del mar entre gaviotas, entre labios, del mar huyendo
y entregando retazos de botellas, entre la impermanencia
de la arena que toma cualquier huella y esconde cualquier ostra
le daré forma de signo, ingresará a la tribu

de la memoria.

INDIAN PAINTINGS

with sand I form this flower that will cease to sink
into oblivion
sand lives for dying, for passing like a sigh
but on this canvas it will remain asleep and when
it awakens there will be a new form for containing
the impermanence of history,
those minutes of sand that always take leave
of the sea between seagulls, between lips, of the sea fleeing
and surrendering scraps of bottles, between the impermanence
of sand that takes any footprint and hides any oyster
I shall give the form of a sign, it will enter into the tribe

of memory.

VASIJA DE TIERRA

esta vasija recién encontrada, que dormía en el fondo de la tierra
que respiraba junto a las raíces, llena de historias
de emperadores muertos, de mercados, de flores perfumadas

vuelve con su ojo curioso a la retina de una vidriera de museo
donde mi ojo la saluda y celebra, envejecida, reconstruida
en parte por la historia,

en el presente es como una viejita que ya no hace trabajos manuales
es una mujer quieta con ojos agrietados, que se sintió curiosa
al ver la luz del sol de las excavaciones

es una pieza de reflexión y estudio y antes, probablemente
era la vasija casera que llevaban riendo las niñas hasta el agua.

EARTHEN VESSEL

this recently-found vessel, that slept in the depths of the earth
that breathed next to the roots, full of histories
of dead emperors, of markets, of perfumed flowers

turns its curious eye upon the retina of a museum showcase
where my eye greets and celebrates it, old, reconstructed
in part by history

in the present it is like a little old woman who no longer does
manual jobs
it is a quiet woman with cracked eyes, who felt curious
upon seeing the light of the sun of the excavations

it is a piece of reflexion and study and before, probably
it was the household vessel that laughing children would carry for
water.

DE CóMO PERDIMOS LAS ESTRELLAS

"Telephones carry your voice around the earth, not up to the Creator."
*Louis Farmer - jefe onondaga**

de una cultura a otra de una forma de comprender el mundo
se deshojan los atardeceres y marcan pasos rojos
avergonzadas las ventanas miran la tarde
vivir es una fuerza más fuerte, uno debe recordarlo

apuntes contra el presente: seré más fuerte, tendré más
ganas, haré todas las cosas imposibles/posibles,
crecerá una mañana donde me levante y me vea coherente

habrá motivos para vivir más adelante, ahora con mis sandalias
mis ojotas, queda por verse un camino nuevo
perder las alas de lo conocido, y empezar a deslizarse

como un pequeño insecto que no vuela por toda la casa
la casa de los signos que construyeron otros, algo prestado

perdimos casi todo,
antes tocábamos los astros con los ojos.

* "Los teléfonos llevan tu voz alrededor de la tierra, no al Creador."
Louis Farmer--Onondagan Chief

Los onondagas vivían en el Lago Onondaga en la parte central del estado de Nueva York, al noroeste de Syracuse, hasta 1795 cuando el estado de Nueva York se lo compró por sus recursos de sal. La tribu formó parte de la Confederación Iroquois o la Lega Iroquois.

ABOUT HOW WE LOST THE STARS

"Telephones carry your voice around the Earth, not up to the Creator."
*Louis Farmer, Onondagan Chief**

from one culture to another from one way of understanding the world
the late afternoons drop their leaves and mark red steps
the shamefaced windows look at the afternoon
to live is a stronger force, one ought to remember it

notes against the present: I will be stronger, I will be
more eager, I will do all things impossible / possible,
a morning will rise where I shall arise and see a coherent self

there will be motives for living further on, now with my sandals
*my ojotas,** a new road remains to be seen*
to lose the wings of the known, and to begin to slide back

like a small insect that does not fly through the whole house
the house of the signs that others constructed, something lent

we lose almost everything,
before we used to touch the stars with our eyes.

---

*The Onondagans lived on Onondaga Lake in central New York, northwest of Syracuse, until 1795 when the lake was purchased from them by New York state for its salt resources. The tribe formed part of the Iroquois Confederacy or Iroquois League.

**Sandal like shoes made of leather or vegetable fiber and used by Indians in Peru and Chile; they are still used by farm workers in some regions of South America.

INDIAN NATIONS* / PARTES DE MI

*el coro donde pasan la águilas, Gallup***
aquí estamos de pie por las naciones indias, 1991
estamos aquí de pies por esos rostros viejos que no se agotan
de danzar, por las plumas de los pájaros que trajeron
trocitos de destellos para iluminarnos la frente
estamos aquí para celebrar que la vida es una continuación
de rostros (y yo viajo entres espejos hacia el mío)
y el creador nos ve multiplicados en los tres tiempos potenciales
ayer - ahora - pasado, como una línea que fluctúa del corazón
a la cabeza, y por eso, porque nos quiere volveremos
multiplicados en hijos y en memorias, a ser parte de flores
y piezas de universo

tal vez, en otra época yo suba como una mariposa de verano.

---

* Naciones indias.

** Gallup, ubicado en la frontera al oeste de Nuevo México al lado de Arizona, es el sitio de un gran festival indígena para las naciones indias.

INDIAN NATIONS / PARTS OF MYSELF

*the choir loft where the eagles pass, Gallup**
here we are on foot by the Indian nations, 1991
here we are on foot by those old faces that do not tire
of dancing, by the feathers of birds that brought
small bits of sparks for illuminating our foreheads
we are here in order to celebrate that life is a continuation
of faces (and I travel in three mirrors towards my own)
and the creator sees us multiplied in three potential tenses
*yesterday--now--the past**, like a line that fluctuates from the heart*
to the head, and because of that, because he loves us we shall return
multiplied in children and in memories, to be part of flowers
and pieces of universe

perhaps, in another epoch I may rise up like a summer butterfly.

---

* Gallup, located on New Mexico's western boundary with Arizona, is the site of a major indigenous festival for the Indian nations.

** The poet is distinguishing between the present and two aspects of the past: the preterite used for completed actions and the imperfect used for description, background action, and ongoing, habitual actions in the past.

CALENDARIOS

este día
para otra cultura un círculo para mí una línea
una manera de señalar las nubes y seguirlas, inviernos
con caras de búfalos afligidos
primaveras que nacen con el olor de la cocina
veranos que tenían el color de las rocas
otoños que nacieron como yo, el mismo día
y por eso perdemos, y perdemos
en una sucesión de desgastes de ocre,
en la pared de una roca duerme un dibujo
que me recuerda a mi si yo hubiera nacido
dentro de mucho tiempo

la poesía lo puede todo/ la poesía es un eco en la garganta
cósmica de una pradera

pasan los días indios/ sube el polvo a estas páginas.

CALENDARS

this day
for another culture a circle for me a line
a way of pointing out the clouds and following them, winters
with faces of afflicted buffalos
springs that are born with the smell of the kitchen
summers that have the color of rocks
autumns that are born like myself, the same day
and because of that we lose, and we lose
in a succession of ocher abrasions
on the wall of a rock a drawing sleeps
        which reminds me of myself if I had been born
                encircled by a long time

poetry can do anything / poetry is an echo in the cosmic
        throat of a meadow

the Indian days pass / the dust rises to these pages.

Oficios y Personas

Febrero, 1994

Roles and Persons

February, 1994

INTRODUCCIÓN

A la distancia, el estudio de las mariposas parece una búsqueda obsesiva y sin importancia. A un nivel metafórico, lo mismo podria decirse de la vida de un escritor.

Robert Michael Pyle *

A cierta edad una mujer se levanta y se conoce a sí misma. Sabe, por ejemplo, cuáles son las cosas que jamás haría, y cuáles son las obsesiones, los sueños, desde los cuales intenta interpretar el mundo. Hoy me encuentro en esta fase de mi vida. Repasando años de escritura silenciosa, me doy cuenta que sería falsificarme si ignorara los proyectos que realmente me interesan: el proyecto de escribir, el proyecto de crecer con un lenguaje, y dentro de ese lenguaje hacer vibrar mi tiempo.

Estas cosas las advierto cuando repaso cientos de hojas de poemas. Cuando esos poemas terminan cancelados en un cajón. Y luego, en una noche de café con amigos, se leen, se refrescan en la superficie del aire, para después encerrarse otra vez dentro de sí mismos, brevemente iluminados por una noche de premio, seguros en el refugio de su soledad. Por un instante, una palabra revolotea viva en la cabeza de alguien. Y es una de mis palabras.

En el proceso se acumulan pequeñas felicidades. El lenguaje es siempre revelador de nuevos planos de la realidad, zonas discursivas emergen a medida que vivimos, palabras que nos tenían sin cuidado se vuelven más fuertes aún dentro de su propia transparencia. Estos rasgos son característicos de la poesía y de los vocabularios que crecen junto a nuestras experiencias. Con el tiempo uno descubre símbolos, señales, que han transmutado para siempre nuestro universo cotidiano. Al encender una lámpara, para escribir en medio de la soledad, la página se llena de visiones y resplandece con ecos conocidos: nosotros somos esas palabras, las palabras se nos parecen.

---

* Robert Michael Pyle es lepidóptero, naturalista, y escritor que se especializa en la zona oeste del estado de Washington . Ha escrito seis libros sobre las mariposas.

INTRODUCTION

At a distance, the study of butterflies seems an obsessive and unimportant search. At a metaphoric level, the same could be said of a writer's life.
*Robert Michael Pyle**

At a certain age a woman arises and knows herself. She knows, for example, what things she would never do, and what are the obsessions, the dreams from which she tries to interpret the world. Today I find myself in this phase of my life. Reviewing years of silent writing, I realize that I would not be true to myself if I ignored the projects that really interest me: the project of writing, the project of growing with a language, and within that language making my time vibrate.

These things I notice when I review hundreds of leaves of poems. When those poems end up cancelled in a box. And then, during an evening coffee with friends, they are read, they are refreshed in the air's surface, in order to be shut up again later within themselves, briefly lit by an evening of awards, secure in the refuge of their solitude. For an instant, a word flutters around, brought to life in someone's head. And it is one of my words.

In the process small felicities accumulate. Language is ever the revealer of new planes of reality, discursive zones emerge to the extent that we live, words that we used carelessly return stronger even within their own transparency. These features are characteristic of the poetry and the words that grow along with our experiences. With time one discovers symbols, signs that have forever transmuted our daily universe. Upon lighting a lamp, to write in the midst of solitude, the page fills with visions and shines with known echoes: we are those words, the words look like us.

---

* Robert Michael Pyle is a lepidopterist, naturalist, and writer who specializes in the area of western Washington state. He has written six books on butterflies.

En este volúmen presento dos trabajos escritos hace ya algún tiempo. ***Oficios y Personas*** recibió el premio *Federico García Lorca 1994*, otorgado por la *Embajada de España* y la *Asociación de Licenciados y Doctores Españoles en los Estados Unidos*. Al escribirlo pensé en la gente que vive estos oficios diariamente, millones de seres humanos cuyas vidas transcurren en algunas de estas estoicas rutinas.

El segundo trabajo lleva el título con que se publicó un libro de filosofía en el siglo XII. Encontré que ***Guía para perplejos*** se ajustaba a este trayecto que planteo a través de una experiencia interior. Estos poemas no pueden leerse como unidades solitarias, ni saltando de página en página como en una rayuela. Comenzando con mi madre, en estos versos identifico mi recorrido con el de otras mujeres, sujetas de una historicidad cotidiana, familiar, histórica, que buscan dentro de sus recursos expresivos, subjetivos, únicos, expresarse y hacer un pequeño espacio para sí mismas y para otros en el mundo.

Remitiéndome a la frase de Robert Michael Plye, puede ser que, a la distancia, mis poemas parezcan búsquedas inútiles. Pero aquí, muy cerca mío, en mis páginas, en mis noches, en los días de mi vida, estos poemas y otros me han ayudado a sobrevivir, a crecer, a darme cuenta.

Uno solamente espera que otros encuentren sus propios poemas, resistiendo a la vida, trazando la geometría personal que traza una sola mariposa, antes de morir.

Otoño de 1996.

In this volume I present two works written some time ago. ***Roles and Persons*** received the prize *Federico García Lorca 1994*, granted by the *Embassy of Spain* and the *Association of Spanish Lawyers and Doctors in the United States*. Upon writing it, I thought about the people who daily perform these jobs, millions of human beings whose lives are spent in some of these stoical routines.

The second work bears the title of a book of philosophy published in the twelfth century. I found that ***Guide for the Perplexed*** suited this trajectory that I set forth through an interior experience. These poems cannot be read as single units, nor skipping from page to page like a game of hopscotch. Beginning with my mother, in these verses I identify my path with that of other women who, subject to daily, familiar, and historical historicity, seek within their expressive, subjective, and unique resources to express themselves and to make a small space for themselves and for others in the world.

Recurring to Robert Michael Pyle's phrase, it may be that, at a distance, my poems may seem useless searches. But here, close within myself, in my pages, in my nights, in the days of my life, these poems and others have helped me to survive, to grow, to give an account of myself.

One only hopes that others find their own poems, withstanding life, tracing the personal geometary that a single butterfly traces, before dying.

Fall of 1996

Oficios y Personas

CONTENIDO

Roles and Persons

CONTENTS

POCO A POCO

de tanto golpear el corazón contra las puertas de uno mismo
se abre una hendija donde una luz dice: *te estaba esperando*
y rayos de sol muerto se filtran, acariciando cosas que perdimos
astillas incrustadas entre las mesas y los platos
el piso empapado de pedacitos de uno: pisadas o gestos
los zapatos gastados y el ojo de los gatos de tres meses

poco a poco el corazón que te miraba rígido se enciende
y formas de ocupar la casa se transforman, papeles perdidos,
botones, bolsillos, este arreglar enchufes en el cuarto
cortar los cables que nos electrocutan de sueños imposibles
envejecemos, somos menos ciertos en el mundo

poco a poco resplandecemos con chispazos de perplejidad
como poner los mismos cubiertos en la mesa y soñarnos más
jóvenes y creer que esas formas de inexperiencia llevan
el sagrado secreto de todo lo futuro

poco a poco, mi oficio es recordar tus ojos frescos,
es una voz de lámpara hacia el amanecer, es un leer
poderes en ausencia: aquello que me diste y compartimos.
Una vida es una vida es una vida.

Poco a poco,
de tanto golpear el corazón contra las puertas de uno mismo
se abre una hendija donde una luz dice: *te estaba esperando*

LITTLE BY LITTLE

from the heart beating so hard against the doors of oneself
a crack opens where a light says: *I was expecting you*
and rays of dead sunlight filter down, caressing things that we lose
splinters encrusted on tables and plates
the floor papered with one's little pieces: steps or gestures
worn out shoes and the eye of three-month old cats

little by little the rigid heart that looked at you flares up
and ways of occupying the house are transformed, lost papers,
buttons, pocketbooks, this arranging receptacles in the room
cutting cables that electrocute us with impossible dreams
we grow old, we are less certain in the world

little by little we glitter with sparks of perplexity
like putting the same place mats on the table and dreaming ourselves
younger and believing that those forms of inexperience carry
the sacred secret of all the future

little by little, my role is to remember your fresh eyes,
it is a lamp's voice towards the dawn, it is a reading
of powers in absentia: what you told me and we shared.
A life is a life is a life.

Little by little
from the heart beating so hard against the doors of oneself
a crack opens where a light says: *I was expecting you*

FRAGMENTOS DE FUTURO

(lectura de las líneas de una mano)

... el viento marino enredado en las plumas de los pájaros
fuerza de las rocas que no tiemblan cuando pasa el viento
el viento que corre hacia un océano de estrellas húmedas
esta vez, alguien te traerá cosas frescas:
como los peces recién nacidos, como las estrellas intactas
debajo del agua, niños que respiran

... cambiará tu vida a fuerza de mareas - *placentas*
que viajan invisibles, batallas de sangre inconclusas -
pájaros agredidos abrirán su boca para tocar el agua
un caracol dibujará un signo brillante con su cuerpo

... algo que no estaba en tu vida, una presencia,
de cáscaras de ayer se quemará la luna, fases de la luna
formas de la luna en tu mano presente

atravesando la soledad de tus verbos

fuerza de las rocas que no tiemblan cuando pasa el viento

y el amanecer tendiendo sus brazos.

FRAGMENTS OF THE FUTURE

(reading of a hand's lines)

. . . the marine wind entangled in the birds' feathers
the force of rocks that don't tremble when the wind passes
the wind that runs toward an ocean of wet stars
this time, someone will bring you fresh things:
like newborn fish, like intact stars
beneath the water, children that breath

. . . your life will change by dint of seasickness--*placentas*
that travel invisible, inconclusive blood battles--
assaulted birds will open their mouths to touch the water
a snail will draw a brilliant sign with its body

. . . something that was not in your life, a presence,
of yesterday's shells will burn the moon, moon phases
moon forms in your present hand

crossing the solitude of your words
the force of rocks that don't tremble when the wind passes

and the dawn holding out her arms.

FOTOS VIEJAS

Uno no condena a una tijera por haber formado parte del trabajo de cortar una fotografía.

El afilador de tijeras pasa con su silbato inundando la tarde
las tijeras son como pájaras dormidas adentro de un cajón
picos que parlotean en silencio, o se duermen sin mar

y pasa la tarde - apretada a sus flores de durazno - pasa
levantando la siesta, rozando con los dedos las ventanas
una mujer mirando fotos viejas, personas que cruzaban el pasillo
restos de sol tocando la espalda de una silla,

cortar una fotografía mientras llora, y el afilador cruza
con su silbato por la esquina, el hombre lleno de potencias:
dividir, cortar, lastimar, organizar de otra manera,
el rompecabezas de líneas que suben y bajan, pedacitos de ella

que caen por la ventana cuando él silba y pasa: en un trabajo
inofensivo de afilar esas bocas de pájara,
y en un inofensivo caer de la tristeza.

OLD PHOTOS

One does not condemn scissors for having formed part of the work of cutting up a photograph.

The scissors sharpener passes with his whistling flooding the afternoon
the scissors are like paper roosters sleeping within a drawer
beaks that jabber in silence, or go to sleep sealess

and the afternoon passes--pressed to its peach flowers--passes
lifting the siesta, brushing the windows with its fingers
a woman looking at old photos, persons that are crossing the corridor
remains of sunlight touching the back of a chair,

cutting a photograph while she cries, and the sharpener crosses
by the corner with his whistling, the man full of power:
to divide, to cut, to injure, to organize in another way,
the puzzle of lines that climb and go down, little pieces of her

that fall through the window when he whistles and passes: in an
inoffensive work of sharpening those bird mouths,
and in an inoffensive falling of sadness.

TRANSPARENCIAS

Podrías inventar un lenguaje en el que el signo sea idéntico al objeto? Inclusive los más abstractos e indeterminados. El infinito. Un perfume. Un sueño.
Augusto Roa Bastos. *(Yo el Supremo)*

entre los vidrios mojados de lluvia (las teclas viajan
hacia adentro, recogen partes de ventanas antiguas, formas
de llaves, y se remontan hacia el universo)

y afuera empapados de día corren los pájaros (y el mundo
secreto de las lámparas leyendo líneas de poemas antiguos
y las mantas, y las habitaciones en silencio)

es posible que el espejo que recoge tu cara (en la ventana
la superficie fresca de un día de invierno) recoja también
esa forma de decir para adentro, secretamente

lo que las palabras dicen hasta apagarse calladamente
como las velas y los fósforos, en el silencio
es posible que el espejo que recoge tu cara (en la ventana
la superficie fresca de un día de invierno, recoja también
esa forma de decir para adentro, secretamente

lo que las palabras dicen hasta apagarse calladamente
como las velas y los fósforos, en el silencio)

TRANSPARENCIES

Would you be able to invent a language in which the sign is identical to the object?. . .
Including the most abstract and indeterminate. Infinity. A perfume. A dream.
Augusto Roa Bastos *(I, the Supreme)*

between the windowpanes wet with rain (the typewriter keys travel
towards the inside, collect parts of old windows, forms
of keys, and soar towards the universe)

and outside soaked with daylight the birds run (and the secret
world of lamps reading lines of ancient poems
and the blankets, and the rooms in silence)

it is possible that the mirror which collects your face (in the window
the fresh surface of a winter's day, collects also
this way of saying from within, secretly

what words speak until going out quietly
like candles and matches, in silence)

it is possible that the mirror which collects your face (in the window
the fresh surface of a winter's day, collects also
this way of saying from within, secretly

what words speak until going out quietly
like candles and matches, in silence)

y textos que emergen, tecla por tecla, hora por hora,
hagan un oficio transparente producir poesía, como si se
fuera a recoger algo: agua en manos abiertas, el brillo
de los deseos escondidos,

un tocar puertas y ventanas que se despiden, personas que
se alejan por una calle sola, empedrados y bicicletas,
un palpitar de la lluvia, la cabellera de la lluvia,
la transparencia de la lluvia,

la línea de un poema.

and texts that emerge, key by key, hour by hour,
may make producing poetry a transparent job, as if one
might go to collect something: water in open hands, the lustre
of hidden desires,

a touching of doors and windows that bid farewell, persons who
move into the distance on a lonely street, paving stones and bicycles
a palpitating of the rain, the hair of the rain,
the transparency of the rain,

the line of a poem.

VERANO, VERANO

el sol: un chorro eléctrico que le atraviesa el cráneo,
verano fracturado de luz, lleno de astillas, pasa
como un pájaro de oro por la frente, transpira
a través de los poros de las flores

el verano, la hierba, mientras pasa la cortadora de césped

hay un encender fuerzas amarillas sobre los pétalos
de las flores desordenadas en el cantero, y el agua
de una manguera que hecha luces y refresca
las alas instantáneas de los insectos transparentes

mientras sube el día, pasando la cortadora de césped

un chorro de luz que atraviesa existencias, la vida
de las plantas y de los organismos en la tierra y
más arriba el hombre que se mueve iluminando una sombra
hamacando una sombra, de aquí para allá

mientras crece el calor, pasando la cortadora de césped.

SUMMER, SUMMER

the sun: an electric spurt that crosses the cranium,
summer fractured with light, full of splinters, passes
like a bird of gold by the forehead, breathes
through the flowers' pores

summer, the grass, while the lawn mower passes

there is a firing of yellow forces on the petals
of the flowers disordered in the rock garden, and the hose's
water turns into lights and refreshes
the instantaneous wings of transparent insects

while the day climbs, the lawn mower passing

a spurt of light that crosses existences, the life
of the plants and of the organisms in the earth and
above the man swinging in a hammock illuminating a shadow
rocking a shadow, from here to there

while the heat grows, the lawn mower passing.

LA CARA EN EL ESPEJO

(espejos, espejos suspirando...)

en el tiempo, con el tiempo
mi cara se parece a otras caras que viajan
del fondo de la noche hasta el útero
rostros llenos de surcos o bocas que cubren el aire
de una memoria que llena las vitrinas, los espejos
el marco dorado y liso del espejo que cuelga
el detalle de los marcos

anunciando rebajas en una habitación que da a la calle
mis espejos detienen multiplicando rostros,
el cuello plegado, las miradas fijas, ojos que brotan
llenos de recuerdos, viajar con los ojos, mojarse

de esa imagen de ayer que sonreía en el interior
de un paisaje secreto, el niño que corre hasta tocar
la humedad de la noche, hasta las sábanas, en la
fuerza futura de un llanto que se abre incierto
después de haber empujado tanto y tanto,
para encontrarse con los brazos de alguien

el detalle de los marcos

...así se va la vida.

THE FACE IN THE MIRROR

(mirrors, mirrors sighing . . .)

in time, with time
my face looks like other faces that travel
from the night's depths to the uterus
faces full of furrows or mouths that envelop the air
of a memory that fills the shop windows, the mirrors
the smooth and golden frame of the mirror that is hanging
the detail of the frames

announcing sales in a room that gives unto the street
my mirrors stop, multiplying faces,
the folded collar, the stares, eyes that sprout
full of memories, to travel with the eyes, to get wet

from that image of yesterday that smiled in the interior
of a secret passage, the child that runs till he touches
the night's humidity, till the sheets, in the
future force of a cry that opens up uncertain
after having pushed so hard so very hard,
in order to find himself in someone's arms

the detail of the frames

. . . so life goes on.

NUEVAS LENTES

And Marco's answer was: "Elsewhere is a negative mirror. The traveler recognizes the little that is his, discovering the much he has not had and will never have."

Italo Calvino, *Invisible Cities* *

revoluciones de olas y de pájaros
hasta llegar a ver el ojo aumentado de la aguja
y enhebrar un hilo azul para surcir una media

(el agua que salpica con hilos abrillantados las sombrillas abiertas)

el óptico dice que con estos lentes se puede ver más lejos
hasta las ostras cuando buscan el fondo de la arena,
o botones de nácar prendidos a una blusa

(la luz del agua cruzando entre las piedras, las burbujas)

con estos otros vidrios - dice el óptico - puede mirar igual
que galileo los primeros planetas, las formas de mañana
que se esconden en aguas de otros mundos

(respiración entre las máscaras, un momento de silencio celeste)

* "Y la respuesta de Marco fue: 'A otra parte es un espejo negativo. El viajero reconoce lo poco que es suyo, descubriendo lo mucho que no ha tenido y nunca tendrá'". Italo Calvino, *Ciudades invisibles.*

NEW LENSES

And Marco's answer was: "Elsewhere is a negative mirror.
The traveler recognizes the little that is his, discovering the
much he has not had and will never have."

Italo Calvino, *Invisible Cities*

revolutions of waves and of birds
until coming to see the augmented eye of the needle
and threading a blue thread to darn a stocking

(the water that splashes the open beach umbrellas with many faceted threads)

the optician says that one can see farther with these glasses
to the oysters when they search the sand's depths
or mother-of-pearl buttons fastened on a blouse

(the water's light crossing among the stones, the bubbles)

with these other glasses--the optician says--one can see
the first planets like Galileo, the morning forms
that hide in waters of other worlds

(breathing between masks, a moment of celestial silence)

o cambiar la visión, a estos gruesos cristales, y encontrarse
moviendo objetos viejos, que vuelven desde lejos

(restos de civilización en el agua, ánforas, paisaje de estrellas
que tendidas en el fondo del mar buscan el cielo)

olas inmensas, agua, confusión de los vidrios, el océano:
esas miradas frescas como la arena.

or change the vision, to these thick crystals, and find
old objects moving, that return from far away

(remains of civilization in the water, amphoras, landscape of stars
that hanging in the depths of the sea search for the sky)

immense waves, water, confusion of glasses, the ocean:
those fresh glances like the sand.

EL SOL SOBRE LA HORA DE VIDRIO

mientras lavo los vidrios de un noveno piso
abajo el mundo parece posible, con hilos de pisadas que se pierden
en el eco de una avenida, a donde pasa el viento con sus sonajas
el partido / partir / del otoño: oro sobre las hojas entonces frescas

ahora el otoño vuela contra las banderas de los bancos
el cielo atraviesa costillas de edificios y pasan aviones a lo lejos
como si fueran vuelos sin retorno, páginas azules de mis días
lavando estos vidrios, reflejos de un hombre en el espacio

sostenido frágilmente por sus propias predicciones, o un esperar
las cinco de la tarde para terminar esta tarea, de quitar insectos
sucios, marcas de lluvia, polvo amarillo sobre superficie plana
de una cara de vidrio, a donde me reflejo contra el cielo

y el aire pasa por la hora de vidrio,
pasa el otoño, un avión, el otoño,
un eco de amarillo.

THE SUN ON THE HOUR OF GLASS

while I wash the panes of a ninth floor flat
below the world looks possible, with threads of footsteps that are lost
in the echo of an avenue, to where the wind passes with its tambourine
the departure / the parting of autumn: gold on the leaves then fresh

now the autumn flies against the banks' flags
the sky crosses buildings' ribs and airplanes pass in the distance
as if they were flights without return, my days' blue pages
washing these panes, reflections of a man in space

sustained fragilely by his own predictions, or a waiting for
five in the afternoon in order to finish this job, of removing
dirty insects, rain spots, yellow dust on the level surface
of a face of windowpane, where I am reflected against the sky

and the air passes by the hour of glass,
the autumn, a plane, the autumn passes
an echo of yellow.

CORTE DE PELO

How are you, kid?

el pelo va cayendo y queda apenas una pelusa
en la silla donde a los seis años cuelgan las piernas
delgado, tímido, sin decir una palabra
se somete a un ritual donde le van cambiando los ojos
y las orejas asoman como las de un perro
frescas de mañana

por esa cabeza van ríos de azul de nubes
corren bosques maduros llenos de hojas potentes
un jugar a los indios, un arco abandonado
el azul de la tira de un cinturón sobre la espalda
a veces llorando solo junto a las hormigas,
tendido en la tierra

Nubes, bosques, arcos, un refregarse los puños
contra la cara, con los ojos hinchados volver hasta la mesa
o perderse en la habitación llena de ausencia
buscando entre cuatro paredes un padre

con el peluquero es distinto,
es la única persona que le acaricia la cabeza
y lo trata como si fuera un niño
como si todavía tuviera intacta la inocencia.

HAIRCUT

How are you, kid?

his hair is falling and scarcely any down remains
on the chair where the six-year-old hangs his legs
thin, timid, without saying a word
he submits to a ritual where his eyes are changing
and his ears emerge like those of a dog
morning fresh

through that head slide rivers of cloud blue
slide mature forests full of potent leaves
playing Indian, an abandoned bow
the blue of a belt lash on his back
sometimes crying alone next to the ants
stretched out on the earth

Clouds, forests, bows, a rubbing of fists
against his face, with his eyes swollen to return to the table
or get lost in the bedroom full of absence
looking between four walls for a father

with the barber it is different,
he is the only person that caresses his head
and treats him as if he were a child
as if he still had his innocence intact.

Guía para perplejos

Guide for the Perplexed

GUÍA PARA PERPLEJOS

CONTENIDO

GUIDE FOR THE PERPLEXED

CONTENTS

Personas perdidas

Lost Persons

PERSONAS PERDIDAS

I am looking for a girl, ten years old, probably pale,
with dark hair and very large, rather melancholic dark eyes.
Heinrich Böll *

Cuando el hielo cae como una paloma partida, como una lengua
transparente
en mi ventana el mundo avanza con formas de invierno,

y a veces, un poema pasa por el mundo como un cometa fugaz y el
mundo
ni siquiera levanta los ojos para maravillarse,

un poema trata afónico de manifestarse pero llega demasiado pronto
y dibuja una línea brillosa de caracol entre las manos de su tiempo,

otros encuentran ese camino después, esa manera de apoyar los ojos
contra las ventanas, de abrocharse una blusa y salir a enfrentar

el resplandor que existe entre el corazón que teme y el que vacila,
pisar o no pisar el hielo endurecido bajo el sol?

Las palomas partidas de la nieve, el fondo de uno mismo
esa imagen de espejo donde yo sonreía cuando tenía diez años.

---

* "Estoy buscando a una muchacha de diez años de edad, probablemente pálida, de pelo moreno y de ojos muy grandes, algo melancólicos.

Heinrich Böll

LOST PERSONS

I am looking for a girl, ten years old, probably pale,
with dark eyes and very large, rather melancholic dark eyes.
Heinrich Böll

When ice falls like a cleft dove, like a transparent tongue
in my window the world advances with winter forms,

and sometimes, a poem passes through the world like a fleeting comet
and the world doesn't even raise its eyes to wonder at it,

a poem tries unvoiced to realize itself but it arrives too soon
and draws a shiny snail's line between the hands of its time,

others find that road later, that way of resting eyes
against windows, of buttoning up a blouse and leaving to confront

the radiance that exists between the heart which fears and that which
vacillates, to step or not to step on the ice hardened beneath the sun?

The cleft doves of snow, the depths of oneself
that mirror image where I smiled when I was ten years old.

EL GRADO CERO DE LA ESCRITURA

...recuerdo a mi hermano con un caracol sobre la oreja
y el ruido del viento mareando las ventanas, salpicados de agua los
pájaros
recuerdo como mi hermano hablaba y se reía solo en los rincones de la
casa
como si tuviera tanto que decirse, se pasaba horas contándose historias
esa fusión de invisibilidad y momento me llevó hasta la página,
poder juntar rastros de vida, como las olas que se mueven
y traen pedacitos de botellas, y de lejos, muy lejos, un chico
de pies rosas sale a buscarlos, creyendo que es el sol.

ZERO DEGREE WRITING

. . . I remember my brother with a shell to his ear
and the noise of the wind hoisting the windows,
splashing the birds with water
I remember how my brother would talk and laugh alone
in the corners of the house
as if he had so much to say to himself,
he spent hours telling himself stories
that fusion of invisibility and moment brought me to the page,
to be able to join traces of life, like the waves that move
and bring little pieces of bottles, and away, far away, a boy
with rosy feet goes out to look for them, believing it to be the sun.

MI TIEMPO, MI NOSTALGIA

Lejos, lejos hasta que la mañana deposite sus
rayos en la cerradura,
y las puertas de la oscuridad se abran de par en par.
Tomas Tranströmer.

tejo y destejo palabras en mi computadora
las pongo en orden, las borro, alternativamente
es una bufanda inacabada para el invierno
una bufanda azul sobre una página eléctrica

y para ponerte al cuello mis gorriones afligidos
"no tomes frío" "no te resfríes" "no corras mucho"
un patio de escuela, una ronda de niñas

tejo la corriente de viento de mis pensamientos
lo que yo quería ser / lo que soy, lo que soñaba
lo que no se sueña ya, un viento aparecido
a las siete de la mañana en invierno

Aquí el invierno es blanco como una flor nacida sin sus pétalos.

MY TIME, MY NOSTALGIA

Away, far away until the morning deposits its
rays in the keyhole,
and the doors of darkness may open wide.
Thomas Tranströmer

I knit and unravel words on my computer
I put them in order, I erase them, alternatively
It is an unfinished scarf for winter
a blue scarf on an electric page

and in order to put my afflicted sparrows around your neck
"don't get cold" "don't catch cold" "don't run too much"
a school patio, the girls' ring-around-a-rosy

I knit the wind's current of my thoughts
what I wanted to be / what I am, what I dreamt
what is not dreamt now, a wind appearing
at 7 o'clock on a winter's morning

Here winter is white like a flower born without its petals.

A LA MANERA DE FRIDA KAHLO

la edad de las muñecas

Yo nunca pinto sueños. Yo pinto mi propia realidad.
Frida Kahlo.

hay muñecas tendidas en el patio con los ojos fijos
como si estuvieran hablando con una nube azul negra
como si estuvieran esperando--desesperanzadas--un flash de sol
sobre la cara--mía/de ellas--un hilo de luz que filtrándose
en la casa abriera las ventanas -no al otoño- sino al dolor
con riñones a cuestas.

a esos charcos de sangre que cuidadosamente se embotellan
y van por los pasillos con mis brotes, mis sueños, mis banderas
ahí voy yo prendida a oscuras, mis abecedarios,

mi parálisis frente a la vida intensa desde donde otras
niñas pueden jugar a las muñecas, ahí voy yo y nadie lo sabe
murmurando entre paredes blancas mis hazañas de libros ilustrados
una literatura mojada de colores que no existen

porque todo es rojo ahora, rojos los dedos pinchados que
al moverse causan dolor, rojos los brazos desparramados
que miran fijamente el techo, manos que no mueven muñecas,
risas que no se escuchan. Juegos abandonados en el patio.
sangre negra

IN THE MANNER OF FRIDA KAHLO

The Age of Dolls

I never paint dreams, I paint my own reality.
Frida Kahlo

there are dolls with fixed eyes strewn on the patio
as if they were talking with a blue black cloud
as if they were waiting--despairing--a flash of sun
on--my / their--face a thread of light that filtering
into the house might open the windows--not to the fall--but to the
pain of kidneys when lying on one's back

to those puddles of blood that are carefully bottled
and go through the corridors with my shoots, my dreams, my
banners there I go dressed up darkly, my ABC books,

my paralysis confronting the intense life from which other
girls can play with their dolls, there I go and nobody knows it
murmuring among white walls my deeds of illustrated books
a literature wet with colors that don't exist

because all is red now, red the pinched fingers that
on moving cause pain, red the open arms
that stare at the ceiling, hands that don't hold dolls,
laughs that are not heard. Games abandoned on the patio.
black blood

A LA MANERA DE FRIDA KAHLO

Ahí cuelga mi vestido

en esa casa con techos de tejas, en el fondo del patio
con broches como bocas de pájaros, contra el sol que estalla
sin dejar caer sus vidrios

ahí cuelga mi vestido

es una fantasía con mangas cortas y botones dorados
es una tela simple comprada en un mercado
sólo para ponerse los domingos

ahí cuelga mi vestido

los ojos verdes de las hojas lo miran hamacarse
ir y venir sin cuerpo, libre de mí
se mueve suavemente

contra los calendarios olvidados, en el fondo de toda astrología
entre los labios secos del verano
cuando yo era una niña y con mis manos,
soltaba dos palomas.

IN THE MANNER OF FRIDA KAHLO

There My Dress Hangs

in that house of tile roofs, at the edge of the patio
with clothespins like birds' mouths, against the sun that explodes
without letting the windows fall out

there my dress hangs

it is a fantasy of short sleeves and golden buttons
it is of a simple material bought in a market
only for wearing on Sundays

there my dress hangs

the leaves' green eyes look at it swinging
back and forth without body, free of me
it moves softly

against the forgotten calendars, in the depths of all astrology
between the summer's dry lips
when I was a child and with my hands,
set two doves free.

A LA MANERA DE FRIDA KAHLO

Retrato con mariposas

cuando me pinto la boca vuelvo hasta la niña con trenzas oscuras
hasta la persona posible que yo era, la infancia resucitada
en enaguas duras de almidón, o esos vestidos con cuello enorme
con flores tan pequeñas, vuelvo en una operación de distancia
frente al espejo a estar fuera de mí/ siendo yo misma
a ponerme a mirar esa criatura juntando mariposas mentalmente
porque generalmente, mansamente, colgaba las piernas en una silla

dejaba que el otoño me llevara de un amarillo a otro, hasta que
el ocre cerraba las ventanas,
acariciaba la piel de las puertas.

IN THE MANNER OF FRIDA KAHLO

Portrait with Butterflies

when I paint my mouth I return to the child of dark tresses
to the possible person that I was, childhood resuscitated
in petticoats stiff with starch, or those dresses with enormous
collars
with such small flowers, I return through a distance operation
in front of a mirror to be beyond myself / being I myself
setting myself to look at that creature mentally joining butterflies
because generally, gently, she was dangling her legs from a chair

I would let the autumn carry me from one yellow to another, until
ocher would close the windows,
it caressed the doors' skin.

A LA MANERA DE FRIDA KAHLO

A veces yo perdía los anteojos

y se me perdía el mundo o daba vueltas la página
y una lágrima me ablandaba la silla o solamente
estaba en medio de una habitación inmaculada
mientras mis riñones soltaban charcos de sangre
y la infancia se hundía con camisones sin florcitas
y pies rosados, y afuera, en la ventana la plaza
aparecía repleta de palomas

yo hubiera olvidado el abecedario por una corona
de manos, por niños haciendo una ronda hasta que
el sol caía, no como una transfusión sino como un
sol cansado, hasta que las mamás volvían con sus
"se acabó el juego" y el juego terminaba inocente
sin muñecas rotas, sin piezas de mecano que se ausentan
con un: "hasta mañana"...

IN THE MANNER OF FRIDA KAHLO

Sometimes I Lost My Eyeglasses

and the world was lost to me or I turned the page
and a tear softened the chair for me or it was only
that I was in the middle of an immaculate room
while my kidneys unfastened puddles of blood
and childhood sank into nightgowns without little flowers
and rosy feet, and outside, in the window the plaza
appeared replete with doves

I would have given up the ABC book for a circle
of hands, for children making a round until
the sun would fall, not like a transfusion, but like a
tired sun, until the mamas would return with their
"the game is over" and the game would end innocent
of broken dolls, without pieces of an Erector set that absent themselves
with a "see you tomorrow" . . .

FOCUSING

en este lugar donde vuelan nubes y horas secas
el vientre del espacio brilla con ojos fijos
a punto de explotar otra estrella fría donde tal vez
mi abuelo viaje con su música, con las corbatas desatadas
tal como era, viaje hasta la memoria de la tierra
donde una vez estuvimos juntos

y tal vez pueda regresando a sus huesos ponerse aquella
cara delgada, esa manera de mirar el mundo, un caminar
nostálgico lleno de desencanto, horas secas, viento
lleno de otoño, una caligrafía en blocks* perdidos
de calles destartaladas

con su cara de Beckett caminaba sosteniendo el sombrero
tenía los ojos tristes, un traje de franela gris oscuro
una fidelidad de puerta vieja a tres o cuatro amigos.

---

* manzanas

FOCUSING

in this place where clouds and dry leaves fly
the womb of space shines with fixed eyes
to the point of another cold star exploding where perhaps
my grandfather travels with his music, with his ties untied
such as he was, travels to the earth's memory
where once we were together

and perhaps regressing to his bones he may put on that
lean face, that way of looking at the world, a nostalgic
walking full of disenchantment, dry leaves, wind
full of fall, a calligraphy in lost blocks
of shabby streets

with his face of Beckett he would walk keeping his hat on
he had sad eyes, a suit of dark grey flannel
a faithfulness of an old door to three or four friends.

COOL MEMORIES

Introducción a las esperas

Dentro de tres horas podremos abrir la heladera
y sentarnos a comer mientras pasa el verano,
hace tres horas mi madre colocó tres cubeteras
repletas de agua y polvo de helado de vainilla.

la espera es más larga, más importante,
es una espera sudamericana que no hace más que
sacralizarlo todo, por ejemplo, esta tarde
mi hermano y yo nos trajimos revistas

para leer cerca de la heladera,
para mirarla de vez en cuando, como si fuera un totem.

COOL MEMORIES

Introduction to Delays

Within three hours we shall open the refrigerator
and sit down to eat while summer passes,
three hours ago my mother put in three trays
full of water and vanilla ice cream powder

the delay is very long, more important,
it is a South American delay which does no more than
sanctify everything, for example, this afternoon
my brother and I bring magazines

to read near the refrigerator
to look at it once in a while, as if it were a totem.

COOL MEMORIES

Graffiti

Mi hermano como un jackson pollock de cuatro años
ilustró la casa con lapices de cera. Una escritura
que en New York hubieran considerado profética
porque los niños saben seguir el rastro del misterio,
de lo imposible, pero a esa altura del mundo
en un pequeño pueblo sobre el mapa, las circunvoluciones
de colores hicieron que mi hermano quedara castigado
tres días con sus noches, y al atardecer del cuarto,
recién entonces, se le permitió volver a la mesa.

COOL MEMORIES

Graffiti

My brother like a four-year-old jackson pollock
illustrated the house with color crayons. A writing
that in New York they would have considered prophetic
because children know how to follow the trace of the mystery
of the impossible, but at that altitude of the world
in a small town on the map, the circumvolutions
of colors brought my brother the punishment of
three days with their nights, and only with the arrival of the fourth
afternoon--
just then, was he permitted to return to the table.

COOL MEMORIES

la piel de un globo

Así terminaremos todos, dice mi tío,
el globo enganchado en una rama termina explotando
el globo que era globo, aire de nuestros pulmones
termina estampado contra las ramas del vecino

mi hermano llorando por lo que fuera un globo
mi tío reflexionando sobre la fugacidad de la vida
los vecinos asomados a las ventanas con un mate en la mano

¿así terminaremos todos? Yo me alejo silenciosamente
del lugar de los hechos. Me alejo como si saliera de un marco,
como si desapareciera de una fotografía

siento un rayo de sol sobre la mente, primeras muertes:
el nacimiento de mi metafísica.

COOL MEMORIES

A Balloon's Skin

Thus we shall all end, my uncle said,
the balloon caught on a branch ended up exploding
the balloon that was a globe, air of our lungs
ended up engraved against the neighbor's branches

my brother crying for what a balloon might be
my uncle reflecting on life's fugacity
the astonished neighbors at the windows with mate* in their hands

thus we shall all end? . . . I moved away silently
from the scene of the events. I moved away as if I were leaving a frame,
as if I were disappearing from a photograph

I feel a ray of sun upon my mind, first deaths:
the birth of my metaphysics.

---

* A South American herbal tea, first drunk from gourds by the gauchos on the Argentine pampas and now drunk in the cities as well.

SERIE DE RETRATOS

a los treinta y tantos años---a mi edad-- mi madre
se parecía a mí, usando ojos negros para mirar el mundo
su mirada perdida en un patio lleno de mariposas,

a veces le faltaban las fuerzas para poder llegar
hasta el final de un día con mangas de camisa,
la tristeza crecía como una fruta azul o un árbol

expandiendo sus ramas en el sur, ocupando la sombra
de una hamaca donde nosotros jugábamos sin comprender
que las mujeres de su generación no tenían imagen

y habían crecido como esos insectos voladores, para
dar vueltas la casa de punta a punta, para revolotear
del mercado a los cuadernos de aritmética sin poder

poner en orden las emociones, esos cometas, que pasaban
rozándola, que pasaban humedeciéndole los ojos
cuando tenía treinta y tantos años, mi madre.

SERIES OF PORTRAITS

at thirty-something years--at my age--my mother
looked like me, using my black eyes to see the world
her glance lost in a patio full of butterflies,

sometimes she lacked the energy for being able to last
'til the end of a day in shirt sleeves
sadness grew like a blue fruit or a tree

expanding its branches in the south, occupying the shade
of a hammock where we would play without understanding
that the women of her generation didn't have an image

and had grown up like those flying insects, to
go through the house from end to end, to flit
from the market to arithmetic notebooks without being able

to put emotions in order, those comets, that passed
brushing her, that passed making her eyes tear
when she was thirty-something, my mother.

SE ACABARON LOS CUENTOS

Imelda Marcos

es una pena que entre tantos pares de zapatos no haya una Cenicienta
o, al revés, que entre tantas noches de príncipe no haya ninguna chica
asustada corriendo entre escaleras para encontrar a una persona menos
maravillosa que los objetos voladores---los mosquitos, las luciérnagas,
los aviones--porque ella no quería tener ciento cincuenta pares de zapatos
tirados en un placard, sino un solo par de snickers para salir a correr
por un parque lleno de gente ocupada hasta quedarse sin aliento
y tirarse en un banco de Central Park y dar con un hombrecito normal
que comentara cualquier cosa, inclusive que la ayudara a abrocharse
el cordón suelto entre la sonrisa y el viento.

THE STORIES ARE OVER

Imelda Marcos

it is a pity that among so many pairs of shoes there is no Cinderella
or, the opposite, that among so many prince's nights there may be
no frightened girl running up steps to find a person less
marvelous than flying objects--mosquitoes, bats
planes--because she didn't want to have fifty pairs of shoes
tossed on a placard, but only one pair of sneakers to go out running
through a park full of busy people until she was out of breath
and tossed aside on a bench in Central Park and came across a little
ordinary man who might say anything, might even help her fasten
the loose cord between the smile and the wind.

SE ACABARON LOS CUENTOS.

Cenicienta

un zapato de cristal abandonado en una escalera
el que lo encuentre se lleva una mujer que al darse vuelta
conoce un poco de filosofía y barre la casa pensando en las
partículas de sol que dan vueltas, mientras la madrastra
habla sola protestando en la sala

un dedo con un dedal son las dos hermanastras que tampoco
la encuentran atractiva, mientras ella se apoya sobre el palo de escoba
y comprende que la distancia más importante existe
no del cielo a la tierra, sino dentro de la misma familia

que las órbitas terrestres le aprietan la cintura como el elástico
de la enagua simple, mientras estas tres mujeres que la conocen
hace tanto tiempo, la hacen tiritas como si fuera un trapo viejo.
Y ella, con ojos alargados de primavera

recuerda esa frase del libro de Buber: "desencuentros" y se dirige
a la cocina, donde piensa trabajar hasta que llegue el príncipe.
Quiero decir, el escritor, y ponga fin a este litigio de mujeres.

THE STORIES ARE OVER

Cinderella

a crystal shoe abandoned on a stair
he who finds it will carry away a woman who on turning about
knows a little philosophy and sweeps the house thinking of
sun particles that turn about, while the stepmother
talks to herself protesting in the living room

a finger with a thimble are the two stepsisters who don't
find her attractive, while she leans on the broomstick
and understands that the most important distance exists
not between heaven and earth, but within the family itself

that the terrestrial orbits tighten her waist like the elastic
of a half-slip, while these three women have known her
for such a long time, they make bandages of her as if she were a rag.
And she, with elongated eyes of spring

remembers that phrase from Buber's book: "disencounters" and goes
to the kitchen, where she intends to work until the prince shows up.
I mean to say, the writer, and puts an end to this female litigation.

CAMBIO DE PALABRAS

Final de juego

según mi padre no nos volveremos a ver nunca más
después de este encuentro no habrá otro. Perderemos
las caras y los ojos, el timbre de la voz, el hemisferio
incluso las llaves en los bolsillos se quedarán sin puertas,
y los pulmones sin ese aire de domingo que vuela por el patio.

como no nos volveremos a ver nunca más, este día
es el único para apretar entre las manos, y las discusiones
son menos importantes que los afectos, y hay que cuidar
a las personas antes de que se apaguen como astros.

En la radio anunciaban lluvia y mi padre preparaba café
una tormenta de emociones había caído sobre nosotros,
el tiempo nos daba roles* como padre e hija y nos repetía,
pero para mi padre yo siempre era una niña,
la chica de ojos negros, Marcelita.

---

* papeles

EXCHANGE OF WORDS

Game's End

according to my father we shall never see each other again
after this meeting there will be no other. We shall lose
hands and eyes, the voice's timbre, the hemisphere
even the keys in our pockets will remain without doors,
and lungs without that Sunday air that flies through the patio.

since we shall never see each other again, this day
is the only one to press within our hands, and discussions
are less important than endearments, and it's necessary to care
for people before they go out like stars.

On the radio they announce rain and my father prepares coffee
a storm of emotions has fallen on us,
time gave us roles as father and daughter and we repeated ourselves,
but for my father I will always be a child,
the girl with dark eyes, Marcelita.

Índigo

Indigo

POEMA CON LOS OJOS LEJOS

Una sola palabra con una encía rosada,
el techo con la luna, la luna dentro de la casa,
habitación en transparencia
la mujer creando apretada a sus huesos
con un manto de sangre recorriéndola
el cerebro y sus verbos
el corazón pesado como una campana de hierro
bello texto nocturno
mirar la habitación con sus bostezos
de neurona a neurona, cuando escribo,
una cadena de significados regresa hasta la silla
la imágen el momento

en que se abrió la vida como un tonel de pájaros
de pájaros del sur, extraviados, secretos.

POEM WITH ITS EYES IN THE DISTANCE

A single word with its rosy gum,
the roof with the moon, the moon within the house,
room in transparency
the woman creating pressed to her bones
with a mantle of blood running over her
the brain and its words
the heart heavy as an iron bell
bello texto nocturno *
to look at the room with its yawns
from neuron to neuron, when I write,
a chain of meanings returns to the chair
the image the moment

in which life opened like a cask of birds
of southern birds, straying, secret.

---

* beautiful nocturnal text

CABELLOS SUELTOS

en los cuadros de Degas, había una mujer cepillándose el pelo
y un hilo de aire fresco cruzando la botella y la vasija de agua
hasta tocar las hebras doradas sobre el hombro, entonces,
por un cambio de signos, entro al cuadro,
corro por ríos de cabello rubio, camino hasta encontrarme
con una frente ancha, donde una mujer guarda un pensamiento
como una mariposa de alas verdes

me desabrocho una camisa, tiro sobre la cama un par de jeans gastados
es el atardecer con sus mejillas tocando suavemente los espejos
caen sobre mi hebras de pelo largo, melancólico, liso
y hay entre las ventanas y las puertas intimidad de días conocidos
un otoño que se queja en óleo pesado y ocre, una manera de mirar
hebillas debajo de una lámpara, el bostezo de un diario personal,
el murmullo de un patio.

un carraspeo de hombre mayor me regresa hasta la habitación
donde otra gente mira admirada las cabelleras de estos cuadros
y afuera en San Petersburgo el día es amarillo, pasan los ómnibus
se barren las calles, varios niños intentan vender algo, y dos
enamorados se pierden al doblar una esquina.

LOOSE HAIR

in Degas' pictures, there was a woman brushing her hair
and a thread of fresh air crossing the bottle and the water vessel
until it reached the golden threads on her shoulder, then,
through a change of signs, I enter the picture,

I run through rivers of blonde hair, I walk until I meet
a wide forehead, where a woman keeps a thought
like a butterfly with green wings

I unbutton my shirt, I throw a pair of beat-up jeans on the bed
the evening is drawing on with its cheeks softly touching the mirrors
threads of hair--long, melancholy, smooth--fall on me
and there between the windows and the doors is an intimacy of known
days
a fall that complains in heavy ocher oil, a way of looking at
buckles beneath a lamp, the sketch of a personal diary
the murmur of a patio.

An older man's hawking makes me return to the room
where other people look admiringly at the manes of those pictures
and outside in Saint Petersburg the day is yellow, the omnibuses pass
the streets are swept, several children try to sell something, and two
lovers get lost upon turning a corner.

MAGMA RISING *

En este atardecer el sol que se rompe dentro de mi vientre
se descompone en nervios y labios, arrastra material virginal
como mis dedos cuando tocaron por primera vez un rostro deseado
cuando se envolvieron en otras manos, ese segundo de inocencia,

arrastra en su magma genial, repetitivo por generaciones,
esa forma que tenemos las mujeres de soportar dolores de cabeza
la depresión de días de sol morado, de sol guinda pasando por
el cuerpo, eclipsando las noches sin poder dormir

y esas fuerzas ocultas aparecen un poco antes de la madrugada
cuando todos sueñan, cuando la casa duerme, con voces de
sueños destruídos, pedacitos, fragmentos de aquella cosa que
iba a ser la vida, la vida potencial, no la vida privada

donde mi escritura es otra forma de fracaso, un signo inverso,
una rebeldía, una forma de caer sobre la página

mi estío imperfecto, mis revoluciones.

---

* Magma levantándose.

MAGMA RISING

As this evening draws on the sun that breaks within my womb
is decomposed into nerves and lips, it drags virginal matter
like my fingers when they touched a desired face for the first time
when they became entangled with other hands, that second of innocence,

drags in its genial magma, repetitive through generations,
that way that we women have of putting up with headaches
the depression of days of mulberry sun, of cherry sun passing through
the body, eclipsing the nights without being able to sleep

and those occult forces appear a little before daybreak
when everyone dreams, when the house sleeps, with voices of
destroyed dreams, little pieces, fragments of that thing which
was going to be life, potential life, not private life

where my writing is another form of failure, an inverse sign
a rebellion, a way of falling on the page

my imperfect summer, my revolutions.

TIEMPO DEL OBJETO

Cézanne made a living thing out of a teacup, or rather
in a teacup he realized the existence of something alive.
Wassily Kandinsky *

en esa taza de café caliente
se pegaron las madrugadas como si fueran besos a la boca
y era solamente una forma de comunicarnos
abriendo correo, despachando sobres con estampillas de próceres
dejando caer el día como una bata sobre la silla,
el pesado día de hierro helado, con portones de hierro
como si la realidad fuera esto, te digo, me digo, un morirse
un descoser palomas para sacarles vuelo
y no una forma de manifestarse, abrirse, protegiendo cosas ciertas
y entonces...
nos pusimos a pensar en el tiempo en que el lenguaje se mordió la cola
y apareció espectral, seguro, monológico
como si todos fuéramos perfectos en este país, te decía mirándote
como si fueras una persona viva,

no esa taza de café caliente
no un objeto húmedo de luna.

---

* Cézanne hizo una cosa viva de una taza para té, o más bien en una taza para té realizó la existencia de algo vivo.

TIME OF THE OBJECT

Cézanne made a living thing out of a teacup, or rather
in a teacup he realized the existence of something alive.
Wassily Kandinsky

in that cup of hot coffee
daybreaks got stuck as if they were kisses on the mouth
and it was only a way of communicating to each other
opening the mail, dispatching letters with politicians' stamps
letting the day fall like a robe on the chair,
the heavy day of frozen iron, with gates of iron
as if reality were this, I tell you, I tell myself, a dying away
a ripping apart of doves to take their flight away
and not a form for manifesting itself, opening itself, protecting certain
things and then . . .
we set ourselves to thinking of the time in which the tongue bit the tail
and it appeared ghostlike, sure, monologic
as if we were all perfect in this country, I told you looking at you
as if you were a living person,

not that cup of hot coffee

not an object wet with moonlight.

PARTES DEL DISCURSO DE LA LLUVIA

Por aquí pasó hace poco un espiral galáctico y se cayeron
dos o tres estrellas que los niños aprovecharon para cerrar los ojos
y pedir deseos,

cayó polvo caído en la garganta del océano nocturno y al derramarse
provocó un cambio en los ojos del hemisferio sur que iluminado
fotocopió mi cuerpo transparente

entonces yo tenía menos años, tantos años menos, y en los
omóplatos un signo de "algo va a crecer", no el mundo afuera
sino el mundo adentro, palabras prohibidas

esa manera de mirar la lluvia me cambió por completo / fue un flash
sobre la cara, ver la humedad de los vidrios, calcar con una mano
la mañana y olerla

esa manera de caer sobre el mundo, algo cósmico, como el surgir
de un poema que termina donde nunca empezó por un paso de
astronauta
una huella de snickers en la tierra mojada

así la adolescencia desnuda / reflejada / inmersa en la calcomanía

PARTS OF THE RAIN'S DISCOURSE

Here a short while ago a galactic spiral passed and two or three stars
fell which the children took advantage of for closing their eyes
and asking for their hearts' desire.

dust fell falling into the nocturnal ocean's throat and upon spreading out
provoked a change in the eyes of the southern hemisphere that,
illuminated, photocopied my transparent body

then I was many years younger, so many years younger, and in my
shoulder blades a sign of "something is going to grow," not
the world outside but the world within, forbidden words

that way of seeing the rain changed me completely / it was a flash
on my face, to see the wetness of the windowpanes, to trace the morning
with one hand and to smell it

that way of falling upon the world, something cosmic, like the surging
forth of a poem that ends where it never began through an astronaut's
step
a snicker's footprint on the wet earth

thus adolescence--nude / reflected / immersed--in the decalcomania

de los astros, en el efecto de la distancia sobre los cuerpos avanzó hasta donde uno se entrega completamente

física, emocionalmente, a las manos del vacío que significa querer por primera vez a alguien, mientras la lluvia moja las ventanas.

of the stars, in the effect of distance on bodies advanced
to where one surrendered completely

physically, emotionally, to the hands of emptiness that means to love
someone for the first time, while the rain wets the windows.

ELLA VA A IRSE DE ESTA PÁGINA

este poema me cuesta como un chorro de índigo en la ventana,
empapando el sillón de mimbre y esos pensamientos que tuviste
sobre las cosas que se pierden, como lápices de labios, como
cintas del pelo, como un cambiar de caras y de afectos
                    la cara en el espejo, la cara con sus gestos
esa sonrisa de gioconda, en la garganta un tobogán para bajar
angustias, mundos que libremente no podrán ser nunca,
partes del esquema de esta historia.

ella va a irse porque las cosas maduran y cambian, y otros
escenarios envuelven mi cabeza, no ya los quince años,
esas conversaciones con las manos en los bolsillos, con
las manos en el pelo, no ya ese pasillo de niños bobos y tiernos
donde tratábamos de entender la vida los domingos,

sino esta hora, que me lleva lejos, que me despeina,
que me arroja signos, que me hace escucharte a lo lejos
la voz en la campera... una tristeza como la marca de un vaso
en una servilleta, y las sillas dadas vueltas en un café vacío.

SHE IS GOING TO GO AWAY FROM THIS PAGE

this poem accosts me like a spurt of indigo on the window
soaking the wicker chair and those thoughts that you had
about things that get lost, like lipsticks, like
hair ribbons, like a changing of faces and of affections
            the face in the mirror, the face with its gestures
that giaconda smile, in the throat a toboggan for lowering
afflictions, worlds that freely shall never be
parts of the scheme of this history.

she is going to go away because things mature and change, and other
scenes envelop my head, no longer fifteen years old,
those conversations with hands in pockets, with
hands in the hair, no longer that corridor of dumb and tender children
where we tried to understand life on Sundays,

but rather this hour that carries me away, that tussles me,
that hurls signals at me, that makes me listen to you distantly
the voice in your jacket . . . a sadness like the wet ring of a glass
on a napkin, and chairs turned upside down in an empty cafe.

CELESTE MADURO

este cielo caerá sobre mí/ salpicado de estrellas
me herirá mañana con su dentadura celestial, como un animal tierno
que no sabe morder, y me muerde las manos y será la distancia
un pliego donde escribo los recuerdos y el poema
volverá a destejerse mientras ando con pullover usado
para comenzar en la otra punta del camino, con una hebra de día
y un ramo de pretéritos

lloré, sentí, maldije a esa chica con los jeans gastados
a la chica leyendo hasta muy tarde y como un don quijote perdiendo
la cabeza, por mundos, esferas, posibilidades que en ese tiempo
parecían absurdas. Por modos de mirar detrás de la ventana.

y amé, perdí, soñé que en otra parte, alguna vez en medio de la ausencia
una literatura de retazos, como de tazas y de platos viejos,
ocupara la página, fuera un escenario donde otros, mis Otros
dejaran una huella.

este cielo caerá sobre mí/ salpicado de estrellas
hasta que se hunda una página con otra, y de las dos surja una puerta.

MATURE SKY BLUE

this sky will fall on me / splashed with stars
it will wound me tomorrow with its celestial teeth, like a tender animal
that doesn't know how to bite, and bites my hands and the distance will
be a pleat where I write memories and the poem
will unravel again while I walk around in a used pullover
to begin at another point on the road, with a thread of daylight
and a branch of preterits

I cried, I felt, I cursed that girl with the beat-up jeans
that girl reading so late and like a Don Quixote losing
her head, through worlds, spheres, possibilities that in that time
seemed absurd. For modes of seeing behind the window.

and I loved, I lost, I dreamt that elsewhere, sometime in the midst
of absence a literature of fragments, as of cups and old plates,
might fill the page, would be a scene where others, my Others
might leave a trace.

this sky will fall on me / splashed with stars
until one page plunges into another, and from the two a door springs up.

Época

para Michel Foucault

Epoch

for Michel Foucault

SI ME ROMPO

Si caigo de boca a la calle como una paloma amarilla
rodando por una ventana humedecida por la noche
y la lluvia encuentra mi abecedario fragmentado
y no sabe distinguir si fue for you* o por nosotros
si hay restos de manos abiertas o verbos atragantados
o luna ocre metida en el fondo del otoño
y fauces que me comieron un trozo de camisón se abren
desprendiendo mi cuerpo lleno de maravillas
--los libros de viaje, marco polo, mandrell--
si al soltar un pie rosado del balcón se caen
también monedas antiguas, magnetic glasses,** old pictures
y fugazmente en buenos aires un corazón hecho de epifanías
se cae y se rompe, te pido
que como un insecto nocturno prendas los ojos sobre
la línea de mi rebeldía, porque tengo que enfrentarme
con la historia -nuestra historia-
y caer
          y caer
                    y romperme. *Si me rompo.*

---

* para ti.

**vidrios magnéticos; brújulas

IF I BREAK

If I fall on my mouth to the street like a yellow dove
rolling through a window wetted by the night
and the rain finds my fragmented ABC book
and doesn't know how to distinguish whether it was for you or for us
if there are remains of open hands or swallowed words
or ocher moon thrust into the fall's depths
and fauces, that eat a piece of my nightgown, open
releasing my body full of wonders
--the travel books, marco polo, mandrell--
if upon letting a rosy foot go from the balcony there also fall
old coins, magnetic glasses, old pictures
and fleetingly in buenos aires a heart made of epiphanies
falls and breaks, I request that you
like a nocturnal insect pledge your eyes to
the line of my rebellion, because I have to meet up
with history--our history--
and fall

    and fall

        and break. *If I break.*

EL POEMA EN MANGAS DE CAMISA

de tarde en tarde mi madre oía la máquina teclear
(aunque estaba muy lejos, el sonido de la máquina rasgaba
el papel, iba desde la casa a los vecinos hasta la panadería,
subía por la cola de los gatos hasta las bicicletas,
llegaba transpirando en el verano al oído de mi madre,
que exhausta la escuchaba persistir)
era una máquina olympia alemana, tecleaba sin pudor
como si saliera de una guerra y se metiera en otra
como si la destrucción de los edificios y lo que eran esquinas
se hubiera subido hasta el teclado y volviera a visitarme
en una tarde pesada de enero, aquellos años,

y, desde el polvo, desde la deconstrucción sistemática
se uniera a esta otra forma de morirse volcando la cabeza
hacia atrás, a esta otra forma de morder los días como lóbulos
hasta lastimarlos: y mi madre lloraba caminando por la casa,
lloraba sonándose la nariz, en sandalias mirando el pasto
los pequeños insectos que sonreían sin saber por qué

y yo seguía tecleando como si no tuviera más que una locura

THE POEM IN SHIRT SLEEVES

from time to time my mother would hear the machine typing
(although it was very distant, the sound of the machine tore
the paper, it went from home to the neighbors to the bakery,
it climbed through the cats' tails to the bicycles,
arrived sweating in summer to the ear of my mother,
who, exhausted, heard it persisting)

it was a German Olympia machine, it typed without shame
as if it were going to one war and butted into another
as if the destruction of the buildings and what were corners
had climbed to the tile roofs and come back to visit me
in a heavy january afternoon, those years,

and from the dust, from the systematic deconstruction
joined this other form of dying tilting the head
back, to this other form of biting the days like lobes
until it wounded them: and my mother would cry walking around the
house, cry blowing her nose, in sandals looking at the grass
at the little insects that smiled without knowing why

and I would go on typing as if I had nothing more than a madness

de hojas escritas, como si el hastío de sentirme impotente
me hubiera dado cuatro manos, y ese taca-taca llegara hasta
los rezos de mi vecina del tercer piso, y esos puntos finales,
irremediables, perforaran la página como una picadura de verano
con el deseo de borrar heridos, con el devaneo de crear
un discurso para los escombros, para los fragmentos de texto

de otras vidas.

of written leaves, as if being fed up with feeling impotent
had given me four hands, and that tac-tac would reach
the prayers of my neighbor lady on the third floor, and those final periods,
irremediable, would perforate the page like a summer prick
with the desire for erasing wounds, with the raving of creating
a discourse for rubble, for the text fragments

of other lives.

ROSTRO SOBRE ROSTRO

(la construcción de una experiencia)

sobre este rostro que sostengo con las dos manos
otro rostro más profundo se extiende, una pregunta avanza
hacia el final de un pasillo donde la luz prendida
la luz anticipada por las sombras, muestra una mujer escribiendo
una mujer pensando, fumando cigarrillos.

sobre este rostro muchos otros rostros pasaron
mirándome descuidadamente o atentamente, pero todos pasaron
y solamente tus ojos permanecieron mirándome
con la sorpresa de un insecto curioso, iluminado por la lluvia

por esa mirada este rostro fue en parte tu rostro y
el arco de mi sonrisa fucsia, se convirtió en la soga donde una
niña de cabellos largos jugaba con el mundo, si podía jugar
en esa hora brillante del anochecer

y este otro rostro, que me tapo con las dos manos
que completa un ciclo de crecimientos y destierros
es un pedazo de ojo mirando la caída de un día de historia
es un pedazo de mano acariciando la página morbosa de un periódico

FACE ON FACE

(the construction of an experience)

on this face that I hold with my two hands
another more profound face is spread out, a question advances
towards the end of a corridor where the turned-on light,
the light anticipated by the shadows, shows a woman writing
a woman thinking, smoking cigarettes.

on this face many other faces pass by
looking at me carelessly or attentively, but all pass by
and only your eyes keep looking at me
with the surprise of a curious insect, illuminated by the rain

because of that look this face was in part your face and
the bow of my fuchsia smile, was converted into the cord where a
child with long hair played with the world, if she could play
in that brilliant hour of twilight.

and this other face, that I cover with my two hands
which completes a cycle of maturations and exiles
is a piece of eye looking at the fall of a day of history
is a piece of hand caressing the morbid page of a newspaper

y mucho más acá este rostro que sostengo con las dos manos hacia la humedad futura de la noche de otro tiempo, en que escribir y pertenecerme no sean la misma cosa, y mis palabras sin mí, sean un camino. Un discurso entre destierros

el norte/el sur: los huesos de mis deseos y mis brotes.

and here much closer this face that I hold in my two hands
towards the future humidity of the night of another time, in which
writing and belonging to myself may not be the same thing, and my words
without me, may be a road. A discourse between exiles

the north / the south: the bones of my desires and my shoots.

ÉPOCA

los verbos de esta parte de mi mundo son verbos esplendorosamente
verbos, eléctricos, azules, desde los árboles llenos de universo
hasta las piedras con sus fuerzas duras, las palabras partidas
en la boca, son mis verbos quiero decir que son mis rebeldías
salpicando la página de poderes ocultos, como poder ver en los
ojos de los vidrios a los otros lastimosamente cargando
el presente.

son mis verbos, repito contra la mesa, golpeando las encías de
las teclas, *son mis potencias*. Mis trozos de espejo fracturado
mis órganos vivos como mis propias células.

pedazos de tiempo, rebeldía iluminada,
mis verbos son los únicos que pueden
romper la transparencia de la historia.

EPOCH

the words of this part of my world are words splendidly
words, electric, blue, where the trees full of universe
even the stones with their hard strengths, the words cleft
in the mouth, are my words I mean that they are my rebellions
splashing the page with occult powers, like being able to see in the
eyes of the windowpanes the others pityingly loading
the present

they are my words, I repeat against the table, hitting the gums
of the keys, they are my power. My bits of shattered mirror
my living organs like my own cells.

pieces of time, illuminated rebellion,
my words are the only ones that can
break the transparency of history.

Una mujer con la mano en la frente

A Woman with Her Hand on Her Forehead

UNA MUJER CON LA MANO EN LA FRENTE

Aquí adentro hay mundos, océanos de llamadas telefónicas,
revoluciones de días de sol y hielo,
voces que se confunden, el collage de los diarios.
Aquí adentro hay palomas respirando dormidas,
un cosmos propio de estrellas que se mueren
y al borde de sí mismas dejan su fuerza blanca,
una capacidad de agujeros negros
atrayendo materia como sillas, poemas, y cucharas
tu cara con tus dientes, las metáforas,
todo lo que no existe pero existió alguna vez
original, perfecto donde estaba.

Aquí adentro hay una persona, yo, pensándote.
Hay también un poco de luna de ayer sobre las sábanas.
Y el sol de esta mañana al despertarme.

A WOMAN WITH HER HAND ON HER FOREHEAD

Here within there are worlds, oceans of telephone calls,
revolutions of days of sun and ice,
voices that become confused, the collage of the newspapers
Here within there are sleeping doves breathing,
a cosmos itself of stars that die
and at the edge of themselves leave a white force,
a capacity for black holes
attracting matter like chairs, poems, and spoons
your face with your teeth, the metaphors,
all that doesn't exist but existed sometime
original, perfect where it was.

Here within there is a person, myself, dreaming you.
There is also a little of yesterday's moonlight on the sheets.
And this morning's sun upon my awakening.

TRANSPARENCIAS

--nadie esperaba que cuando ella terminó su taza de café
y se dirigía a la ventana, un rayo de sol la atravesara
mostrando la columna vertebral y una parte del cráneo
donde guardaba mariposas del verano pasado,

nadie esperaba, por ejemplo, que en ese momento de verdad
saliera de adentro suyo un gesto como de mujer desamparada
no por el otoño o por la claridad, sino por esa manera
que él tenía de decir las cosas, casi murmurándolas

nadie esperaba que él siguiera ocupando un lugar dentro
de la estructura ósea, y asomara los ojos entre olas eléctricas
del cerebro, saludando con la mano, como si fuera a despedirse
de la muerte.

TRANSPARENCIES

nobody expected that when she finished her cup of coffee
and turned to the window, a ray of light would pass through her
showing her vertebral column and a part of her cranium
where she kept butterflies from last summer

nobody expected, for example, that in that moment of truth
a gesture like that of a helpless woman would come out from within
not because of the fall or because of clarity, but because of that way
that he had of saying things, almost murmuring them

nobody expected that he would continue occupying a place within
her bony structure, and would appear in her eyes like electric brain waves,
waving with his hand, as if he were saying goodbye
to death.

SCHMETTERLING *

Conversaciones de mujeres

como una mariposa atrapada por el vidrio
como una mariposa atrapada así corría mi vida por un hilo de noche
y el viento frío empapaba las hojas, el viento que se lleva los papeles
en medio de la calle -en el silencio de los otros- entre puertas

una cara debajo de una máscara sonriendo, pero la tristeza con patios
con aros dorados de naranjas, con higueras, abría sus pétalos agrios
como si fueran pétalos de mujer forzada a contemplar las cosas
sin poder moverlas de lugar, como una casa prestada

como una mariposa que hace piruetas para escapar
atrapada por la luz artificial de la lámpara y el brillo de una estrella
atrapada por otras vidas, por otros cuerpos ajenos,
por úteros, gorjeos, pisadas en la arena

como si no fuera a despertarme de esta pesadilla
así corría mi vida

---

*"Schmetterling" es la palabra alemana para mariposa.

SCHMETTERLING*

Women's Conversations

like a butterfly trapped by the windowpane
like a trapped butterfly my life was running thus by a night's thread
and the cold wind soaked the leaves, the wind carries the papers
into the middle of the street--into the silences of others--between doors

a face beneath a mask smiling, but the sadness with patios
with golden rims of oranges, with figs, opened its bitter petals
as if they were petals of a woman forced to contemplate things
without being able to change their place, like a borrowed thing

like a butterfly that makes pirouettes in order to escape
trapped by the lamp's artificial light and the brilliance of a star
by wombs, warblings, treads in the sand

as if I were not going to wake up out of this nightmare
thus ran my life

---

* "Schmetterling" is the German word for butterfly.

HER/STORY

Conversaciones de mujeres

Después de leerte los ojos:
si yo tuviera un hijo detenido, secuestrado, desnudo, maltratado
en cualquier parte de este mundo, en este mundo,
yo saldría a buscarlo debajo de los dientes de la tierra,
a buscarlo contra puertas cerradas, autoridades, celdas
yo saldría a buscarlo cerca de las piedras sin importarme
los escarabajos,
saldría a quemarme las noches contra archivos de rastros,
de pies húmedos, de caras fracturadas, de trozos de recuerdo.

dicen que fue un accidente y se perdió,

yo saldría del dormitorio con hebillas brillantes, con camisa
desabrochada, con inquietud de pájara, con almohadas húmedas.
Me abrocharía el mundo contra mí.

y saldría a buscarlo.

HER/STORY

Women's Conversations

After reading your eyes:
if I had a child detained, sequestered, naked, mistreated
in any part of this world, in this world,
I would go out to find him beneath the earth's teeth,
to find him despite closed doors, authorities, cells
I would go out to find him near the stones without the black beetles
mattering to me,
I would go out to burn the nights up despite archives of vestiges
of wet feet, of fractured faces, of pieces of memory,

they say it was an accident and he was lost,

would go out of the bedroom with brilliant buckles, with
an unbuttoned shirt, with a bird's disquiet, with wet pillows.
would button up the world against myself

would go out to find him.

FOTOGRAFÍA DE VERANO

la espalda contra la silla la silla de espaldas
con mi camisa abierta, sin corpiño mirando el mundo
los dedos son mariposas efímeras, tocan un ojo y otro,
miran la superficie dorada de un vaso un día de verano

yo estoy como esas vagabundas que buscan tesoros
en la raya de luz que dibuja la línea de un poema
como si fuera a sacar ostras de esos diálogos y esas cartas
que se acumulan como animales raros con estampillas extranjeras

y pasan abejas a rayas, las moscas con sus pétalos verdes
hermosas todas las frases de la arena que no se repiten
en cada pisada de mujer joven corriendo detrás de un perro
o de una vida, quien sabe

y entonces me doy vuelta y sonrío, con una mano sostengo el sombrero
estas piernas largas, estos ojos tristes, y allá abajo
sombrillas y niños, labios de mar corriendo.

SUMMER PHOTOGRAPH

my back against the chair the chair behind me
with my shirt open, without a brassiere looking at the world
my fingers are ephemeral butterflies, they touch one eye and the other,
they look at the golden surface of a glass one summer's day

I am like those bag ladies who search for treasures
in the ray of light that a line of a poem draws
as if I were going to extract oysters from those dialogues and those letters
that accumulate like rare animals with foreign stamps

and striped bees pass, the flies with green petals
beautiful all the sand's phrases that are not repeated
in each step of a young woman running behind a dog
or a life, who knows

and then I turn around and smile, with one hand I hold my hat
these long legs, these sad eyes, and there below
beach umbrellas and children, sea lips running.

LEYENDO CARTAS

(las estrellas interrumpen mi lectura), carraspea
la noche con mi techo, y mi ventana cerrada
hace señales de mundo: afuera los autos, pasa el viento,
una extraordinaria nube de hojas se produce
por el otoño que cae, irremediablemente.

(el tiempo interrumpe mi lectura) porque mientras yo
estoy aquí con los pies fríos allá está tu almohada
de hemisferio a hemisferio cambiamos signos
como si fuéramos animales o letras de otro abecedario

(tu caligrafía interrumpe mi lectura) y cruzan lagartijas
indescifrables contándome algo sobre una tía, trato
de recomponer la frase como un trozo de texto antiguo
y el frío interrumpe mi lectura:

voy a buscar café y unas tostadas.

READING LETTERS

(the stars interrupt my reading), the night
speaks hoarsely to my roof, and my closed window
makes worldly signs: outside the cars, the wind passes,
an extraordinary cloud of leaves is produced
by the autumn that is falling, irremediably.

(time and the season interrupt my reading) because while
am here with cold feet there is your pillow
from hemisphere to hemisphere we change signs
as if we were animals or letters of another ABC book

(your calligraphy interrupts my reading) and indecipherable
lizards cross telling me something about an aunt, I try
to recompose the phrase like a bit of ancient text
and the cold interrupts my reading

am going to find coffee and some toast.

TEXTOS DEL ATARDECER

Conversaciones de mujeres

Algunos escritos aparecieron después de los cuarenta años
como una manera de saludar esa marea de mar rojo que se
despide para siempre. Tocando por última vez el sentido
de lo posible, el útero que se cierra, la escritura que se abre
la vida que no desaparece pero esfuma paisajes con un ciclo
de adioses, con cajones de fotos desparramadas
casas que se pierden, muebles que se regalan o se cambian
retratos de familia, persistencias al ver crecer las flores

algunos escritos justifican un largo camino de transgresiones
donde las palabras decían no, pero los sueños decían sí
y sueños y palabras, mucho más seguros de sí mismos,
se aprietan contra el destino final de una idea expresada
no para resplandecer contra el universo, sino para brillar
en el pequeño espacio de la propiedad privada: el cuerpo

el rincón con los libros, las tazas de café secas y sucias
esas cosas--dijo ella caminando con un libro en la mano--
se saben después, nunca antes, se conocen a una cierta altura
del mundo y del sufrimiento, y entonces yo -dijo ella-
reemplazo la gloria por un minuto de comprensión

TWILIGHT TEXTS

Women's Conversations

Some writings appear after forty years
like a way of greeting this nausea from the red sea that
says farewell forever. Touching for the last time the sense
of the possible, the uterus that closes up, the writing that opens up
the life that doesn't disappear but tones landscapes down with a cycle
of goodbyes, with drawers of photos of open
houses that get lost, furniture that is given away or family
portraits are changed, persistence upon seeing flowers grow

some writings justify a long road of transgressions
where words say no, but dreams say yes,
and dreams and words, much more sure of themselves,
press against the final destiny of an idea expressed
not to glitter against the universe, but to sparkle
in the small space of private property: the body

the book corner, the dry and dirty coffee cups
those things--she said walking about with a book in her hand--
are known later, never before, become familiar at a certain altitude
of the world and of suffering, and then I--she said--
replace glory for a minute of comprehension

donde bajando las persianas, acariciando objetos conocidos
la casa que me contiene, la cáscara de nuez que es mi reino
se balancee suavemente, en una línea abierta por los otros.

where lowering the Venetian blinds, caressing familiar objects
the house which contains me, the nut's shell which is my kingdom
may be balanced softly, in a line opened by others.

ESTANDO SOLA

Conversaciones de mujeres

cuando la casa esta sola me muero de miedo, siento como si los muebles
estuvieran en forma inconsciente pensando cómo mudarse
y el otoño con ojos alargados cambiara las nubes, las hojas sucias
de cobre y de amarillo, todo me parece frágil

y las pulseras radiantes sobre una cómoda se convierten en una boca
abierta, los espejos copian las llaves para encerrarme en la habitación
a oscuras. Un vecino no podría oírme. Casi todos escuchan la televisión
hasta muy tarde.

En suma, las cosas más ínfimas se desdoblan en otra realidad,
y es porque si estuvieras yo me enredaría a tu cuerpo, soltaría el cabello
movería los brazos debajo de tu almohada,

me metería en tu piel como en un sueño. No me saldría azul por la
garganta

BEING ALONE

Women's Conversations

when the house is alone I die of fright, I feel as if the furniture
were unconsciously thinking about changing place
and the fall with elongated eyes were changing clouds, the dirty leaves
of copper and gold, everything seems fragile to me

and the radiant bracelets on the dresser change into an open
mouth, the mirrors copy keys to enclose me in the dark
room. A neighbor couldn't hear me. Almost all of them
listen to the television until very late.

In sum, the humblest things duplicate themselves into another reality,
and it is because if you were here, I would wrap myself around your
body,
I would loosen my hair, I would move my arms beneath your pillow,

I would get into your skin as in a dream. Blue would not come
out of my throat.

Cerrando los Ojos

Closing My Eyes

BASEBALL

como corren los jugadores en un campo bajo las estrellas
ignorantes de las estrellas porque están iluminados por las luces
más altas, en un estadio--tu vida, mi vida-- vamos todos
detrás de las cosas menos bellas, porque lo que no vemos:
deseos, posibilidades, derrotas, son fuerzas más profundas
y al movernos detrás de la gloria, al apuntar un triunfo
al equipo, con camisetas rayadas, con cuerpos transpirados
con el hurra que aparece emocionado como una boca abierta

perdemos noción de dónde estamos. De cuál es el porcentaje
de lluvia de lágrimas que inundaron el mundo, de cuánta gente
no llegó a ninguna parte por no tener a donde llegar

y al apretar un objeto sagrado: tu mano con mi mano
la gloria se desvanece no por la muerte no por el tiempo
por los parámetros históricos que nos limitan y nos endurecen,
sino por esta forma de ignorar lo presente:

ese brillo de los ojos de las luciérnagas.

BASEBALL

as players run in a field beneath the stars
ignorant of the stars because they are illuminated by the highest
lights, in a stadium--your life, my life--we all go
after the least beautiful things, because what we don't see:
desires, possibilities, defeats, are more profound forces
and upon trailing after glory, upon aiming for a triumph
for the team, with striped shirts, with sweaty bodies
with the hurrah that shows up excited with an open mouth

we lose the notion of where we are. Of what is the percentage
of the rain of tears that flooded the world, of how many people
never got anywhere for not having anywhere to get

and upon squeezing a sacred object: your hand in my hand
glory vanishes not because of death nor because of time
nor because of historical parameters that limit us and harden us
but rather because of this way of ignoring the present:

that shining of the fireflies' eyes

JUEGOS DE MARIPOSAS

el parloteo en un garden party,* el parloteo de las mujeres
y mi propia conversación riendo y gesticulando, esa manera de
mirar por el rabillo del ojo la camisa de un hombre
esa manera de hacer planes enormes o pequeños,
un vaso de limonada, vestidos que son prácticos y bellos
y una valija medioabierta: este episodio.

y luego volver a casa y sacarme las medias, tirar los zapatos
tocar la oreja del teléfono y seguir parloteando. Si,
casi todas las mujeres necesitamos mujeres para sobrevivir
y hombres que, como las comas en los párrafos,
marquen una pausa, suave, firme, breve
y detengan el texto de la muerte.

---

* fiesta en el jardín

BUTTERFLY GAMES

the chatter at a garden party, the chatter of women
and my own conversation laughing and gesturing, that way of
looking out of the corner of my eye at a man's shirt
that way of making enormous or small plans
a glass of lemonade, dresses that are practical and beautiful
and a half-opened suitcase: this episode.

and then to return home and take off my stockings, to toss my shoes
to put my ear to the telephone and continue chattering. Yes,
almost all of us women need women to survive
and men that, like commas in paragraphs,
may mark a pause--soft, firm, brief--
and may stop death's text.

4th OF JULY*

y mi cuatro de julio es una mujer que traspasa las puertas de vidrio,
tan joven, con tacos, y deja un par de lentes en un bolsillo
y un bolso con una máquina de escribir. Esas cosas pasaron en mi vida
y casi no las puedo creer, llegar a encontrarme con nadie
con mi sombra, temblar de miedo al cruzar una calle,
pedir instrucciones en una ventanilla.

a veces me da miedo pensar en la forma sencilla y solitaria
con que junté mis cosas y descansé en la noche americana: pedacitos de
hielo y todo tan desconocido como el destino de estos poemas
por eso ahora, cuando los imprima, cuando los deje irse
sé lo que ellos sentirán,

millones de mariposas en el estómago
un vértigo al entrar en la vida de otros, al pasar por los ojos de otros
al no tener mamá que venga a consolarlos.

---

* 4 de julio.

4TH OF JULY

and my fourth of july is a woman who passes through glass doors,
so young, with high heels, and keeps a pair of glasses in her pocketbook
and a bag with a typewriter. Those things happened in my life
and I almost cannot believe them, to find myself at last with nobody
with my shadow, to tremble with fear upon crossing a street
to ask directions at a window

sometimes it makes me scared to think of the simple and solitary way
that I got my things together and rested in the american night
little pieces of ice
and all so unknown like the destiny of these poems
because of that now, when I publish them, when I let them go
I know what they will feel,

millions of butterflies in the stomach
a vertigo upon entering others' lives, upon passing through others' eyes
upon not having a mama who comes to console them.

Fuerza blanca

White Force

MORNING MANUSCRIPT*

a veces prendo la luz y con las cortinas corridas no sé en que ciudad
estoy,
es una sensación de que la geometría fracasa
que las distancias forman una red invisible y ese perro que cruzaba
un cuento de Chejov, o cualquier otro cuento sudamericano
o el cuento de un buen cuentista inglés,
pasan desvalidos o felices sobre un pedazo de vereda y se pierde
el concepto de que estamos divididos -o eso quiero pensar

a veces siento entre las sábanas que la mañana podría ser
esa otra mañana dentro de veinticuatro horas que mi madre vivirá
al levantar las sábanas y sacudirlas en la cama, previamente
haber dejado un sueño volando por la habitación y un camisón
sobre una silla o que,

al abrocharme una camisa o un reloj, mi madre se cubrirá
las piernas con medias transparentes o con esas medias de lana
pesadas y nostálgicas del sur

---

*Manuscrito para la mañana

MORNING MANUSCRIPT

sometimes I turn on the light and with the curtains closed I don't know
what city I'm in,
it is a sensation that geometry fails
that distances form an invisible net and the dog that crosses
a story of Chekhov, or some other South American story
or the story of a good English storyteller
they pass helpless or happy on a piece of sidewalk and the concept
that we are divided is lost--or that is what I want to think

sometimes between the sheets I feel that the morning could be
that other morning within twenty-four hours that my mother will live
upon lifting the sheets and shaking them on the bed, previously
having left a dream flying through the room and her nightgown
on a chair or that,

upon putting on a shirt or a watch, my mother will cover
her legs with transparent stockings or with those wool stockings
heavy and nostalgic of the south

cosas de mujeres, pero el texto se extiende de un lugar a otro
de un óvulo a una idea, y hasta las flores en sus trompas
tienen recuerdos de otras flores y al levantarme, al abrir la
puerta,
posiblemente entro en la memoria de un suspiro,
que mi madre dará al mirar mis fotos.

women's things, but the text spreads out from one place to another
from an ovule to an idea, and even the flowers in their trumpets
have memories of other flowers and upon getting up, upon opening
the door, perhaps I enter into the memory of a sigh,
that my mother will give upon looking at my photos.

ESTADO DE LUZ

como oler la tormenta con el aire repleto de manzanas
y un viento que se levanta haciendo volar las cortinas
y una nervadura brillante anunciando lluvia, algo que va a caer
y todavía es un presentimiento

en alguna parte en este momento ese disco espiral que busca
voces en el espacio, está atento como una oreja sin poluciones
a cosas que nosotros ignoramos en este juntar los juguetes
de los niños, afuera, en el patio

y eso lo supe siempre, eso inició un camino a contramarcha
no es el agua la que viene a mí, yo voy al agua, me traslado
al borde de una nube, paso por anillos de viento hasta que de
mi casa hago solamente una estructura mental: puertas y ventanas

pero yo siempre supe, que en esta tarde como en cualquier otra
el poema que se está por escribir deviene como una pintura
abstracta y llena de interrogantes, como una iglesia vacía de
expectativas y llena de deseos, deviene como una madeja de

hilo azul brillante, no la de las mujeres tejiendo, sino las
de las horas, salpicando ventanas, el agua fresca en mi cara

STATE OF LIGHT

like smelling the storm with the air replete with apples
and a wind that rises making the curtains fly
and a brilliant nervure announcing rain, something that is going to fall
and still is a presentiment.

somewhere at this moment that spiral disk that searches
for voices in space, is attentive like an ear without pollution
to things that we don't know in this gathering together
of children's toys, outside, on the patio

and that I knew always, that initiated the marching to a different drum
it is not the water that comes to me, I go to the water, I transport myself
to the edge of a cloud, I pass through rings of wind until
I make my house just a mental structure: doors and windows

but I always knew that in this afternoon as in any other
the poem that is about to be written happens like a painting—
abstract and full of question marks, like a church empty of
expectations and full of desires, happens like a skein of

brilliant blue thread, not that of women knitting, but rather those
of the hours, splashing windows, the fresh water on my face

en tu cara: el poema que yo siento todavía no ha nacido
es un presagio, es una nostalgia al mirar fotos de galaxias

al pensar que mis dedos dejarán de ser dedos, mi computadora
desparramará el agua, las compotas, los árboles

el poema que está por venir dejará atrás a la mujer con blusa,
a la mujer con lápices de labios, a la mujer que en una calle
compra pan, mira las vidrieras, corre por la lluvia.

on your face: the poem that I feel still has not been born
a presage, is a nostalgia upon looking at photos of galaxies

upon thinking that my fingers will cease to be fingers, my computer
will spill out water, compotes, trees:

the poem that is about to be will leave behind the woman in her blouse
the woman with her lipsticks, the woman that in the street
buys bread, looks in shop windows, runs through the rain.

HEMISFERIO BLANCO

la luz que entra por mis oídos,
rompe la ventana con su hora más clara, es el sol que se hunde
en las costillas de la casa, el principio del amanecer
escribiendo

la seducción es blanca como una hoja sola
que extiende su vacío de neurona a neurona hasta que los dedos
se mueven como las pájaras inseguras

una página de computadora
una mujer descalza, la luz que viene del sol a buscar palabras
a revolver el útero

para encontrar intermitencias de comas, suspiros de puntos,
un cajón lleno de máscaras

metáforas,

ojos llenos de sueño y las manos desnudas.
Pedacitos de vidrio iluminado, anteojos.
La garganta, una avenida llena de luz. La saliva, los astros.

WHITE HEMISPHERE

the light that enters through my ears,
breaks the window with its clearest hour, it is the sun that buries
itself in the house's ribs, the beginning of dawn
writing

the seduction is white like a single leaf
that extends its emptiness from neuron to neuron until fingers
move like insecure female birds

a computer page
a barefoot woman, the light that comes from the sun to find words
to stir the womb

to find intermittencies of commas, sighs of periods,
a drawer full of masks

metaphors

dream-filled eyes and bare hands.
Little pieces of illuminated glass, eyeglasses.
The throat, an avenue full of light. Saliva, stars.

CREANDO/VIVIENDO

tazas desnudas de sus manos, días desvestidos de sus sombras
dedos que se olvidaron los anillos, entre las tardes que pasaron
segmentos de amarillo, pétalos enjuagados por la lluvia, piedras
brillando solas con sus ojos, angustias de domingos

potencias que se fueron, siento, pienso, tiemblo como las hojas
estos poemas no son más que partes de mí misma, incompletos,
complejos, silenciosos

pétalos de hombros, pétalos de bocas, estos poemas se descienden
fosforescencias de la noche, ventanas oprimidas, como una galería
de cuadros en silencio mi vida, pechos, manos, dedos,

la cavidad solar del día se duerme, en las líneas de un sueño.

CREATING/LIVING

cups denuded of their hands, days divested of their shadows
fingers that rings forgot, among the afternoons that passed
segments of yellow, petals soaked by the rain, stones
shining alone with their eyes, Sunday anguish

power that went away, I feel, I think, I tremble like the leaves
these poems are no more than parts of myself, incomplete,
complex, silent

petals of shoulders, petals of mouths, these poems descend
night phosphorescence, oppressive windows, like a gallery
of pictures in silence my life, breasts, hands, fingers

the day's solar cavity goes to sleep, in the lines of a dream

ALASKA

los días blancos

los que vinieron antes que yo cosieron con hilos de agua el borde
de esta historia. La luz no termina jamás, por las ventanas la luz
entra como un traje de noche lleno de lentejuelas. La luz, aprieta
los objetos y los hace desvelarse, sacando los cuerpos de sus túnicas,
los objetos de sus antiguas manos, perdiendo los pies
en la maravillosa página de historia oral donde las focas ríen
levantando los ojos hacia el cielo boreal, hacia los celestes empapados.

en esta parte del mundo, yo enuncio la palabra Yo partida en hielo
viajando suavemente sobre el agua escarchada, y ese trozo de mí
viaja con el recuerdo, hacia los ojos amarillos de un perro
hacia las alas moradas de un cuervo, hacia una multitud de aguas
donde la vida se enreda con los dedos tiritando de fríc

y es un poema el que pasa por el mundo con su traje polar
es un poema inmenso como una sola raya de arco iris, y poner
una mano junto al vidrio para tocar la mañana se convierte en un acto
sagrado, porque detrás, afuera, entre los pasos del
agua mis propios pasos se pierden,
este día se pierde,
yo comienzo a perderme en esta página.

ALASKA

the white days

those who came before me sewed the edge of this story with threads
of water. The light never ends, through the windows the light
enters like an evening dress full of sequins. The light squeezes
objects and unveils them, taking bodies out of their tunics,
objects out of their ancient hands, losing their feet
in the magic page of oral history where the seals laugh
raising their eyes towards the boreal sky, towards the blue-soaked sky

in this part of the world, I enunciate the word I split in ice
traveling softly over the frosted water, and that piece of myself
travels with memory, towards a dog's yellow eyes
towards a crow's mulberry wings, towards a multitude of waters
where life becomes entangled with fingers shivering from cold

and what passes through the world is a poem in a polar suit,
an immense poem like a single strip of rainbow, and putting
my hand on the window to touch the morning becomes
                                        a sacred act, because behind, outside, between the
water's steps my own steps are lost:
                                        this day is lost,
                                                I begin to lose myself on this page.

RESPLANDORES Y AUSENCIAS

circulan en el espacio millones de sonidos
en mis huesos hay voces de otras tantas voces
es como escuchar los niños del pasado besando ardillas
o tocando flores con la curiosidad de los recién llegados
y yo nado, paso las páginas de esta noche cósmica
donde mi vegetación es una maraña de libros, y hojas
caídas en la tierra que me dan papel blanco,
y montañas de puntos y de comas como arañas fugaces

yo nado abrazando una multitud de otras voces,
otros poemas, que nacieron de mujeres con vestidos simples
y hombres que al apoyar anteojos en la mesa
sintieron caer el mundo como caerse sobre una montaña
de escombros

y pierdo los zapatos, me desato el cabello, me siento
en la zona sagrada donde todos hacemos el poema
donde porque yo nací otros murieron, y todavía mi abuelo
triste, largo, flaco, habla solo en voz baja
a sus consabidos fracasos con la vida,

SPLENDORS AND ABSENCES

millions of sounds circulate in space
in my bones there are voices of others so many voices
it is like listening to the children of the past kissing squirrels
or touching flowers with the curiosity of the recently arrived
and I swim, turn the pages of this cosmic night
where my vegetation is a thicket of books, and leaves
fallen on the earth that give me white paper,
and mountains of periods and of commas like fleeting spiders

I swim embracing a multitude of other voices,
other poems, that were born of women with simple dresses
and men that upon resting eyeglasses on the table
felt the world fall like falling on a mountain
of rubbish

and I lose my shoes, I untie my hair, I move
into the sacred zone where we all make the poem
where because I was born others died, and yet my grandfather-
sad, long, thin--speaks to himself in a low voice
of his well-known failures in life,

y espera que yo pueda sobreponerme

mirando las estrellas, saludándolo con la mano en alto.

and expects that I may be able to triumph
looking at the stars, greeting him with my hand on high.

PALABRAS DEL CAMINO

To think is to confine yourself to a single thought

that one day stands still like a star in the world's sky.

*Letter on Humanism--Martin Heidegger**

alguna vez esta misma palabra para otro será pronunciada
sin romperse los labios en la boca, sin tener que dormir
sobresaltada, esta misma palabra en otros labios será
un camino suave, brilloso, transparente
como deslizarse en la nieve formando figuras con esquís
y ese jeroglífico blanco los ojos llenos de sonrisas
esa palabra se encuentre con el mundo.

Hay textos radiantes que en su tiempo fueron oscurecidos
por una gran indiferencia, que en su tiempo descansaron
sobre los nervios de un poeta, otro poeta, otro poeta

de alguna manera escribiendo uno quisiera crear un espacio
para esos textos que silentes fueron de un cajón a otro cajón
de un invierno a otro. Para esas grandes mareas de luz

---

*"Pensar es confinarse a un solo pensamiento que un día queda quieta como una estrella en el cielo del mundo." *Carta sobre el humanismo* de Martín Heidegger.

WORDS ON THE ROAD

To think is to confine yourself to a single thought

that one day stands still like a star in the world's sky

Letter on Humanism–Martin Heidegger

sometime this very word will be pronounced for another
without breaking my mouth's lips, without having to sleep
fitfully, this very word in other lips will be
a smooth, shiny, transparent road
like sliding in the snow forming figures with skis
and that white hieroglyphic, the eyes full of smiles
that word will meet the world.

There are radiant texts that in their time were obscured
by a great indifference, that in their time rested
on the nerves of a poet, another poet, another poet

in some way writing one wants to create a space
for those texts that went silent from one drawer to another drawer
from one winter to another. For that great seasickness of light

que podían encandilar y descomponer el presente

y que solo mucho tiempo después y por casualidad
fueron leídas, transformando el ayer en materia profética
desempolvando mañanas, escuchando el hilo de universo

que corría entre páginas rebeldes, esas mujeres
esos hombres, para quienes el tiempo de su tiempo no significó
un espejo, para quienes solamente el futuro

podía devolverles un rostro.

that could dazzle and disturb the present

    and only much later and by chance
they were read transforming yesterday into prophetic matter
dusting tomorrows, listening to the thread of the universe

    that ran among rebel pages, those women
those men, for whom the time of their time did not mean
a mirror, for whom only the future

        could give them a face.

Las formas del espejo que regresa

La luz me dure para siempre.

René Char

The Forms of the Mirror That Returns

Let the light last for me forever.

René Char

ESFERAS DE PODER

Poder reconocer debajo de la lluvia mi rostro que levanta una capa
invisible de universo: esta edad con mis manos y mis vocabularios,
la forma de un anillo sobre un dedo, todo esto es la historia
y la emoción: el tiempo, sus desgajos, las piedras de un camino

de neurona a neurona viaja el deseo, del hemisferio cerebral
derecho al hemisferio izquierdo, de la crisis de lluvia caída
en las ventanas, hasta las flores deshechas e inocentes
la primera verdad partida en dos: somos nosotros mismos,
nuestras contradicciones

si te fueras--me digo a mi misma, esa mujer delgada contra la pared·
si te fueras entonces se podrían abrir los baúles de estas membranas,
el ejercicio de esta sangre metida en rincones de mundo
un completo despertar de verbos fuertes, rebeldes, sumergidos

si te fueras, aún con el sueño, aún en medio de las sábanas
estarían esas formas de encandilar los objetos y averiguarlos
como la filosofía, la religión, el mundo, la sabiduría de los humildes
y si no me voy.

SPHERES OF POWER

To be able to recognize beneath the rain my face which lifts an invisible
cape of universe: this age with my hands and my vocabularies,
the form of a ring on a finger, all this is history
and emotion: time, its divisions, the road's stones

from neuron to neuron desire travels, from the cerebral right
hemisphere to the left hemisphere, from the crisis of rain fallen
on the windows, to the flowers uninterested and innocent
the first truth divided in two: we are ourselves alone,
our contradictions

if you went away--I say to myself alone, that slender woman against the
wall--if you went away then the trunks of these membranes could open up
the exercise of this blood smuggled into corners of world
a complete awakening of strong, rebellious, submerged words

if you went away even with sleepiness, even in between the sheets
there would exist those forms of dazzling objects and verifying them
like philosophy, religion, the world, the wisdom of the humble
and if I do not go,

es porque estamos juntos, mis dos hemisferios, mis pasiones
el mundo del sur y el del norte, las ramas de la primavera y
el polvo dorado del otoño, y afuera en la calle que se desdobla
ingreso como mujer madura hasta la niña y de la niña al útero

transgresiones y vértigos, horas de trabajo. La madurez de
las lámparas, el resplandor de los vidrios. Un ir y venir de
afectos y desencuentros,
alguien sagrado como el interior de una página.

it is because we are together, my two hemispheres, my passions
the world of the south and of the north, the branches of spring and
the golden dust of autumn, and outside on the street that splits
I enter as a mature woman into the child and from the child into the
uterus.

transgressions and vertigos, hours of work. The maturity of
lamps, the splendor of windowpanes. A coming and going of
affections and disencounters,
someone sacred like the interior of a page.

SKY MIRROR

mis hijos, mis poemas serán astronautas, they will see me inside,*
y el cielo será transparente como una lágrima, impotente como
una lágrima, duro como una lágrima

estados cósmicos del agua, renovación del agua sobre las manos,
escuché tu pensamiento como una forma de llamarme en el futuro
(en la oreja había peces sueltos, arena mojada, hebillas)

esta cara se rompe se hace astillas frente a la tempestad y surgen
en la superficie pedazos de cielo: ahí van las líneas debajo de los ojos
navegando en busca de un camino que se llama experiencia

el pensamiento sopla, como una vela de barco sopla

estoy mirando el cielo lleno de cielo,
y porque pienso en los dos, bajo los ojos.

---

* Me verán por adentro.

SKY MIRROR

my children, my poems will be astronauts, they will see me inside,
and the sky will be transparent like a tear, impotent like
a tear, hard like a tear

cosmic states of water, renewal of water on hands,
I listened to your thought like a way of calling myself into the future
(in my ear there were loose fish, wet sand, buckles)

this face breaks apart it becomes splinters before the tempest and
on the surface pieces of sky surge: there go the lines beneath your eyes
navigating in search of a road that is called experience

the thought blows, as a boat's candle blows

I am looking at the sky full of sky
and because I think about the two, I lower my eyes.

LA FIESTA / METÁFORA PRIVADA.

"A veces mi vida abria los ojos en la oscuridad"

y tímidamente, sutilmente, aparecían metáforas como radiografias de
un tiempo de dolor: fotocopias de ojos tristes, de hombros caídos.
así vino la vida, con sus fuerzas oscuras, como escribió el poeta sueco

y vino así la vida con su vestido de pliegues brillosos
con este aire de verano que cruza las ventanas, con un espiar hacia
adentro para que nadie me vea alzar la copa a una luna fresca,
que cae como agua congelada sobre el mundo

y así vino la vida, te digo/me digo, como si pudieras escucharme
una carrera de burbujas que sueltan cometas, un chocar de vidrios
mientras otros saludan y conversan
fuegos artificiales, arcos de luz como estrellas perdidas
celebrar otro año más, por la vida, por la vida

hacia la duda, hacia el resplandor final,
hacia la vida que me despedirá,
con un vestido lleno de preguntas.

"A veces mi vida abria los ojos en la oscuridad"

T. Tranströmer.

LA FIESTA/PRIVATE METAPHOR

"Sometimes my life opened its eyes in the dark"

and timidly, subtly, metaphors appeared like radiographs of
a time of pain: photocopies of sad eyes, of fallen shoulders.
so life came, with its dark forces, as the Swedish poet wrote.

and so life came with its dress of shiny pleats
with this summer air that crosses the windows, with a spying towards
the inside so that no one sees me lifting a drink to a fresh moon,
that falls like congealed water on the world

and so life came, I tell you / I tell myself, as if you could hear me
a course of bubbles that set comets free, a collision of windowpanes
while others waved and conversed
fireworks, arches of light like lost stars
celebrating one more year, for life, for life

towards doubt, towards the final splendor
towards life which will take leave of me
with my dress full of questions.

"Sometimes my life opened its eyes in the dark"

T. Tranströmer.

TIEMPOS PARALELOS

gracias tiempo
porque yo nunca estuve en una iglesia más hermosa
que estos brazos que tengo rodeando las rodillas
mirando pasar las hojas
en la vereda de mi casa que en aquella época
y en ésta es como la vereda del mundo

gracias tiempo
porque mientras pasan las hojas aquellos sonidos
éstos, los del pecho / la paloma escapada / la hoja reseca
resuenan como si me conocieran
repiten fugamente mi nombre

hacen gestos transparentes como detrás de la hoja de vidrio
de un aeropuerto, desde donde me vuelo
con un ramo de lámparas, con una pulsera iluminando
la cara que entonces tenía / la que tengo

oh tiempo, abrazándome, deconstruyéndome como a las hojas
polvo, ruido seco, manta de suspiros
trayectos de los átomos
el dorado / el oro / el amarillo / el viento.

PARALLEL TIME

thanks time
for I never was in a more beautiful church
than these arms that I hold encircling my knees
looking at the leaves passing
on the sidewalk of my house that in that epoch
and in this is like the sidewalk of the world

thanks time
for while the leaves pass those sounds
these, those of my breast / the escaped dove / the dried up leaf
resound as if they knew me
they fleetingly repeat my name.

they make transparent gestures as if behind the glass pane
of an airport, from whence I fly
with a branch of lamps, with an illuminated bracelet
the face that I had then / the one that I have

oh time, embrace me, destroy me like the leaves
dust, dry noise, cloak of sighs
trajectories of atoms
golden / gold / yellow / wind.

GUIA PARA PERPLEJOS

I.

Este magma azul el celeste de la tarde pálida
me recuerda ese monasterio donde se encontraron signos de otra
época, el asombro de mi cara frente al resplandor de los vidrios
al detenerse el coche, y la tarde tan seca de sonidos
que mis propios pasos resonaban en lo que llaman un lugar sagrado
las paredes blancas, mi campera pesada, tocar las puertas
que otros tocaron, hilos de luz de vela silenciosos

II.

al darme vuelta una pared blanca de hospital y sin dibujitos
el día se come mi día como si yo fuera nada más que materia
comestible y mi sangre hubiera crecido para recorridos de tubo de
vena plástica, sin poder mover los pies o las manos

mi cabeza fijamente mira el resplandor de las ventanas. Aquí
estoy quieta, y no sabía que tantas generaciones han estado
quietas con la inquietud de lo que no se puede hacer, decir,
pensar. A los cuatro años, un río de sangre lleva pedacitos
de libros ilustrados, bocas de crayon azul.

GUIDE FOR THE PERPLEXED

I.

This celestial blue magma of the pale afternoon
reminds me of that monastery where signs of another epoch
were found, the wonder in my face before the splendor of the windows
when the car stopped, and the afternoon so dry of sounds
that my own footsteps resounded in what they call a sacred place
the white walls, my heavy backpack, touching the doors
that others touched, silent threads of candlelight

II.

upon turning about a white hospital wall, one without little drawings
the day eats my day as if I were nothing more than digestible
matter and my blood had been raised for runs in a tube of
plastic vein, without being able to move my feet or my hands

my head stares at the splendor of the windows. Here
I am quiet, and I didn't know that so many generations have been
quiet with the disquiet of what cannot be done, said
thought. Just four years old, a river of blood carries little pieces
of illustrated books, mouths of blue crayon.

III.

en el río de tinta que han significado mis labios cerrados
y mis cartas, papeles, poemas, cruzando el océano aéreo algunas
veces mirando por la ventana el jeroglífico de luz que se enciende
ante una ciudad desconocida. Bajando por la noche a aeropuertos
donde uno sabe que nadie lo espera

esa soledad multiplicada por uno, que no hace más que uno lleno
de adioses, lleno de puntos vacíos, entonces recordar que la poesía
como una aguja que busca sangre nos busca, aún en ese momento
en que, por la madrugada, adormecidos, contamos los rayos
del sol como si fueran mágicos, desdoblando la infancia
en instantes secretos, íntimos de alegría.

IV.

y al volver al presente, a este rostro con estas manos con
estos anillos. Hacer que la tierra se empequeñezca porque estamos
juntos con esta posibilidad verbal y alucinante del recuerdo
con el Otro: tiempo y espacio de Einstein, donde nosotros somos
los que nos dispersamos para reunirnos, para poner en orden
ese pasar puertas y metáforas,

para llegar a definirnos no como lo que teníamos que ser
sino lo que somos, para nada más que nosotros mismos.

III.

in the river of ink that my closed lips have meant
and my letters, papers, poems, crossing the airy ocean some-
times looking through the window at the hieroglyphic of light that is
turned on before an unknown city. Coming down at night to airports
where you know that nobody is waiting for you

this solitude multiplied by one, that doesn't make more than one full
of goodbyes, full of empty periods, then to remember that poetry
like a needle that searches for blood is searching for us, even in that
moment in which, through daybreak, asleep, we count the rays
of the sun as if they were magic, doubling infancy
in secret instants, intimate with happiness.

IV.

and upon returning to the present, to this face with these hands with
these rings. To make the earth grow small because we are
together with this dazzling verbal possibility of the remembrance
of the Other: Einstein's time and space, where we are
the ones who scatter in order to come together again, for putting order in
that passing through doors and metaphors,

for coming to define ourselves not as what we had to be
but as what we are, for nothing more than ourselves alone.

Cultivar la propia extrañeza (René Char)

V.

y con haces de luz repartidos en la casa, salgan mis hebillas,
salgan mis corpiños, aparezca una enagua enjuagada en la soga
una mariposa de occidente y de oriente, sacarme los días
que no se van, se quedan debajo de los ojos,

deshojarme social e individualmente en la mano frágil de
mi poema próximo.

VI.

alguna vez las llaves encontrarán las puertas.

Eso pensé, mientras avanzaba por la vereda de un monasterio del
siglo XII, y cuando acariciada por la tarde pálida, me di cuenta
que estaba viva, como si volviera a un recuerdo de mi primer llanto
en el mundo, a esa primera sacudida y ese: estoy aquí

no sé si por asociación de recuerdos, por pensar que hay algo sagrado
en cada cosa que hacemos o decimos, o que a través de la civilización
estamos bendecidos por otros hombres y otras mujeres
somos parte de la respiración de otros sueños, materia ósea convertida
en astros, el resplandor de la nieve, el tocar las ventanas moradas de frío
este escenario de adioses con que daré el punto final a mis pensamientos

To cultivate one's own strangeness (René Char)

V.

and with faggots of light spread out in the house, may my buckles leave,
may my brassieres leave, may a rinsed slip appear on the clothesline
a butterfly of west and east, to take from me the days
that do not go away, they remain beneath my eyes,
to defoliate myself socially and individually in the fragile hand of
my next poem.

VI.

sometime keys will find doors

I thought that, while I was advancing along the sidewalk of the twelfth-
century monastery, and when caressed by the pale afternoon, I realized
that I was alive, as if I came back to a memory of my first cry
in the world, to that first shaking and so: I am here

I don't know if by memory association, by thinking that there is
something
sacred in each thing that we do or say, or that through civilization
we are blessed by other men and other women
we are part of the breathing of other dreams, bony matter converted
into stars, the snow's splendor, the touching of windows mulberried
with cold, this scene of goodbyes with which I give the final period
to my thoughts

VII.

alguna vez las llaves encontrarán sus puertas

y si en el camino restos de mí se fueron perdiendo como en una arqueología de destellos, si algo se fue muriendo poco a poco entre blocks* de poemas, dientes rotos, alas de mis pulmones,
controversia de toda mi familia, fotografías viejas, en un cajón las llaves
las metáforas, las ventanas, el viento

sí, yo sé que un día, alguien,
alguna vez encontrará las puertas.

Benediktbeuren, Alemania, 1993

---

*bloques

VII.

sometime keys will find doors

and if on the road remains of myself were being lost as in an archeology
of flashes, if something was dying little by little among blocks
of poems, broken teeth, my lungs' wings,
controversy of all my family, old photographs, in a drawer the keys
the metaphors, the windows, the wind

yes, I know that one day, someone
sometime will find the doors.

Benediktbeuren, 1993

INDEX OF TITLES

[Page numbers in roman refer to the text; those in italics, following poem titles, refer to the introduction or the preface.]

INDEX OF PROPER NAMES